Chicago's Public Wits

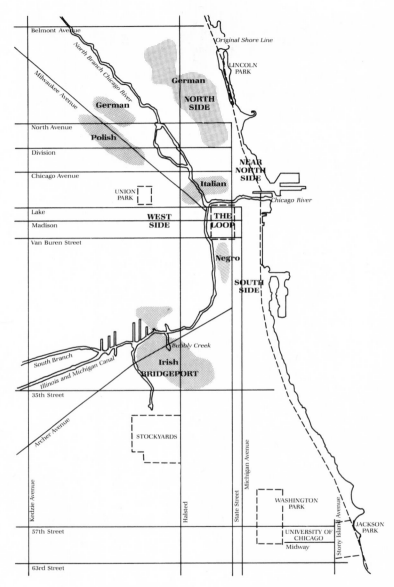

Post-fire Chicago, with approximate principal locations and ethnic groupings. Adapted from *Historic City: The Settlement of Chicago* (Chicago: City of Chicago Department of Development and Planning, 1976).

Chicago's Public Wits

A Chapter in the American Comic Spirit

Edited, with Commentaries, by
Kenny J. Williams and Bernard Duffey

Louisiana State University Press
Baton Rouge and London

Designer: Patricia Douglas Crowder
Typeface: Linotron Zapf Book
Typesetter: G&S Typesetters, Inc.

Library of Congress Cataloging in Publication Data

Main entry under title:

Chicago's public wits.

    1. Chicago (Ill.)—Anecdotes, facetiae, satire, etc.   2. American wit and humor—
Illinois—Chicago.   I. Williams, Kenny J.   II. Duffey, Bernard I., 1917–
F548.36.C48 1983   817′.008′0977311   82-9876
ISBN 0-8071-1043-4   AACR2

Contents

Illustrations

Preface

The literature of Chicago has been a significant one, but to single out its humor may seem an attempt to do either the impossible or the unimportant. Such a task is burdened by the widely held assumption that only straight-faced efforts to view life merit serious literary concern. However, it is our belief that a collection of humor—ranging from parodies and caricatures to satire and wit—also has value. Understanding what makes a community laugh at a given moment in its history can go far in revealing the nature of that locale and ultimately can give insight into the human condition. From Henri Bergson to L. J. Potts and Wayne C. Booth, theorists have examined the comic impulse in world literature, and scholars of American literature from Constance Rourke to Walter Blair and Hamlin Hill have addressed the issue of humor in our national writing. Few, however, have concentrated their attention on the urban Middle West.

Louis D. Rubin, Jr., in his introduction to *The Comic Imagination in America*, offers a suggestion that can be useful in relating humor to the more universal spirit. Our national laughter, he theorizes, has often arisen out of a great American joke briefly statable as an interplay between "the cultural ideal and the everyday fact"—a phrase that will serve as an introductory guide to this volume. His observation implies an awareness amenable to the personal and pragmatic insight urban experience demands, just as it presumes the life of a democratic culture to be one stretched between the more studied attitudes of aspiration and upwardness, and the basic—if less edifying—truths. All humor, it may be, is somewhat "lowering" and in that sense ironic in its pressure. Certainly our urban humor often responded to its world by a recasting, again in Rubin's terms, of "ornamental" pretensions into the terms of individual and more "elemental" perception.

American humorists seized upon this gambit and expanded it into a virtual industry during the late nineteenth century and into the twentieth. Professional humorists were everywhere, supplying large quantities of newspaper and magazine writing. Although it was thus part of a national wave from its inception, Chicago humor has at the same time possessed some unique characteristics. To begin with, it was almost wholly rooted in local newspapers and magazines rather than in aspirations toward the national "lecture" circuit. Comic writers, consequently, had to develop appropriately durable and flexible modes. Furthermore, as Chicago humor pointedly analyzed the incongruities of a city life wanting to define itself, it assumed many forms. Underlying much of it was a seriousness designed to expose mankind's foibles within the vagaries of an urban environment affected both by its own newness and its sense of competition with older cities. This emphasis undoubtedly was related to the notion that an ideal society could be created on the shores of Lake Michigan. It is not surprising, then, to note a strong satiric element in the city's humor as the public wits viewed men and women in a world occupied with establishing itself. There were no sacred cows; no one escaped the scrutiny of the humorists. The high, the low, the immigrant, the native-born, the Democrat, the early Whig and later Republican were subjected to the comic writer's "superior eye." Finally, although Chicago's publications supported independent cartoon efforts like those of Charles Lederer and John T. McCutcheon for the *Tribune* and T. E. Powers for *America*, the writers remained true to a freestanding verbal humor, one substantially independent of the great appeal of the integral or adjacent illustration which was a mainstay, for example, of New York's comic weeklies.

We have arrived at our sense of Chicago's urban humor by surveying the publications generated by the city's wits in order to select what seems most indicative of such writing from the early days to the present time. Many of our authors, beginning in Chicago, later received wider recognition. But both those who made this transition and those who did not are included here for the wit that the city of Chicago and the writer's presence in it, taken together, made possible. Our humorists are at once representatives of the urban world with which they deal and commentators on it for an audience that is, at least in part, also their subject matter. Theirs is the humor of a city knowing itself in its time. The city's "public wit," we may say, is one who speaks for and to an audience itself encountering the unpredictability of an urban experience in the making.

Such an achievement was a wholesome one for the city's culture, and this is certainly not less true when, with the kind of ambitious and ruthless struggle for success that marked Chicago's history, the humorist exposed those aspects of reality that a comic sense of incongruity alone can perceive. The wit is often a debunker. His very debunking, however, when held at the comic level, is an affirmative act offering the feel of a time and place. Chicago humor moves toward individualized perception. Although the city's motto declares it to be an "*urbs in horto*," Chicago's unofficial statement of mood is the declaration "I Will," and the city's history has to a great extent been an acting out of that bold assertion. But contained within the "I Will" spirit is the more harshly or more gently skewed declaration "I spy," and the ideal is refocused by the critical eye.

So much has been made of the southwestern humor of the nineteenth-century frontier that the early urban humor of the Middle West has been neglected. Whereas for many, Chicago humor is dated from 1883 and the appearance of Eugene Field in the city, our selections begin in the 1840s. At first, perhaps, the city itself looked much like a simple extension of the familiar rural town and its world, but extension soon bred complication, and early written comedy exhibited an unusually serious bent for such a pioneering community. Chicago— despite its heralded growth—was in the days before the Civil War clearly identified with the spirit of western sectionalism. That conflict marked an increased sense of involvement with national issues, and this was played out against the backdrop of a divided city. The town seemed doomed after the Fire of 1871, but those who uttered words of despair had not counted on the indomitable will displayed during the period of rebuilding. By 1893 Chicago had not only become one of America's major cities but an international center as well.

The humorist's concern with his city's transitions becomes apparent as the reader moves from a traditional locus in political and social satire invoking well-defined values, toward a more amorphous sense of the awkwardness the swelling polyglot town presented, and from there toward its lurch—still fledgling and awkward—into a metropolis. Our earliest examples show Chicago writers closely involved in their history, viewing with a mixture of gusto and hard realism the impact of canal, railroad, and factory on their trading post, arguing the orthodoxy of one political interest against another, making jokes about the raw sprawl of their unceasingly multiplying neighborhoods, taking pride in their size, protecting what they considered to be theirs against the onslaught of "foreigners," and enjoying or questioning the fruits that urban success had ripened. The World's Columbian Exposition, in its time dubbed the "White City," generated admiration for its splendor, yet visitors and humorists were quick to note the ironic contrast between the "White City" and the "black city," or real Chicago, which had produced the spectacular international fair.

The spread of writing across these years is distinguished in the later nineteenth century by a humor moving more surely onto a base of its own—a humor marked by the appearance of George P. Upton as "Peregrine Pickle" and Charles Harris as "Carl Pretzel" and continuing through the advent of Eugene Field in the early eighties and of Finley Peter Dunne and George Ade in the nineties. With such figures, urban wit in Chicago may be said to have come into its own; the humorist's first achievement would thus be to find an individual voice that defined his own attitudes toward the city and the times. Allegiances—political and otherwise—might be maintained, but they would be subjected to the wit's terms and interests.

The nineteenth century's vision did not yet run deeply counter to the city's dominant concerns. It allowed Upton to construct a world of personal observation and reaction, but one, still, to which every reader was invited. It allowed Field to design a privately conceived city in his writing but one happily manufactured from ingredients that Chicago itself put at his disposal. It allowed Ade to draw characters from originals he observed in the life of "the streets and town" about which he first wrote. And it allowed Dunne to make his own choice of a spokesman, but one he offered as Chicago's and then America's ideal—if only potential—everyman viewing the publicly engrossing events of the day.

As years passed, however, the angle of vision widened, and by the early twentieth century Chicago's wits had begun to regard the city with a less congenial eye. The town became more incidental to the vision, though it was still utilized as a point of departure for assessments of, and interests in, the urban experience. The directions of wit multiplied. In our most recent authors, wit's vantage seems almost reversed from its Chicago beginnings, placing the humorist in a self-defined attitude detached from loyalty to the city (which is still his). Consequently, Chicago wit has moved with the times but perhaps has done so to remain faithful to the perennial obligation of humor to amuse, to perceive with a sense of discovery, and ultimately to offer the reader a hold on a particular world.

Acknowledgments

Finley Peter Dunne, "Things Spiritual" and "The Big Fine," in *Mr. Dooley Says*. Copyright © 1910 by Charles Scribner's Sons; copyright renewed. (New York: Charles Scribner's Sons, 1910.) Reprinted with the permission of Charles Scribner's Sons.

Extracts from *You Know Me, Al* by Ring Lardner. Copyright 1916 by Charles Scribner's Sons; copyright renewed 1944 by Ellis A. Lardner. (New York: Charles Scribner's Sons, 1916.) Reprinted with the permission of Charles Scribner's Sons.

Extracts from "Gullible's Travels" by Ring Lardner, in *Round Up*. Copyright © 1929 by Charles Scribner's Sons; copyright renewed 1957 by Ellis A. Lardner. (New York: Charles Scribner's Sons, 1929.) Reprinted with the permission of Charles Scribner's Sons.

From the Chicago *Daily News*: Alfred Kreymborg, "The Stevens Fadeaway"; Morey Schwartz, "A Lowbrow Blinks at Literary Lights"; Carl Sandburg, "A Middle-West Man"; Keith Preston, from "The Periscope"; Ben Hecht, from "Boob Babble." Copyright © Field Enterprises. Reprinted with permission.

From the Chicago *Tribune*: Burton Rascoe, from "The Intellectual Autobiography of Francis Hackett"; from "On a Certain Condescension in Our Natives"; from "Do, Re, Mi, Fa, So, La"; from "Olla Podrida." Bert Leston Taylor, from "A Line O' Type or Two." Reprinted with permission of the Chicago *Tribune*.

Reprinted by permission of Hill and Wang, a division of Farrar, Straus and Giroux, Inc.: "Feet Live Their Own Life" from *The Best of Simple* by Langston Hughes. Copyright © 1961 by Langston Hughes.

"In the Dark" by Langston Hughes, from *Simple Speaks His Mind*. Copyright © 1950 by Langston Hughes; renewed 1978 by George Bass, executor for the Estate of Langston Hughes. Reprinted by permission of Harold Ober Associates, Incorporated.

"How the Devil Came Down Division Street," copyright 1944 by Nelson Algren, from his book *The Neon Wilderness*. Reprinted by permission of Doubleday & Company, Inc.

"When Slats Caught Santa," "Ma's Quiet Tax Revolt," "Alinsky Not in Their League," "Dent Leads to a Wipe-Out." From *Slats Grobnik and Some Other Friends* by Mike Royko. Copyright © 1966, 1968, 1970, 1971, 1972, 1973 by Mike Royko. Reprinted by permission of the publisher, E. P. Dutton, Inc.

"San-Fran-York on the Lake" by Mike Royko, from *I May Be Wrong But I Doubt It*. Copyright © 1968 by Mike Royko. Reprinted by permission of The Sterling Lord Agency, Inc.

"Talkin' Chicawgo" by Bill Granger, from *The Chicagoan*. Reprinted by permission of Bill Granger.

"A Middle-West Man" by Carl Sandburg, reprinted by permission of the Sandburg Family Trust.

Poems and Prose by Keith Preston reprinted from *Pot Shots from Parnassus* by Keith Preston, copyright 1929. Used by permission of Crown Publishers, Inc.

Three illustrations by Herman Rosse reprinted from *1001 Afternoons in Chicago* by Ben Hecht, design and illustration by Herman Rosse, copyright 1922. Used by permission of Crown Publishers, Inc.

Part One
Early Chicago and the Comic Spirit

The South Water Street Market, from an illustration by
John T. McCutcheon for *The Chicago Record's Stories of
the Streets and of the Town* (1894). The view suggests the
prevailing appearance of Chicago's business district before
the advent of the modern city.

Introduction _____

What became the city of Chicago was for many years an active part of the American frontier. The establishment of Fort Dearborn in 1803 was one means by which the government of the United States thought it might police the various border skirmishes between the Indians and the few settlers who had ventured that far westward. Furthermore, the fort served notice (or so it was imagined) that the new nation would tolerate no nonsense from the British, who were accused of inciting the Indians. Among frontier military outposts, however, Dearborn had the least activity and did not enter the folklore of the nation until the massacre of 1812. The destruction of the fort ended the existence of the small settlement that had huddled about it.

With the defeat of the British in 1815 the midwestern frontier offered a safer territory, and westward expansion seemed assured with the opening of the Erie Canal in 1825. The little village of Chicago was first incorporated in 1833, but—in spite of various rhapsodic claims by the city's apologists and defenders who were convinced that the territory was destined for greatness—nothing about that village distinguished it substantially from the multitude of towns springing up all over the nation. By the village's 1837 incorporation as a city, however, the small settlement gave evidence that it was indeed different from other communities. It had pizzazz and gutsy confidence—some later called it *chutzpah*—and was known for its phenomenal growth.

Population rose from less than 5,000 in 1837 to 298,977 by 1870, reaching 1,698,575 by 1900. Foreign immigrants were among those who flocked to the city. Many found work on the Illinois and Michigan Canal, others staffed the various industries. Whatever problems the Civil War produced in the rest of the nation, Chicago prospered and by 1871

was thought of as a major American city. Then, within a two-day period in October of that year, the city was destroyed by fire. Perhaps at
no period in Chicago's history has the population demonstrated such
determination as in the gigantic undertakings that led to the city's
restoration.

During the nineteenth century the city had suffered—as had the
rest of the nation—several severe financial panics, but the "I Will"
spirit had long been part of the place, and each depression only re-
inforced the desire to succeed. Chicago's rapid growth, the success of
so many of the early settlers, the creation of a number of fortunes in a
short period, the vast wealth that came from such industries as lumber, railroading, and meat packing, the almost miraculous recovery
from the Fire of 1871 in a few short years, and the magnificence of the
World's Columbian Exposition of 1893 remain very substantial elements in the city's history.

Eugene Field's move from Denver to Chicago in 1883 is important in
the annals of the city's humor, but whatever significance is attributed
to Field must be tempered by a recognition that a strong comic tradition had been created before the Fire of 1871. The earlier humor bears a
strong resemblance to that of later writers, displaying an urbane sophistication and wit that belie the essentially rural nature of the young
city. As Chicago's early humorists viewed life around them, they exper-
imented—entertaining little notion of posterity—with various comic
forms. Hence, the city's humor is marked by a wide diversity of techniques and types.

One of the first—albeit accidental—manifestations of Chicago's
meeting with the frontier resulted in the "urbanization" of the long-
familiar tall tale, whose techniques were used by local historians to
record the story of their city. Gross exaggerations and emphases upon
super-heroes were employed to convince others of Chicago's unique-
ness. The optimism of the tall tale eventually was accompanied by
a strong sense of disillusionment, which seemed even more pronounced because of the city's high expectations. The comic impulse
thus initially produced an abundance of satires, though the object of
ridicule was not consistently the same. Many conditions evoked satire:
local and national politics with the inevitable political campaigns, the
country bumpkin's first forays into the city, the westerner who could
outsmart the easterner, the obvious stupidities of the nouveaux riches,

the incongruities of life, and the new city's nervous self-analysis. Even so serious a situation as the Civil War provided an avenue for humor— grim though it was.

The early city also saw the rise of a group of journalists who were observers of and commentators on the urban experience in America. Frequently hiding behind the mask of a created persona, these writers laughed at themselves and at the foibles of their city as well as at the nation. In so doing, they often pointed out some of the terrible truths of human existence. Most of their work appeared with a degree of regularity even before Eugene Field joined the *Daily News* and made his "Sharps and Flats" an important regular feature of the newspaper.

During the course of the nineteenth century, the Chicago *Tribune*, for example, used a group of writers whose created characters commented on the city, the state, and the nation. In addition to George P. Upton's "Peregrine Pickle," the 1860s saw the publication of the work of "Gath," a creation of George Alfred Townsend (1841–1914), the *Tribune*'s Washington correspondent. Joining him in the nation's capital was "Nix," whose columns became popular during Andrew Johnson's impeachment trial. From the Boston area came the letters of a correspondent who signed his *Tribune* columns "Revere," and the work of "Vigo" dealt with postwar conditions in the South. In the 1870s the work of "Raconteur," "Lynn," "Harryth," "Ouisel," "Sangamon," "Aaron About," "Reno," and "Fern Leaf" prefigured Finley Dunne's "Martin Dooley," without themselves achieving "Mr. Dooley's" lasting national popularity. Franc B. Wilkie's "Poliuto" and Charles Harris' "Carl Pretzel," however, joined "Peregrine Pickle" to appeal to wide audiences in the city and in the nation. They were successful observers whose comic postures shifted with their concerns.

The humor of early Chicago was seldom provincial and much of it had an underlying purpose. This was especially true of the attacks upon foreign immigrants. The mocking of "those who were different" was initially coarsely done but gained a frightening smoothness toward the end of the century (all the more fascinating when one considers that Chicago prided itself on being "the most American city"). The business tycoons, politicians, social climbers, and foreign immigrants who first understood what it meant to live in America when they attempted to survive in Chicago are recognizable as distinct urban types. Thus to understand the humor of early Chicago ultimately helps to foster a knowledge of the modern American city. That such a comic tradition and spirit should have developed in Chicago is somewhat inexplicable; certainly there were other cities on the middle border that were far more sophisticated.

Although the early humorists are not as familiar as those of the latter part of the nineteenth century, the city's first public wits still provide a background for the study of the more popular journalists who became major voices in American literature. If for no other reason than that they served as forerunners, the early humorists of Chicago have an abiding significance.

Political Satire in Early Chicago

Early Chicago produced some coarse and often vitriolic political satires during the nineteenth century. These caustic works at first glance seem to be a legitimate outgrowth of the rollicking humor of the frontier, but upon closer examination they display a distinct urbane sophistication and reveal that there were those in the city who recognized the faults of society. Consequently, these works furnish excellent historical documentation for the problems of the period, often representing the seemingly universal attack of the "have-nots" against the "haves."

Do satires of a bygone era continue to amuse? Certainly much depends upon an understanding of the conditions that led to the ridicule in the first place. Although allusions may be dated, satires ordinarily live because certain character types are still recognizable. The crooked politician and his cronies are part of the folklore of American humor, and the possibility that a defeated politician may "go to hell" or become—as in the case of the "Magician"—part of the demon world is an event often devoutly desired.

The political satires produced in early Chicago may not be "great" literature. But though many are rough, they often reveal their authors' knowledge of the mechanics of literature. Much of the poetry, for example, suggests a familiarity with the heroic couplet as well as with the mock heroic forms and the techniques of parody. The writers also recognized the effectiveness of using well-known allusions for comic purposes. Although the humor of satire is dependent upon its cutting edge, there is always the possibility that the underlying motive will destroy any literary sensibility. Well-developed characters are too frequently replaced by caricatures, and the episodes are too obscure to be meaningful; these, however, are expected problems of the genre. Devices often used by later political observers to lessen the sting, such as the use of dialect for comic effects, were not commonplace in early Chicago. In the final analysis, these works are seldom funny in the usual sense of the word, but all of them display great wit.

By the end of the 1840s, just a few years after the incorporation of the city, several types of political satire had been produced in Chicago. Some were rather sophisticated in spite of the frequent crudity and coarseness of the allusions. Political satire was also closely associated with the numerous local campaign papers. Although these newspapers were concerned with showing the local relevance of their material, *Hard Cider Press* (1840), *Field Piece* (1848), *Free West* (1856), and *The Rail Splitter* (1860) supported national candidates by frequently lampooning the opposition. Even the daily newspapers published satires on occasion. Another type commonly issued independently as either a broadside or a pamphlet was far more "literary" in its origin and appeal. That many of these works reduced serious considerations to farce should surprise no one familiar with political literature.

Still another satiric form—best represented by the political concerns of the Civil War and the expressed animosity between the *Tribune* and the *Times*—is better understood today although much of it is not funny in the modern sense. There were, in addition, some social satires produced which were neither as popular nor as prevalent but which in many ways complete the chronicle of the development of this genre in early Chicago. Such works as the anonymously published *Age of Humbug* (1869) and John Chamberlain's *Cotton Stealing* (1869) are examples of the sense of pessimism that swept the country as the Gilded Age became more than a convenient name for a period. Both works examine and ridicule the lack of moral precepts caused by faithfulness to the dictates of big business. Although published in Chicago, these works were designed to appeal to a national audience.

Although these satires and the spirit that produced them were well known during the nineteenth century, no evidence exists to suggest that these works exercised an influence upon the later developments in the Middle West. By the 1880s political satire was far more closely associated with ethnic humor; however, as early as the 1840s writers were clearly aware—at least in their own minds—of the close relationship between politics and foreign immigration.

The satiric spirit still flourished in the post–Civil War era. Chicagoans maintained an interest in national politics as the city's journalists continued to ridicule the purveyors and dispensers of political power both in the city and in the nation. Sometimes their work was as pointed as that of Juvenal, sometimes it displayed the gentle ribbing of Horace; but by implication the journalists were committed to the notion of ridicule in order to change conditions—if not for the better, at least to another political party.

Two Satires of the 1840s

Although Chicago was only a few years old in the 1840s, the period produced a variety of satires in the city. For example, what some historians have called the first "lampoon" in Chicago was written in 1843. Much of what motivated that attack has been lost to history, but the humorous jabs at the representatives and elected officials of the young municipal government, the urban elite, the foreign immigrant, and the newly installed judicial system are clearly understandable. The author, who signed himself "Rocky Mountain, Esq.," used the noisy serenade often given to bridal couples as the basis for the farcical action of *The Charivari*, ominously subtitled: "What Took Place and What Didn't Take Place on the Evening of January 19, 1843, in the City of Japan, Kamschatka Co., Ills., What Was Done and What Wasn't Done by the Sheet Iron Band. A Full Report of the Apprehension of the Rioters, and Their Examination, Including What Was Said and What Wasn't Said on That Occasion."

The following two works represent a range of satiric wit in early Chicago. From the burlesque drama of *The Magician* to the restrained heroic couplets of "Isaac Arnold," the anonymous authors displayed a variety of techniques not frequently associated with the Middle West of the 1840s.

The Magician

[One of the first satires published in the city appeared in the *Daily American*, a Whig newspaper.[1] Written in 1840 by J. T. C. of Ottawa, Illinois, *The Magician* ran for two days—May 5 and 6.

During the administration of Andrew Jackson (1828–1836) the Whigs had attracted all political dissidents, but the party was not strong enough to unseat the Democrats; hence Martin Van Buren had won the presidency in 1836 and ran for reelection in 1840. Van Buren's name was anathema to many Chicagoans. He had been responsible for—or so it was imagined—President Jackson's veto of the Maysville Road Bill in 1830, and as a senator Van Buren had joined others in rejecting the notion of supporting internal improvements within the various states. Chicago citizens who felt that the improvements they sought would also benefit the nation could not understand the lack of federal support for many of their projects. Then when Van Buren became president, the panic of 1837, which severely affected the western businessman, did little to endear the chief executive to Chicagoans.

Local politics frequently reflected the viciousness and slanderous appeals of national contests. The presidential campaign of 1840 (for reasons that seem mild today) was extremely bitter. Both candidates were at times victims of relentless attacks which resulted in a strange, but predictable, reversal of roles. William Henry Harrison, the wealthy elitist public servant, was presented as "the man of the people." Martin Van Buren, a commoner and actual product of the American middle class, was presented as a decadent aristocrat who spent his days trying to imitate every unsound fiscal policy destined to weaken the nation and benefit his many political cronies. His nights, according to this portrait, he spent drinking wine with his pseudo-aristocratic buddies in the White House, which these men viewed as their personal palace rather than as the "people's" house.

Everywhere could be heard "Tippecanoe and Tyler Too!" In rejecting Van Buren, commentators made much of the tastes that he had al-

---

1. *The American* (1835–42) was founded by Thomas O. Davis, and William Stuart became the editor in 1837. In 1839 the *American* became the first daily newspaper in Illinois. Very supportive of Whig principles and strongly opposed to Van Buren, the newspaper took an active role in the campaign of 1840 with the publication of *The Magician*.

legedly acquired abroad when he served as secretary of state. He was accused of sleeping in a Louis XV bed, of perfuming his whiskers with French fragrances, of eating such delicacies as *soupe à la reine* and *pâté de foie gras*, and of riding in a British-made carriage. Andrew Jackson had campaigned earlier on these same premises when he accused John Quincy Adams of having imperial tendencies. Now the Whigs could use the same argument against the Democrats. The popular campaign song of the period avowed:

> No ruffled shirt, no silken hose,
> No airs does Tip display;
> But like "the pith of worth" he goes
> In homespun "hodden-grey."
> Upon his board there ne'er appeared
> The costly "sparkling wine,"
> But plain hard cider such as cheered
> In days of old lang syne.

In a moment of pique, so the legend goes, an eastern Democratic journalist supposedly announced that if Harrison were given a choice of a barrel of cider with a log cabin or a chance to live in the White House, "Old Tip" would choose the log cabin. The Whigs immediately seized upon the symbols of log cabin and cider, and they continued to sing:

> Let Van from his coolers of silver drink wine,
>   And lounge on his cushioned settee;
> Our man on his buckeye bench can recline,
>   Content with hard cider is he.
> Then a shout from each freeman—a shout from each State,
>   To the plain, honest husbandman true,
> And this be our motto—the motto of Fate—
>   "Hurrah for Old Tippecanoe!"

Act I of *The Magician* appeared on May 5, 1840. Act II appeared the following day.]

• • •

Dramatis Personae

    Magician[2]

    Levite, a Soothsayer

    Amos, Toperus, Demons, &c, &c.

---

2. The adept political maneuvering of Martin Van Buren earned him the nickname "the little magician."

"THE UNION OF THE WHIGS FOR THE SAKE OF THE UNION."

For President,
WILLIAM H. HARRISON,
Of Ohio.
For Vice President,
JOHN TYLER,
Of Virginia.

Illustration from the Chicago *American*, May 5, 1840.

Act I.

Scene 1. *A room in the White House—Magician solus, holding in his hand a newspaper containing an account of the Harrison meeting at Columbus, Ohio. Time, night.*

Mag.—'Tis strange, this fantasy which haunts my brain!
  The clock on yonder dome has tolled the hour
  Of one, and yet I cannot quiet so
  My agitated brain to find the sleep
  I so much need. Why am I so disturbed?
  Where is the unshaking and unshaken soul
  Of which I once could boast. It is as I
  Have sometimes guessed, that 'twas not of itself
  So firm, but my all grasping, uncontrolled
  Ambition, for the moment made it such?
  Alas! I should have pondered this more deeply
  The man who seeks to set his foot on some
  Precarious height, beneath which yawns in dire
  And fearful aspect the dread precipice;
  If he ascend not with a cautious step,
  But rushes to the top; when he surveys
  The scene below, fearful and wild in its
  Obscurity, the glance will bring a chill
  And dizzy sickness on his brain, till his
  Unsteady feet shall seek in vain to hold
  Their place upon the rude rock's verge; his eyes
  See not, his blood grows cold and down he sinks
  Down, down, down—Help! help! I'm gone.

(He falls from his chair in a swoon. The servants rush in and endeavor to restore him.)

1st Servt.—One of you go for the Levite—quick! You know it is our master's orders to have him called on every occasion of importance.
  (Exit one of the servants.)

2nd Servt.[3]—Je ne sais pas, mais, I am vara sure dat someting is de mattaire de mon maitre, dis long temps. He no eat, he no sleep,

---

3. The Second Servant's combined use of French with the German-American dialect and the Third Servant's Irish accent are indicative of "the foreign vote" which allegedly put Van Buren into office.

he grow poor toutes les jours. Mon Dieu, vat will come of mon pauvre maitre.

1st Servt.—I don't know. I have watched him anxiously for weeks— something is heavy on his mind. For many nights past I have heard him walk up and down in this room after he has sent us all away, and he would talk and mutter to himself, and then I would think I heard other voices besides my master's; and with my hair on end for very fright—for I knew nobody else could be there but ghosts or some such things—I would steal to the key-hole and watch to see if there really were spirits talking to him.

2nd Servt.—Mon Dieu! Did you see dem?

1st Servt.—No. When I would come to the key hole and look at my master he would be walking and muttering and scowling and sometimes he would stop and start as though he had seen something, and sometimes he would answer as though some-body had spoke to him; but I could see no living soul with him; and always after a while he would call me, and send for the Le-vite the soothsayer, who would soon quiet him.

3rd Servt.—Our masther brathes! By the sowl of Saint Patrick, if ye dont lave off palavering, and hilp to put him on yon bid, I'll taich your eyes to forget day light, sure I will. (*Exit servants, bearing off the Magician—Scene closes.*)

Scene 2. *The Magician reclining on a splendid couch—the Levite by his side.*

Levite.—I joy to see your excellency so Recovered.

Mag.—Thank you good Levite.

Lev.—What heavy thoughts laboring in your mind,
    So shakes your You, who hitherto
    Have turned all time and circumstance to your
    Account and kept your fortune in good time
    With pop'lar favor,—do you now begin
    The first to tremble and distrust your power
    To keep the vantage you have gained? O fie,
    Do you not know the very way to lose
    Is to betray the fear you will?

Mag.—Did I not know the spirits those possess
    With whom I have to strive, I yet might hope.

Had I deceived them not, or only once
I might deceive them still—or had it been
My fortune, as I hoped, to keep them blind
With flattering words, until my plans were ripe
And with your aid, good Levite, I possessed
Both purse and sword, my will the only law
And constitution; then let them awake,
And I would laugh in mockery at their threats.
But they have seen my treachery while yet
They have the power to thwart it, and they will.

Lev.—You would not thus have reasoned some years since.

Mag.—Have you not heard there comes a period
To every villain, when remorse will prey
Like harpies on his soul,—when his black deeds
Will scowl like spectres round, or sit
Like fire upon his brain, and make him tremble?

Lev.—For shame I: Shake from your mind these gloomy thoughts;
Have you forgot the artifices we
So oft have used, and been successful, too?
Have you not often told me you despised
The people, condescending to make use
Of them alone as stepping stones to that
High pinnacle of power and fame which your
Ambitious spirit aims at? Why then remorse?
Has not your favorite scheme "The National
The Independent Treasury," been passed
Already by the Senate? Cannot gold
And promise of high place and favor at
Your hands bear it with equal triumph through
The House? Believe me sir, it must and will.

Mag.—I fear your zeal to serve me makes you blind:
Read that (*handing him a paper containing an account of the
Columbus meeting*) and see if I have nought to fear,
You see by that the people are awake,
And should the bill you speak of pass, it will
Not, cannot bring them that relief we need,
And which, they well know, we have promised long.
To fix myself in power beyond the reach

Of law, and aggrandize my friends, was all
I ever contemplated it could do.
Lev.—But you must tell them benefits as great
As those, in your extreme solicitude,
For their prosperity you're striving for,
Come never like the sudden gushing of
The mountain torrent. If they would possess,
They must patience wait till the broad plans
You lay, have time to yield their glorious fruit.
Mag.—Too much already have I promised them.
Did I not tell them when I took my seat
Upon the chair of state, retrenchment in
Th' expenses of the Government, and in
Their taxes, a reduction great should follow?[4]
Was not economy—economy—
In all my speech? Yet see how sadly that
Word chimes with facts, which now, in bold relief,
Stand out in open view of friend and foe.
Twelve millions was, when Adams left the chair,
Th' amount it took to keep the simple and
Yet mighty springs of Government in play.
And now the hungry maws of those who suck
The life-blood of the body politic,
Will hardly be content with thirty-five.
If they would crush the bank, and gratify
Both me and him, proud in whose steps I tread,[5]
Gold, too, I promised them should fall in showers—
Thick as the manna which the Hebrews fed.
And when they yielded to my pettish wish,
And madly threw away the currency,
The wisdom of their fathers gave to them,
Did I not give that same gold to my friends,
And tell the people they were "apt t' expect
Too much at the hands of the government."

4. A great speculative element led to the panic of 1837. Hard money was withdrawn from banks. In the meantime the U.S. government had transferred many of its deposits and had used large sums of money to buy western lands. The depression which followed was caused—according to the people—by the Democrats, the party in power.
5. Van Buren followed Andrew Jackson's fiscal policies.

> And think you Levite, they'll forget all this?
> And suffer me to wheedle them, and lead
> Them still with promises, they see I do
> Not mean to execute? Believe it not.

Lev.—Rouse, rouse your mind—these childish fantasies
> Become you not. Are there not thousands here
> (Thanks to the goodly policy we have used,)[6]
> And thro' the broad extent of this fair land,
> Whose being almost hangs on your success?
> I grant our opponents have chosen well,[7]
> Of all the world; the very one we could
> Least wish that they would choose. But where is fled
> The tact which we have hitherto employed?
> What though his character be unimpeached,
> Were it as stainless as the purest saints
> In heaven, have we not among us those
> Who soon could make it blacker than a fiend's?[8]
> —Is not the morrow the appointed day,
> Of invitation for your friends to meet
> And feast with you in public audience?

Mag.—To-morrow—yes, it is. To-morrow and
> To-morrow, and a few to-morrow's more
> In this proud mansion will our feasts be o'er.
> My heart forbodes it, and my mind misgives.

Lev.—Whatever be your fears, to-morrow throw
> At least this gloom aside, and let the smiles
> Of former days give brightness to your eye.

Mag.—Am I not always thus before the world?
> My pride hath not yet reached so low an ebb,
> As to exhibit to the vulgar gaze
> The torments which may rack us when alone.

Lev.—The midnight moon her greeting long has paid,
> Till at the least we meet, I take my leave. (*Going*)

6. Spoils system.
7. William Henry Harrison, a war hero and Indian fighter, was such a popular figure that it would be difficult to beat him in a political campaign.
8. Smear tactics.

Mag.—Adieu! good Levite, you shall find me then,
>   Not what I am, but what I seem to be. (*Scene closes*.)

Scene 3. *A room in the Magician's House. The Levite, Amos, Toperus,*
and other guests sitting around it—The Magician at the head.
Mag.—Welcome, good friends. It gives me great delight
>   To meet you here with such plain marks of gay,
>   And joyous spirits stamped upon your brows.
>   I hail it as suspicious, and a fair portend
>   Of the good fortune, and that sure success
>   Which shall attend our cause. C__n[9] how takes
>   This masterly and unexpected stroke
>   Of policy, this compact we have sealed,
>   Among your proud and haughty nullifiers?
C.—Most excellently well. On me and all
>   Advancement of preferment on me placed,
>   They look with joy and pride, regarding me
>   As their most favorite, though hitherto
>   Somewhat unlucky son; and when I told
>   Them their long hopes would prove reality
>   In this grand scheme, and hinted further too
>   That it might not prove altogether dry
>   And profitless to them, they drank success
>   Almost with one accord to all our schemes.
>   Fear not, my noble state will aid you well.
Mag.—I cannot doubt it, when the assurance comes
>   From you, for which accept my hearty thanks.
>   Among the favors which kind fortune has
>   On me bestowed, I count it not the least
>   That she has given friends, on whose zealous
>   Fidelity I could rely with quick
>   And well placed confidence. Amos have you
>   Heard aught by post, to day, how our affairs
>   Are thriving in the land?

9. John Calhoun of South Carolina. Van Buren tried to bridge the gap between the nullifiers of South Carolina and the northern Democrats. As a result, he pleased neither group.

Amos.[10]_____The last night's mail
   Brought papers from Chicago, which contain
   The cheering news that that queen city of
   The Prairie State, has borne our ticket through
   Triumphantly, and "as Chicago goes.
   So goes" (*But that's a lie—aside*) say they—"the State."
Mag.—That is indeed, good news. Come, gentlemen,
   Fill up your glasses to the very brim,
   In such proportion as ye all shall drink,
   Both deep and long, success to our good cause
   In that proportion shall I hold you friends—
   The greatest he who longest, deepest drinks.
Toperus.—If that be the criterion whereby
   You test us, then am I d__m'd sure that I
   Shall be in favor high.
Mag.—We long have felt,
   To you indebted, in a long account
   Of gratitude. Your worth is so well known
   You need not praise from us. Your deeds have tongues
   Which speak your praise transcendently beyond
   All that of which our lips are capable.
   The people know you well, and when they see
   Your last grand effort,[11] happily complete,
   And feel its lightning stroke, you need not fear
   Your immortality will be secure
   As long as men shall bow at Freedom's shrine.
Top.—You praise me, sir, by far beyond desert.
   I know not better how I should reply
   Than filling high once more my empty glass.
   Fill, gentlemen, I give you with good will
   Our noble President, with three times three.
All.—Our noble President. (*They drink.*)
Amos.—(*To Toperus, perceiving that he was drinking from the bottle
   instead of his Glass.*)

---

10. Amos Kendall was one of Van Buren's cronies and confidants.
 11. Proposal of an independent treasury or—in reality—a government bank was defeated until 1840 by those who were in favor of state rather than federal banks.

> Should that mistake be frequent, you will make
> Us jealous of the favor you may win
> Thereby from him whose favor is our life.

Top.—Confound me, gentlemen, if I dont beg
> Your pardon. 'Twas the zeal the toast inspired
> Which caused the cursed blunder. Let us quaff
> Another glass to drown its memory. (*They drink.*)
> There's nothing like good wine to cheer the heart—
> Except it be—good brandy!

C.—Who of our number will, with good song
> Regale our ears. Music and wine ever
> Should be consociate.

> 1st.—Top.—*Sings.*
> Hurrah, hurrah for the Kinderhook[12] seer,
> He has promised success, and we've nothing to fear;
> We have gold in our pockets and gold in the mint,
> And the promise of more without measure of stint,
> Though the people are pennyless, who care we,
> They have borne it too long to "dare now to be free."
>> The whigs may rise,
>> Till earth and skies,
> Re-echo their shout for Old Tippecanoe.[13]
>> Their efforts are vain,
>> To the seer again,
> As the needle to magnet, his friends shall prove true;
> Then fill up your glass to the Kinderhook seer,
> He has promised success, and we've nothing to fear.
> 2.
> In the name *democrat* there's a powerful charm,
> 'Twill allay all excitement, and quiet alarm;
> With a union of strength, in the day of our need,
> And with that as our watchword, we're sure to succeed.
>> From hill and glen,
>> Shall rally men,

---

12. Kinderhook, New York, was the birthplace of Van Buren.
13. Harrison ran unsuccessfully against Van Buren in 1836.

Who are ready to conquer or die in the field;
>   For while our watchword,
>   Can make itself heard,
To the *petticoat granny*, we never will yield.
>   Then fill up, &c.

3.
Who, who would not strive, where there's so much to win,
For the way we'll get office, will then be a sin;
We will wait till our pockets with specie run over,
And then like friend Swartwout, we'll "cut stick for Dover."
>   Then fill up your glasses,
>   While merrily passes,
The time that we riot on victory's
>   Let no thought intrude,
>   For the people's good,
Or in how much commotion our land
But first of all, fill to the Kinderhook
For he's promised success, and we've no fear.
>   (*End of Act 1st.*)

Act II.

Scene 1. *A room in the White House. Time, night before the 4th of March, A.D. 1841.—The Magician and Levite in conversation.*
Mag.—Did I not tell you, Levite,'twould be so?
>   To-morrow, aye to-morrow, must I bid
>   Adieu to this good mansion, and with it
>   To all my golden dreams of future fame.
>   Where now is the fulfilment of the soft
>   Insinuating flatteries, my friends
>   With such address, have whispered in my ear?
>   Fools! did they think that I believed them all?
>   In pity, no! I'd scorn to have it thought
>   That I was born to be deceived by such
>   Vile trash as any thing that wears the face
>   Or form of human. They were willing I
>   The people should deceive, whose interests

And weal they were entrusted to defend,
Because they thought they were deceiving me,
While I (—I've nothing now to gain or lose
By the *expose*, and make it fearlessly—)
Made use of both as yielding, quiet tools
To bring about my own ambitious views.

Lev.—The tide of our good fortune now has ebb'd,
Never again, I fear, alas! to flow.

Mag.—Fear! fear! (*scornfully*) 'tis ever thus with vulgar minds,
They fear, and doubt, and halt, while they should act.
Think you, if I had been to doubt and fear,
So sickly sensitive, I should have played,
For some time past, the desperate game I did?
Since first the field of civic strife awoke
My energies, I've had the goal in view
And short of which I never meant to stop.
Farther, if might be, so far I would go.
I used all means both fair and foul; I turn'd
All circumstances to my good account
To reach that goal—that goal at last I reached.
It was the highest, guided by the shield
The Constitution throws around to guard
Their liberty the people had to give.
I sought for more, but wisely they refused,
The only wise act they have done for years.
They now may hate or praise, I scorn alike
Their hatred as their praise; they're both more apt
To be misplaced than guided by desert.

Lev.—Too sanguine, too confiding, aye, and more,
Too honest have I been. I've been a fool!
I have let others hoard their fortunes from
The public purse, until that purse is dry,
And nothing left for me but poverty,
Embittered by contempt and ridicule.

Mag.—You had the fitting opportunities,
If you neglected them you do deserve
To suffer for your folly.

Lev.—Power I loved
    Too much to let it lightly slip my grasp.
    I lost the substance, while I grasped the shade.
Mag.—Madness! Did you not know that gold was power?
    (*A sudden light from without illumines the room, and shouting
    is heard.*)
    Note that, and tell me what you think of fame
    Among a set of changelings, such as these?
    How long is it since these illuminations
    Thus welcomed in the day *I* took my seat,
    And now they blaze for one in every way
    Antipodes to me. *I* made myself,
    In doing which, I learned to *love myself,*
    While *circumstances* made him what he is.
    He served his country well, and how was paid?
    By poverty and negligence! And if
    He serve it well again and get its praise,
    What has he gained? A vain and idle breath—
    An idle nothing. It will neither warm
    Nor clothe, nor lull to rest a single pain.
    Let others seek for praise, so will not I,
    If ever I have seemed to love its glare,
    Be sure it was to further some design.
    Who'd guide the state must humor its caprice,
    But guiding so he cannot help despise.
    To-morrow here will come an honest man,
    Let those who go, protect themselves who can.

Scene 2. *An old ruined house in the vicinity of Kinderhook. The Magician is discovered sleeping on a couch. Time, midnight. Enter a number of demons.*
1st Demon.—Fitting time is this to meet,
    While howls the wind, and drives the sleet,
    In tempest's wrath and cannon's roar,
    My pinions best delight to soar.
2nd Demon.—Since we cannot the "White House" keep,
    Here will we meet, but not to sleep;
    Were it my nature to be quiet,

I have good reason now to try it.
A nation where there once reigned gladness,
I've driven to the verge of madness.
I've scattered wide distress so dire,
'Twill be an age ere it expire.
It was so great that even I,
Who feast on human misery,
Was almost touch'd with sympathy;
But rest would be a hell to me,
E'en as I have been, must I be.

3rd Demon.—(*Looking upon the Magician.*)

I've seen sleep come to the warrior's breast,
When tired he laid him down to rest
Upon the plain, which an hour before,
Had flowed with torrents of human gore.
I've seen the weary traveller sink,
To quiet rest on the crater's brink.
But that a man whose life was spent,
And all his energies intent
To work destruction to his kind,
Should such a gentle slumber find,
Is strange, even to my demon mind.
A soul like that should not be chained,
Nor be by earth's dull clay restrained,
'Tis better fitted far to be
One of our goodly company.—
Mortal awake! (*The demons approach the Magician.*)

All.—Awake! (*He awakes.*)

Mag.—My old companions! Do I see you here?
What would ye with me now, our reign is o'er?

1st Demon.—Mortal wouldst thou like to live
The life which we alone can give.
Wilt thou make one of our number
Where thou no longer shalt need slumber,
Where thou shalt not feel again
The pains which rack the forms of men,
But immortal as we are
Be a bright though fallen star?

2nd Demon.—Mortal, come, our revels want thee,
>Let visions dim no longer haunt thee,
>But burst thy shell, and hail the light
>Which breaks in splendor on thy sight.

3rd Demon.—Our path is over the world's expanse,
>We take it in at an easy glance;
>When the winds and waves in fury meet,
>On the wings of the storm we take our seat.
>And when the ship with its snowy sail
>Is strown like reeds on the whirling gale,
>And the shriek of the dying to heaven is cast,
>Our laugh is heard in that tempest blast.

1st Demon.—Mortal, to our revels come.

2nd Demon.—Come and make with us thy home.

Mag.—There's one thing ye know well; the time is past
>When I should fear you, or mistrust ye would
>Exert your power to work me harm. 'Tis true
>I long have looked with scorn upon the dull
>And plodding souls with which I have been forced
>To mingle my proud spirit.—Can ye make,
>In all respects, me even as yourselves?

Demons.—We can.

Mag.—I am prepared for anything. Proceed!

1st Demon.—Mortal clay which long hath bound him
>And thrown thy fettering links around him
>Mingle with thy mother earth,
>As thou wert before his birth.
>His spirit thou no more shalt guide,
>No more in thee shall it abide,
>But free as ours it hence shall be,
>Immortal in eternity.

All.—We command thee, mortal dust—
>Hasten to give up thy trust!

(*The body of the Magician gradually disappears, and he stands forth among the demons as one of them. They all dance around him.*)

1st Demon. (*Singing*)
>Welcome, welcome, to our number,
>Earth shall no more thy soul encumber

Now thy soul shall taste the pleasure
Of seeing misery without measure.
Merry is the life we lead
As through the earth our way we speed
And leave a trail of human wo
Along our path, where'er we go.
All. Chorus
    We ride
    On the tide,
    We sail
    O'er the gale,
  But wherever we go
    There's wail
    In our trail
  Among mortals below.
Welcome, welcome, to our number.
Earth shall no more thy soul encumber.
    (*The Demons vanish.*)

Isaac N. Arnold: A Satire in Two Cantos

[Isaac Newton Arnold (1815–1884), who became a nationally known jurist, arrived in Chicago in 1836 and immediately became involved in the political and cultural affairs of the city. He did much toward developing the Young Men's Association in 1841, an organization that served as the forerunner of the public library movement in Chicago. His commitment to the city eventually won for him a seat in the state assembly. He became active in the Republican party when it was formed and eventually became a congressman and a vocal supporter of the American body politic. He was not only a lover of books and a prolific writer but also one of the earliest biographers of Abraham Lincoln.

To many of his detractors—including the unidentified author of this poem—Arnold was the epitome of municipal corruption in the young city because he had served as the local agent and lawyer for Arthur Bronson, whose role in the life of Chicago was odd indeed. Bronson, a New Yorker, had apparently visited the city in 1833. He saw, as did other New Yorkers such as William B. Ogden (Chicago's first mayor), the enormous possibilities of making money in local real estate. But unlike Ogden, Arnold, and others, Bronson never moved to

Chicago. Instead he became a silent partner and manipulator in a number of financial schemes which ultimately involved some of the "best people" in the city. He lent money at high rates of interest to those who wished to invest in the city. At the same time he gave willingly to the underprivileged. In essence, he was an early example of the Chicago philanthropist who bilks the people with one hand and soothes their ruffled feelings with the other. Bronson's ultrashady land dealings made fortunes for many but also involved him in several lawsuits, which were ably argued by Isaac Arnold.

The author of "Isaac N. Arnold" was undoubtedly a person of scholarly bent. The poem suggests his knowledge of classical literature as well as an understanding of the neoclassical tradition in writing. Clearly he resented Arnold's climb to power through an association with Arthur Bronson and other political puppets; neither was he shy in his treatment of a man who was one of the powerful and highly respected public figures of the day.

There is a strong possibility that this satire, published April 30, 1843, was written by David D. Griswold, who owned *Quid Nunc*, a Chicago daily newspaper that existed for just over thirty days in 1842.]

• • •

Canto I.

Isaac N. Arnold!—Phoebus what a name!
To fill, as Byron says, the trump of fame.
To fill indeed, as erst, when treason gave,
A namesake traitor, to perdition's grave.
But what's a name?—an onion, cabbage, rose,
By other titles, cannot cheat the nose,
Tho' words of linked sweetness lend their sound,
And Araby's rich odors, breathe around.
I cry ye mercy—Smith, or Jones, or Brown,
Or any one, of com'ner name, in town.
I'll ask you, would you change? How would you trade
For instance, Smith, for Judas!!—woulds't, if paid
The wealth of Indus, so endure the scorn
Of christian men?—The race of woman born?
And to association's tyrant pow'r.
Yield thee to such an odor for an hour?
Iscariot! or Arnold!—Of the two,

I swear I'd take my chances with the Jew.
It is great misfortune to be sent,
Into this breathing world, 'gainst our consent,
With taint, and taunt, upon a harmless name,
Lacking no merit, and yet feeling shame!
Hard, hard our fate; to be "conceived in sin,"
And curs'd with nicknames, as we're ushered in.
"Original" indeed, that sorry lot,
To die—and not in mercy be forgot.
For scent the name of Arnold as you will,
The *traitor-stench*, will hang around it still
Can it be merit, Isaac, in thy case?
Traits of great genius, join'd to match'ess grace?
That in thy mind and person so unite,
To set thee up, in very fate's despite;
For up, you are:—full, in the public eye,
At once, a *wonder*! and a *mystery*!
It were an easy task, to show thy track;
To trace thy mean, and tricky pathway back.
Detect the frauds,—the times from which you date,
Your public honors, and your cares of state.
How soon from being Arthur Bronson's tool,
You yearn'd for honors of a higher school.
And from a servile, of the humblest aim.
The people's representative, became!
How, with single mind, "the discerning few,"
Threw Caesar's conquering mantle over you;
And deck'd you out, "for better or for worse,"
Lieutenant! in company of horse!![14]
Great Caesar!—Alexander!—Bonaparte!
Types of the noble blood, and lion heart,
Burst not your cerements:—'twas *mock'ry* all;
A joke, a trick, the sport of "cup and ball";

14. In the spring of 1842 the Chicago Cavalry, one of several independent military companies in the city, was organized. Arnold was immediately honored by being commissioned first lieutenant. The company paraded in its new uniforms on July 4, 1842. Arnold's experience with horses, however, was limited to his days as a circuit-riding lawyer in Illinois!

We swear it, for the honor of the State,
By heav'n, we *are* not so degenerate.
And yet—we do remember as a dream,
That clamorous shout, that deafening scream,
That pour'd from every rude and rabble up,
It's coarse, broad humour on thy horsemanship.
Some merry fellows, venturing to suggest,
A *side-saddle*, might suit Miss Nancy best,
Some called for pouncet-box, some for cologne,
Some greeted with a hiss, and some a groan.
Some said, the glory of the Black Hawk war,
Would pale, before the splendor of thy star.
Others, that *much discretion* would control,
The vaulting aspirations of thy soul.
Bearing thee *safely* through the battle-fray—
And let thee live, "to fight another day."

Canto II.
Omnipotent Democracy! are these,
The triumphs, thy heroic fancy please?
Where are your leaders? Garrett, Hoard, stand forth;
I'st possible, there is no man of worth,
Among your boasted "*bone and muscle*" class,
More apt, and able, than this braying ass?
Is Dr. Eagan of no consequence,[15]

15. Augustus Garrett (1801–48) was an early land speculator who in the 1830s, according to the Chicago *American* (October 31, 1835), took in more than $1,800,000. Arnold worked in his office. By the 1840s, however, Garrett emphasized "integrity" in government. When this poem was published, he had just become mayor of Chicago. From 1842 to 1844 Samuel Hoard was a state senator, representing Lake and Cook counties, and was a handy tool in the hands of Chicago's financial establishment. Among the politicians named by the anonymous poet, no one is more fascinating than Dr. William Bradshaw Egan (1808–60). He was born in Ireland, studied medicine in England, and arrived in Chicago in 1833. As early as 1842 the Irish had formed a significant political bloc in the city, and Dr. Egan was one of their favorite sons, though he was also involved in various real estate maneuvers. At one point the Irish joined forces with other foreign immigrants and substituted the name of Egan to replace Arnold as the party nominee for the state legislature. This caused an early rupture in the party between the foreign- and native-born.
William Onahan described the Chicago of the 1850s in his article "Sixty Years in Chicago" (*Transactions of the Illinois State Historical Society*, XXII, 1916, 79–88). According to

The scholar, gentleman, and man of sense?
Nor Mark Skinner,[16] (the lachets of whose shoes,
Your puppet, is not worthy to unloose;)
Were claims like Dickey's, Strode's, and Judd's forgot,[17]
In all the secret hatchings of the plot?
Oh shame! when every selfish, mean pretence,
When falsehood, ignorance, and impudence,
Against the public good are falsely weighed,
And honest men, deserted and betrayed.
How in the world, this simpleton became,
Enamour'd in his own conceit, of fame,

---

him, Dr. Egan was a "physician . . . more given to real estate than to pills and potions." Among the many apocryphal stories that have been circulated about the good doctor, Onahan recalls:

At the opening of the Illinois and Michigan Canal a grand celebration was planned to be held at the Chicago end, or beginning—in Bridgeport at the time and for long afterwards settled by the Irish—many of whom had been engaged in work on the canal. For this celebration Dr. Egan (a man of fine education, a classical scholar, and an attractive public speaker) was selected as the orator of the occasion. The time was mid-summer, and naturally a crowd was expected. The Doctor had taken thought as to the conditions and being largely interested in Bridgeport lots he conceived a plan for unloading a few.

The night before the celebration he sent out a barrel of Bourbon whiskey—which then was very cheap, and had it dumped into a well that had been opened to provide the thirsty and perspiring crowd with liquid solace.

The heat of the day and the crowds quickly drew people to the well—and there sure enough it was flowing with a tempting toddy! This was a revelation and a temptation—and it is said every Irishman in the crowd—hurried to the Doctor's agent, who—providently had a real estate shanty nearby—in order to secure a lot in the near vicinity of the wonderful well!

16. Mark Skinner (1813–87) was born in Manchester, Vermont, and graduated in 1833 from Middlebury College. He studied law and moved to Chicago in 1836. Admitted to the bar in 1839, like the other men mentioned in the poem he was also a member of the Democratic party. In 1840 he became the city attorney and eventually became a judge. He was an outstanding and active politician.

17. Hugh Thompson Dickey (1811–92) was born in New York City. After completing his studies at Columbia, he read law and was admitted to the bar. He first visited Chicago in 1836 and decided to settle there in 1840. Until 1885—when he returned to New York City—Dickey served as a lawyer then a judge in the city. James M. Strode (ca. 1808–64), began as a circuit-riding attorney in the state. He served as register for the U.S. Land Office in Chicago in the late 1830s and early 1840s and was later very active in city politics. Norman Buel Judd (1815–78) was born in Rome, New York, where he read law and was admitted to the bar. He moved to Chicago in 1836 and soon became extremely influential. After holding various jobs in city government, he was a member of the Illinois state senate from 1844 to 1860. He was a personal friend of Abraham Lincoln, who appointed him minister plenipotentiary to Prussia, where he served until 1865. In 1870 he was elected to the Forty-first Congress.

Is passing strange!—Philosophy may show,
How sturdy oaks, from little acorns grow;
How, too, of conscience, but a single gleam,
May dash the spirit, of a maniac's dream;
How all things, to their nat'ral level tend;
How bubbles burst, and humbugs have an end
But how contrive, to make wise men of fools,
Passes the cunning, of our modern schools.
But, turn we, from this sick'ning theme the while;
Fain would the muse, these party griefs beguile.
Fain point "the people" to a cheerful spot,
Where deep disgrace, like this, may be forgot.
That lane is long, that hath no turning in't;
Surely, there's hope, and comfort in the hint.
Soon, may they find him out, and "*set him back*,"
The humble drudge, upon his humble track.
Perhaps, like other dogs, he's had his day;
Grant it, Kind Heav'n!—"and we will ever pray."
And now,—farewell to thee, thou luckless wight;
To all thy bastard honors—a good night.
Spurn not, our ruder manners in thy wrath,
We'll mend them—*when we write thy epitaph.*

The *Times* and the *Tribune* Fight the Civil War

By the 1850s both political parties were in a dilemma. The passage of the Fugitive Slave Law (1850) and the Kansas-Nebraska Act (1854) created a need for a strong antislavery party. The Republican party, founded in July of 1854, was composed of former Whigs and those northern Democrats who felt they could not support either the law of 1850 or the act of 1854.

The northern faction of the Democratic party was truly "over the barrel" in the days before, during, and immediately after the Civil War. Even the so-called "War Democrats" suffered. To support the party meant going against the goals of the Union and the presidency of Abraham Lincoln. The Republicans and their supporters, in order to maintain the political clout that had been gained with the election of Lincoln, equated any opposition with treason and suggested that the Democrats—usually referred to as "Copperheads"—were in favor of a violent overthrow of the government. Northern Democrats, however, felt that the party could settle any conflicts and aimed for a return to power in order "to set things straight." Those Democrats who were not enthusiastic about this possibility were viewed as being disloyal and accused of covertly supporting the Republicans. Perhaps nowhere in the nation did the animosity between the two political parties become more apparent than in Chicago, as the two leading newspapers—the Chicago *Tribune* and the Chicago *Times*—hurled charges and insults at each other. Much of the consequent humor was indeed grim.

As might be expected, Lincoln came to represent for both newspapers the best and the worst (depending upon the editorial point of view) of the Civil War period. When the two newspapers carried the news of the Lincoln-Douglas debate on August 23, 1858, the *Times* headline read: LINCOLN BREAKS DOWN—DOUGLAS SKINS THE LIVING DOG. The *Tribune* reported: DRED SCOTT CHAMPION PULVERIZED. The *Times*'s violent opposition to Lincoln caused Carl Sandburg to conclude, in his *Abraham Lincoln: The War Years*, that if John Wilkes Booth had read the *Times* "he would have felt himself correct and justified to go forth to put a bullet through Lincoln's head." [18]

As the two newspapers reported war activities, each tried "to scoop" the other. Wilbur Storey's admonition to a journalist during this period tells a great deal about his "news sense." When the journalist asked what to do about dispatches during any lull in fighting, Storey reportedly answered: "If there is no news, send rumors."

18. Carl Sandburg, *Abraham Lincoln: The War Years* (New York: Harcourt, Brace, and World, 1939), 304. The fact that Wilbur Storey, as many other northern Democrats, wanted to maintain the Union whereas such Republican journals as the *Tribune* berated Lincoln for not moving fast enough toward the emancipation of the slaves has frequently been ignored. What is remembered are the various attacks made upon Lincoln and the Union by the Democratic press. It was not, however, until Lincoln issued the Emancipation Proclamation, which was to become effective on January 1, 1863, that he lost the support of many northern Democrats. While many Chicago Republicans were attacking Lincoln, Storey voiced the opinion of the city's Democrats when he editorialized on June 26, 1861, "the war has no relation to slavery. What becomes of the negro is of no importance." A few days earlier he had said, "Mr. Lincoln will not make this an anti-slavery war," and promised that as long as the president avoided doing so "a united nation will strengthen his arms." At the same time he cautioned against any support of the abolitionists and threatened that if Lincoln forgot the importance of the Union "the spell of patriotism which has, so far, saved the republic" would be broken (June 22, 1861).

Wilbur F. Storey (1819–1884) obtained control of the Chicago *Times* in 1861 and made the newspaper one of the outstanding Democratic dailies in the Northwest. Horace White (1834–1916) went to the *Tribune* in 1857, became associate editor in 1863, and was editor-in-chief from 1864 to 1874. In some ways the antagonism between the two newspapers went beyond political parties and represented the differences between Storey and White.

Both men were originally from New England. Storey was born in Vermont and decided in 1838 to try the West. In 1853 he purchased an interest in the Detroit *Free Press* and remained in Michigan until he took over the Chicago *Times*. Fiery, vindictive, a yellow journalist before that type of journalism became popular, Storey made the *Times*. His assertion "I am the *Times*" aptly explains the control he exercised over all phases of the newspaper as well as over the journalists who worked for him.

Horace White was not such a colorful figure, but he was one of the outstanding journalists and administrators of the period. Born into a book-oriented family in New Hampshire, he was brought as a youngster to Wisconsin where his father founded Beloit College, from which Horace graduated in 1853. In January of the following year he arrived in Chicago as the city editor of the *Journal*, and for twenty years the city's journalism benefited from his commitment to lucid, good prose. Under White's leadership the *Tribune*'s columns were examples of some of the best writing in the city.

By the 1850s the *Tribune* had become a powerful newspaper, and through a series of judicious mergers (such as with the *Gem of the Prairie* in 1852, *Free West* in 1855, and *Daily Democratic Press* in 1858) it had a distinguished roster of men and women associated with it. Politically the *Tribune* was one of the earliest supporters of the candidacy of Abraham Lincoln for the presidency of the United States; yet—like many other northern newspapers—the *Tribune* became disenchanted shortly after Lincoln began his term. Horace White, however, remained closely attached to Lincoln, and the newspaper staunchly supported the tenets of the newly formed Republican party.

From 1865 to 1883 James W. Sheahan (1824–1883) served as one of the chief editorial writers for the *Tribune*. He had had a long and varied career in journalism beginning in Washington, D.C., as a congressional reporter. He then moved to Springfield, Illinois, and finally to Chicago where, in 1854, he accepted—at Senator Stephen A. Douglas' urging—the editorship of *Young America*, a forerunner of the Chicago *Times*. In 1860 he established the *Morning Post*, which eventually became the vehicle for the "War Democrats" who opposed the position taken by the *Times*. Although he had not made a complete political reversal, his animosity toward the *Times* was real and he did much to bring balance to the editorial page of the *Tribune*. On September 4, 1866, his editorial "Coming to the Funeral" appeared. Certainly it is not "funny," but its knifelike wit and use of understatement illustrate another kind of 1860s newspaper humor. Marked by the bitterness displayed toward President Andrew Johnson in many northern cities, the editorial became a classic in its own day and can serve as an example of the journalist's role as the conscience of a community. The restrictions of today and our surface display of good manners would probably render such an approach to humor unacceptable, but occasionally one sees vestiges of this humorless humor on the editorial pages of modern newspapers. For many years after the editorial's publication, Sheahan's hard-biting wit was recalled by his associates.

The following selections from the Chicago *Tribune* and the Chicago *Times* are illustrative of the political satire used by the journalists of the era.

Song of the Democracy—Selected for the Chicago Times

[From a political point of view, the announcement of the Emancipation Proclamation came at an importune time. The 1862 congressional elections were to be held, and the Democrats rejoiced at the prospect of sweeping into office those who supported the Union but diametrically opposed abolition in any form. Northern Democrats began to believe that the majority of the American people would oppose any war designed to set the slaves free, and the election of 1862 was to be a test of Lincoln's northern support. On election day (November 4, 1862) Wilbur Storey published a parody of "We Are Coming Father Abraham, Three Hundred Thousand More." The popular recruiting song had appeared anonymously in July of 1862 but was later ascribed to James Sloan Gibbons (1810–1892), an outstanding abolitionist.

Storey's parody, "Song of the Democracy—Selected for the Chicago

Times," made the position of the northern Democrats clear. How effective were his efforts is a moot point, although the Democrats made appreciable gains during the 1862 election. From this point on, Storey assumed an anti-Lincoln position that grew more and more vindictive and did not subside until the president's assassination.]

• • •

1

We are coming Father Abraham, Three Hundred Thousand
    Strong.
To save you from the clutches of the abolition throng.
You've heard from Pennsylvania and from Indiana, too,
And Ohio has been speaking through her ballot box to you!
The sturdy men of iron, from the Furnace and the Mine,
When the Hoosiers and the Buckeye boys are swinging into
    line!
They are marching to the music of the Union as of yore,
And Illinois is coming after them, Three Hundred Thousand
    more.

2

We are marching Father Abraham, to that familiar tune
With which, so often, in former years we've reared the same
    old coon!
Once more from hill and valley, it rings forth with cheering
    sound,
To gladden every household where a loyal heart is found.
See! Every star is blazoned with the banner we unfold;
For the Union that our Jackson saved, our SHERMAN will
    uphold!
To scatter all the nation's foes—the Union to restore.
We're coming Father Abraham, Three Hundred Thousand
    more.

3

We are coming Father Abraham, and as we march along,
We'll relieve you of the "pressure" of the abolition throng!
You told them that you couldn't make a pig's leg of its tail,
And that against the comet papal bulls would not avail.
They wouldn't heed your anecdotes or listen to your pleas,

They swore that white men should be slaves and niggers
    should be free.
But you need not mind their ravings now, nor trouble at their
    roar,
For we're coming Father Abraham, Three Hundred Thousand
    more.

4

We are coming Father Abraham, to cast away your fears,
'Tis the democratic "slogan" that is ringing in your ear!
They pretend to call us traitors! But we point you to the blood
That soaks into Virginia's soil, or—that dyes Potomac's flood—
That stains the hills of Maryland, the Plains of Tennessee—
Such "traitors," Father Abraham, the Union loves to see.
It's a growing "traitor" army that is thundering at your door,
And Illinois'll swell the columns by Three Hundred Thousand
    more.

5

We are coming Father Abraham, to vindicate the laws,
To hold the Starry Banner up—to guard the Nation's cause;
Our motto is "The White Man's Rights"—For this we've battled
    long—
For this we'll fight with sinewy arms, with earnest hearts and
    strong—
For this we'll burst Fort Warren's bars, and crumble
    Lafayette—
For we'll crush the Nation's foes and save the Union yet.
Thus speaks the North! Oh, Abraham, you'll heed its mighty
    roar,
When Illinois shall swell the chorus by Three Hundred
    Thousand more.

The Abraham Laudamus

[According to the Chicago *Times* (March 2, 1864), the Union soldiers
were disenchanted with Lincoln as the commander-in-chief, but they
had not lost complete faith in him. Following the president's reelection,
the soldiers allegedly recited the following adaptations of the *Te
Deum* and the Lord's Prayer.]

I.

We praise thee, O Abe. We acknowledge thee to be sound on
the goose.

All Yankee land doth worship thee, everlasting old joker.

To thee all office-seekers cry aloud, "Flunkeydom and all
power therein."

To thee *Stanton* and *Welles* continually do cry, "Bully, Bully,
Bully, boy with the glass eye." [19]

Washington and Illinois are full of the majesty of thy glory.

The glorious company of political generals praise thee.

O Abe, save thy people, and bless thy parasites. Govern them
and increase their salaries forever.

Day by day we puff thee.

And we exalt thy name ever in the daily papers.

Vouchsafe, O Abe, to keep this day without a change of
Generals.

O Abe, have mercy on the army of the Potomac.

O Abe, let thy mercy be upon us, as our trust is not in *Stanton*.

O Abe, for thee have I voted, let me never be redrafted.

II.

Our Father who art in Washington, Uncle Abraham be thy name; the
victory won; thy will be done at the South as at the North; give us this
day our daily rations of crackers and pork; and forgive us our short-
comings as we forgive our quartermasters; for thine is the power, the
soldiers and the negroes, for the space of three year. Amen.

On Abraham Lincoln

[The *Times* would have cause to regret this July 1, 1864, statement and
other similar attacks upon Lincoln. And lest the public be fooled by

---

19. Edwin McMasters Stanton (1814–69) was a Democratic appointee. As the attorney general he feared that Buchanan was not dealing correctly with the threat of se-
cession and covertly met with leaders of the Republican party. When Simon Cameron
was dismissed as the secretary of war, Lincoln appointed Stanton to assume that position in January of 1862. Stanton was extremely unpopular with the military forces. Gid-
eon Welles (1802–78) was originally a Democrat but broke with the party and aided
in the 1854 establishment of the Republican party. He was highly supportive of Lincoln
and held that the Emancipation Proclamation was an important war measure. As the
secretary of the navy he was responsible for the highly successful blockade of the
Confederacy.

Storey's regret at the assassination, the *Tribune* republished this statement on April 29, 1865, a few days after Lincoln's death.]

• • •

[Lincoln] could not be more worthless dead than living, but would be infinitely less mischievous, and his corpse, repulsive as it would be in its freshest state and richest and most graceful habilments, would yet be the most appropriate sacrifice which the insulted nation could offer in atonement for its submission to his imbecility and despotism.

The Times *"Defines" the* Tribune

[Wilbur Storey decreed that the *Tribune* should never be referred to by name but rather by the term: "*the poor old morning abolition newspaper concern of this city.*" Finally in February of 1864 the *Tribune* ceremonially lodged a public complaint against the *Times* for refusing to use the newspaper's name. Storey announced the following "definition" on February 10, 1864.]

• • •

The poor old morning abolition newspaper concern of this city [objects] to being called the poor old morning abolition newspaper of this city. . . . We style it poor old morning abolition newspaper concern of this city because it is "wanting in good, valuable, or desirable properties," and is "not good, excellent, or proper" as a newspaper. For these reasons it comes squarely within the definition of our first adjective appellative. Old is a relative term. It claims to be the oldest newspaper established in Chicago. It is issued in the morning, and is devoted to abolitionism. It is a concern because it is "an establishment or firm for the transaction of business." Our definitions are taken from standard authorities, and, with the facts, not only justify, but we think, commend the appropriateness of our nomenclature. If it is objected that the title is cumbersome and inelegant, we can only reply that our habits as democratic journalists, as well as the rule of our party, compel us to sacrifice all other considerations to accurate and truthful statement.

The Tribune *Retaliates*

[On March 15, 1864, the *Tribune* reacted to the fact that the *Times* building was under police protection because of threats to the editor, the building, and the newspaper.]

• • •

Loyal men of this city look at that sheet [Chicago *Times*] and the establishment whence it emanates as very much like a skunk and they are loathe to foul themselves by touching it, even to kill. But Storey's guilty conscience magnifies the molehill of threats into a mountain of danger.

[Even the weather was not free from political attacks. As early as March 15, 1861, the following appeared in a *Tribune* editorial.]

•••

Spring is coming. The trees have caught a hint of it and are quietly busy with their buds. In little summer nooks paths of turf wax fresher and greener every day. Yellow daffodils in the gardens are getting impatient in their imprisoned folds and the first kiss of sunshine will bring them out. The other day we heard a frog. Nature goes right on year after year, not in the least mindful of the fortunes of the states or the plots of statesmen. The buds burst in their season whether human governments burst or not. Thank Providence that this is all kept out of the hands of the voters.

[The winter of 1863–1864 was particularly harsh, and some of the streets were still impassable in April when the *Tribune* held "Copperhead street cleaners" responsible for the conditions. The articles that appeared are reminiscent of those in 1979 that attributed the defeat of Mayor Michael Bilandic to the snow!]

The Tribune *Defines a "Democrat"*

[In spite of the influence of the *Tribune* and some outstanding businessmen who openly supported the paper, Chicago was essentially a Democratic city. Seldom could the Republicans garner enough strength to win a municipal election. On October 20, 1868, the *Tribune* ran the following.]

•••

A true Democrat is never so delighted as when he has one hand upon your throat and the other in your pocket. Brought forth in sin, baptized in ignorance, cradled in dirt and swathed in rags, the great majority of the self-styled Democrats of Chicago come forth from their foul abodes full fledged to prey upon the better portion of society, sometimes to do a little honest work in our tunnels and canals, to vote, to nominate themselves by universal acclamation as candidates for the Bridewell and state prisons, and to give our good-natured police functionaries all the trouble they can. That is Chicago Democracy.

"Laugh and the World Laughs with You"_____

Initially, much of Chicago's humor was devoted to political satire; however, the earliest newspapers in the city used jokes as filler and eventually inserted nonpolitical cartoons between serious articles. Comic verse also became a staple item.

Although the use of specialized columns and columnists is associated with the latter part of the century, Chicago newspapers frequently served as an outlet for those outstanding journalists who were comic observers of the local as well as the national scene and whose work was frequently little more than a collection of humorous tales and observations. By 1854 W. W. Danenhower's *Literary Budget* was featuring a column of humor entitled "Quirks and Quiblets." In 1857 the Reverend A. C. Barry's "Whittlings from the Chimney Corner" appeared in the *Sunday Leader*.

By the 1860s both George P. Upton of the *Tribune*, who used "Peregrine Pickle" as his *nom de plume*, and Franc B. Wilkie of the *Times*, better known to many of his readers as "Poliuto," were being featured weekly by their respective papers. The letters of Peregrine Pickle appeared in the Sunday *Tribune* from 1867 to 1869 and covered a wide range of subjects. From 1867 to 1869 the Sunday *Times* issued the weekly essays by Wilkie that were eventually published in 1869 as *Walks About Chicago*. Both men showed a perception of urban life, yet each was willing to laugh at those Chicagoans who took themselves too seriously. The observation has been made frequently that the line between comedy and tragedy is thin; to move from Wilkie's description of "the Westside" to those of later periods which emphasize the slums is to cross that narrow line. Although there are some elements of humor in later descriptions, it is humor generally devoid of mirth.

The post–Civil War period saw a decline in the animus that had sparked much of the disagreement between the *Tribune* and the *Times*. But the newspapers continued to battle each other over inconsequential issues. By the time, however, of Storey's death in 1884 the two newspapers had entered a period of quiet coexistence. The postwar era also saw Chicago writers beginning to turn their attention to other aspects of American life. Of especial interest during this period was the growing popularity of the railroad, the subject of many humorous, albeit realistic, tales; but perhaps no one was as perceptive as Benjamin Taylor, who considered this newest phenomenon in his *The World on Wheels and Other Sketches* (1874).

On the surface the serious nature of such journals as *America* (1888–1892) overshadowed the comic element that appeared in every issue. Yet the work of Harry B. Smith and the other poets of light verse did much to balance that particular journal and keep it from being merely a weekly bitter diatribe. From the romantic wits of the 1840s to the realistic wits of the 1880s comic writers demonstrated their sincere belief in the universal and appealing quality of laughter.

Horatio Cooke

As early as 1843 there was issued from the printing firm of Ellis and Fergus a slim volume by Horatio Cooke entitled *Gleanings of Thought; in a Series of Poems and Miscellaneous Pieces*. This work, which has the dubious distinction of being the first collection of poetry published in Chicago, was done—according to Cooke—"merely for amusement."

Little is known of Cooke's life, but it is safe to assume that he was an eastern artisan who did not remain in Chicago. As might be expected, most of the poems—which vary in intensity and appeal—are didactic and trite with little to recommend them to posterity. Cooke did, however, demonstrate an ability to deal lightly with subjects of some seriousness.

On Alexander Pope's Famous Line,
"A Little Learning Is a Dangerous Thing."

I do not pretend to criticise the great poet, Pope; for surely he was a great poet. But I do mean to rebuff this line, as it is frequently quoted by mere pretenders to taste and judgment. H. Cooke.

> "A little learning is a dangerous thing"—
>> So says Pope, and who will dare deny it?
> I will, for one; and so my battery bring
>> Of thought or reason, as you will, to try it.
> My long gun, charged with double-headed shot,
>> Shall blaze away to prove the thing all wrong,—
> An emanation from misguidance got,

And thence ejected on the careless throng;—
Who, ever apt to countenance fam'd greatness,
    Cares very little for the matter's strength,
So it be worded quite precise in neatness,
    And to a syllable exact in length.
That I feel sorry for this lack of judging
    The throng of reading votaries among,
I will evince, for once, by fearless nudging
    Their memories, to show them where they're wrong.
But first, my dear, dear Pope, as clever poet
    As e'er ten-syllabled or jingled rhyme,
Though it be dangerous, I mean to show it
    Was sometimes false to sense, though true to time.
If little learning is a dangerous thing,
    I wonder what the mass of men must be,
Who, spite of modern learning's wide-spread wing,
    Do pass with little quite contentedly.
I've seen a John Bull o'er plumb-pudding smiling;
    I've seen a Yankee whittling a stick;
I've seen a Frenchman with his mistress whiling;
    I've seen a Scotchman a red herring pick;
Yet all of these, though they'd a little learning,
    Did seem quite peaceable and clever folk.
And each was satisfied with his discerning,
    For all except the Frenchman seldom spoke;
And he, good man, did speak so blithe and gay,
    And danc'd about and smack'd his chops at kissing,
You would have thought it was his wedding day,
    And that dull Care had been forever missing.
Not Brother Jonathan, nor Johnny Bull,
    Shrewd Sawny, or the son of sunny France,
Did seem with danger quite so brimming full
    As this quaint text so boldly does advance.
Shrewd Sawny and John Bull stuck to their victualing;
    The Frenchman blithely kiss'd his girl and danc'd;
And Brother Jonathan kept on his whittling;
    But not an eye of either danger glanc'd.
Though this don't prove precise that learning scant

Be dangerous or not, yet still I must think that
A little's better than an utter want.
    A little must be gain'd, to form a link that
Shall cling to more, and so, proceeding on still,
    Foot quick, past foot, or mayhap hand o'er hand,
Shall quick become what Wisdom smiles upon still,
    A beacon bright to guide to her own land.
"A little learning is a dangerous thing"—
    A famous line for those who poor folks fetter;
But those who stick by Freedom, back will fling
    The nonsense-breeder; every word and letter
Then rallying array, to this truth cling—
    "A little learning's good, but more much better."

A Civil War Chaplain Speaks to the Lord

Because of the nature of the Civil War and because much of the knowledge about it came through dispatches sent to such newspapers as
the *Times* and *Tribune*, little of the humor of the war became a significant part of Chicago's journalism. There were the inevitable jokes and
—after the war—the expected tales of unusual exploits, but there was
not a significant or lasting comic tradition from that period.

Interestingly, many of the war stories—and this was not peculiar to
the city—began with insistent assertions that "God is on our side."
This found expression in a multitude of jokes and humorous tales
which are distinguished by their similarity. The following tale was
apparently rather popular in wartime Chicago in spite of its many
variations.   • • •

The 19th Illinois Division from Chicago was stationed outside of Missionary Ridge during a particularly heavy battle. When a lull in the
fighting occurred, the chaplain suggested that the soldiers join him in
a divine service of song and prayer. The chaplain selected for singing
the hymn which begins:

> Show pity, Lord, oh Lord forgive;
> Let a repentant rebel live . . .

He had barely finished "lining" the song when the small voice of a soldier—a zealous Christian—cried out: "No Lord, not unless they all lay

down their arms." At the end of the service, the chaplain prayed again. This time shots were heard in the distance as fighting was resumed. The devout chaplain said as his benediction:

> "Lord, if those are Union shots, send the
> bullets straight; an' if they ain't, hit
> a tree with 'em, Lord."

George Putnam Upton

Born in Boston in 1834, George P. Upton had, by the time he reached his twentieth birthday, completed his studies for the M.A. degree from Brown University. After spending a year as a teacher, he set out for Chicago in 1855 where he became affiliated with the newspaper world. He began with a position on the *Native Citizen*; six months later he became the city editor of the Chicago *Evening Journal*, where he initiated the first musical columns to appear in the city. In 1862 he joined the staff of the Chicago *Tribune* and remained with the paper until his death in 1919. During his fifty-seven years with the *Tribune* he did much—as the music, drama, and art critic—to make Chicagoans aware of the city's potential as a cultural center. At the *Tribune* he also served in a number of specific capacities, some of which overlapped. He was, for example, a city editor and war correspondent (1862–1863), then he became the main music critic (1863–1881), worked as an editorial writer in 1870, and was associate editor from 1872 to 1905.

Upton was a prolific writer and beginning in the 1880s produced a number of reference works still used by those interested in the general subject of music history. Interestingly enough, many of these went through several editions, which suggests that some may have been used as "subscription" books. Among the more important are: *Women in Music* (1880), *Standard Operas* (1886), *Standard Oratorios* (1887), *Standard Cantatas* (1888), *Standard Symphonies* (1889), *Musical Pastels* (1902), *Standard Light Operas* (1902), *Standard Concert Guide* (1908), *Standard Concert Repertory* (1909), *Standard Musical Biographies* (1910), *In Music Land* (1913), and *The Song, Its Birth, Evolution, and Functions with Numerous Selections from Old English Lyrics* (1915).

In the wake of the Chicago fire many writers used their talents to "recall" the history of the city in order to "replace" lost records. Upton, collaborating with fellow *Tribune* colleague James Sheahan, made a notable contribution to this effort. He also coauthored with another *Tribune* columnist, Elias Colbert, *Biographical Sketches of the Leading Men of Chicago* (1876). Upton's edition of *Theodore Thomas: A Musical Autobiography* (1905) is still considered one of the best works on the career of Thomas. His own autobiography, *Musical Memories* (1908), tells a great deal not only about his involvement in such groups as the Apollo Music Club but also about the city of Chicago during the last half of the nineteenth century. In addition, he found the energy to become an outstanding translator, and his work was in demand.

A gentleman and a renowned classical scholar, Upton brought to nineteenth-century Chicago and to all of his work an urbane sophistication that sometimes seems strange in a commercial marketplace. At the same time, his work as "Peregrine Pickle" presents a variety lacking in his other work and illustrates his ability as a wit.

The weekly letters of Upton's created character appeared in the Sunday *Tribune* and covered a wide range of topics. Begun by Upton shortly after joining the *Tribune* staff, the letters gave him a forum. This was not his first attempt to use such a character. His first adventure with the creation of an observant character was his "Gunnybag Papers," which he did while on the staff of the Chicago *Evening Journal*, shortly after his arrival in Chicago. The "Gunnybag Papers" and his "Letters of Peregrine Pickle" antedate the work of Eugene Field, Finley Peter Dunne, and George Ade.

The popularity of Peregrine Pickle was sufficiently strong that at the end of 1869 the Western News Company issued a collection of the letters subtitled "This and That and the Other." The book is significant as a forerunner of *The Line Book* and the ephemera from "In the Wake of the News," both of which have offered in the twentieth century selections from the notable *Tribune* column originated by Bert Leston Taylor. Upton recognized the difficulty of such a collection and attempted to select for inclusion those letters that might have appeal beyond a particular time and place. In his introduction, he presents the nine characters who appear with some regularity throughout the work and who lend it an aura of unity. The cast is headed by Old Blobbs who is described as "large-hearted, large-handed," a plain speaker who "hates shams." His wife is a "good woman when left alone and her idea of etiquette is not shocked." There are three young girls: Aurelia who is "plain, practical, well-educated[;] . . . she shed all of her nonsense when her first baby made an appearance." Celeste is a "little flighty," and "would be a Girl of the Period if that did not involve vulgarity." Mignon, the "pet of our set," is "keenly alive to whatever is beautiful, always lively and always graceful." Finally, there is Blanche, "her companion," who is a "quiet and lovable girl." Boosey is a "good-hearted, weak-kneed, young fellow, quite harmless and very self opinionated while Fitz-Herbert is an incapable we cannot shake off." The last character is Maiden Aunt who has "gone to a better world than this."

Mrs. Grundy

Let me whisper in your ear and tell you that Mrs. Grundy is a humbug. I think it would be the most blessed thing that could happen in this vale of tears if Mrs. Grundy should die. What a relief it would be to all of us! Existence would be a boon instead of a bore.

While Mrs. Grundy lives, every man and woman is an arrant hypocrite. While that fearful woman stands looking at us, every man and woman is an arrant coward. We flatter ourselves, or attempt to flatter ourselves—for there is not a man or woman who really believes it—that we are saying and doing things from principle, when in reality we are saying and doing them because Mrs. Grundy, in the shape of our next door neighbor, is looking at us and talking about us. You and I go to church and sit through services which may be the essence of stupidity, and we put on serious faces, and sit very primly, and regard our mortal enemy in the next slip with a lenient face, and pretend to listen to Dr. Creamcheese's commonplaces, and go out very solemnly—and all because Mrs. Grundy is looking at us from every direction, and when we get home, out of Mrs. Grundy's sight, we are ourselves again. We go through the formalities of a fast, and rigidly abstain from the good things while Mrs. Grundy's eyes are upon us, but the moment they are removed, we go into the larder and indulge in the best it affords. Celeste meets with another Dear Creature and lavishes all her affections upon her, when she does not care a snap of her pretty little finger about her, merely because Mrs. Grundy is looking at her. We are all of us, every day of our lives, going through with tedious conventionalities, which we know are conventionalities, which we do not believe in, merely because that woman Grundy is looking at us. She makes us hypocrites in every function of life. Thackeray struck

Mrs. Grundy a blow in the face when he drew with his satirical and powerful pencil Louis XI in his royal robes and Louis XI in *puris natu-ralibus*. In one picture we saw Louis XI in the light of Mrs. Grundy. In the other we saw him as himself. We wear a double suit; one which we know is a lie, for the world; the other, which we know is the truth, for ourselves.

The world will get very near to the millenium when Mrs. Grundy dies. Until that time the lion and the lamb will not lie down together. If they do, the lion will try to convince himself that he is a lamb, al-though he is aching to breakfast on him, and the lamb will try to con-vince himself *he* is a lion. [November 30, 1867.]

The Old

[In the spring of 1869 the *Tribune* moved from its dingy location at 50 Clark Street to a new building at Dearborn and Madison streets. The four-story structure, advertised as "fireproof" and as the "classic Roman (style) adapted to business," was the pride of the staff. Pere-grine Pickle, however, wrote of his visit to the former building on May 1, 1869.]

•••

I did not see any spirits in the old building; quite the contrary. There was a great deal of life there. It was night when I went there, but by the moonlight I saw some strange sights. Our late co-tenants, the rats, mice, cockroaches and spiders, were holding a general mass-meeting in the various rooms, discussing the changed aspect of affairs. An an-tique rat, of venerable appearance and gray whiskers, covered with the scars of many a hard-fought fight, and with a tail sadly mutilated by the numerous inkstands and paper-weights which had followed him into his hole many a time and oft, occupied the Managing Editor's old desk, the empty pigeon-holes of which brought him into admirable perspective. He acted as Chairman of the meeting, and presided with dignity, holding a dusty document in his hand for a gavel, which had been laid away fifteen years ago as of immense value, and never thought of since—just as you and I, you know, who think we are of so much value, will be laid away shortly in a pigeon-hole, and never thought of again. Several rows of rats, who had come down from a for-mer generation, occupied an old table, sitting erect, and manifesting a proper appreciation of the spirit of the meeting. The younger rats were compelled to shift for themselves, and were sprinkled about the floor. The gas pipe running up the wall was festooned with mice who looked down upon the assembly with interested countenances, while the three blind mice of song notoriety could be distinguished by their tails, that is, as much of their tails as escaped the carving knife, which protruded from a hole in the wall. Being bereft of the blessing of sight, it was but natural that they should make the mistake of turning their backs upon the Chairman, but they could hear all that was said. The rat who lived in a well, and who, when he died, went to a warmer climate, you may not be aware returned from that place some time since. He was present as an invited guest from the Museum. The cockroaches looked out of the cracks in every direction, and balanced themselves dexterously on shreds of wall paper. The spiders occupied the centres of their webs, apparently asleep, but in reality wide awake, as one unfortunate blue-bottle fly found, who got caught, and was immediately served up and sent to the spiders of the Local-Room as a present. Besides these, there were a few score of old fogy mosquitoes, left over from last year, and a handsome representation of those quiet little brown bugs addicted to bedsteads, and pronounced odor, whom I do not like to mention by name. The Chairman was listening to the complaints of the multitude, for famine was staring them in the face, and some means must be adopted for self-preservation. A motion to serve out an injunction on the TRIBUNE Company, and compel them to replace the goods they had carried away, was canvassed, but failed of rat-ification. One large, portly rat, with a very benevolent face, and getting gray, whom I at once recognized as an old friend I had seen on my old desk many a time, banqueting on paste, was complaining particularly of me. He characterized such conduct as despicable in the highest degree. It was a betrayal of friendship, a breach of confidence, and he would never again repose trust in a biped. All that he had found in my desk, during a visit that evening, was a dried up bouquet or two, rusty pens, one scissor blade, a photograph of a superannuated prima donna, a paper of pins, and a huge package of tickets to amateur concerts. There was a time when he was young and strong. In those days he could gnaw a file, and derive considerable culinary consolation from a paper-weight, but now he was obliged to conform his diet to a weakened digestion and disordered liver. He spoke more in sorrow than in anger, and regretted that Pickle should be fickle.

At this point, a young mouse, perched upon the top of the gas pipe, in a piping voice complained that he had just commenced going through Abbott's History of the War. It was slow work, but he had got through the covers, and part way through the introduction, and he didn't like to be interrupted in this manner. It was true he hadn't derived much sustenance from the thing, but it was a matter of principle when he commenced a piece of work, to keep at it if it killed him. Some fifteen or twenty old fossilized rats, with their wrinkled faces, scanty hairs and shrunk shanks, made the same complaint with reference to the Patent Office Reports and commercial statistics. To be sure they had not thriven well. One of them had devoured half the Georgian Bay Canal; another had swallowed two Board of Trade Reports, and had got as far as lard in the third, to which he was looking forward with great expectations, being then unprofitably engaged upon lumber; a third had almost exhausted himself with devouring a census table, and was just in sight of some quotations of cheese; a fourth had swallowed the Smithsonian Institution, and put the Covode Investigation on the top of it, and was just ready to attack the American Cyclopedia, in which he was sure to find something to agree with him and repay him for the time he had wasted. A sentimental little mouse complained that she had just got into Mrs. E. D. E. N. Alphabet Southworth's "How He Won Her," and was interrupted, at a critical moment, when "he" and "her" were about to say something nice. She was dying to know "how he won her," and she might go down to a premature grave without the knowledge of that interesting secret. A grave looking rat, with a streak of white fur around his neck, and troubled with a slight cough arising from an affection of the throat, announced that he had devoted several nights of hard labor, in getting through the back of a Biblical Cyclopedia, and had just reached the title page. All the world was before him. Vistas of Hebraic and other sorts of lore, opened before his longing eyes. He was about to enter, when the prize was snatched away. He consoled himself with the reflection that all earthly matters are illusions, but he could not help thinking now and then how pleasant that Cyclopedia would have been. There was one wretched old rat who had eaten up a volume of Swinburne, two duplicates of Walt Whitman, and was feasting upon a gorgeous picture of the spectacle of Undine. He had eaten up four blonde wigs, sixteen legs of ballet girls, and left eight coryphees with a leg apiece. He was very indignant over his disappointment, and even swore about it, for which he was called to account by the grave-looking rat with a slight cough. The wicked rodent growled out something in broken Rattish, and retired to his hole, out of which he shook his tail in defiance. Presently four or five good little mice, whom I had not observed before, with their faces very clean, and their fur smoothed down very sleekly, made their complaint in a weak kind of utterance. It was to the effect that they had discovered a little stock of Sunday School books in a paper box, which were very affecting, and narrated how "Little Freddie" and "Good Teddie" and others, committed forty feet of texts in one day, which disagreed with them so that they died very early, not being good enough for this world. They had just succeeded in getting into the box, and now the books were gone.[1]

In this manner, complaint after complaint was made, and the meeting adjourned to another evening without taking action. You should have seen the assembly after adjournment. The whole mass of rats and mice rushed pell-mell through the dusty heaps of papers on the floor. One set danced a polka on fragments of editorials touching the finances and internal revenue, taxation and other topics. In the local room a rather spare rat, with long reddish hair, mounted the City Editor's desk, and read off, to the edification of the crowd, several mutilated fragments of a "Horrible Murder," "Atrocious Villainy in Bridgeport," "Destructive Fire in Holstein," "Scandal Case on Michigan Avenue," "Religious Announcements," etc.[2] In the Commercial Room several casualties occurred. One unfortunate mouse was nearly choked to death with a column of figures which he found on the floor, and attempted to swallow. Another, of a sentimental turn of mind, went insane trying to understand some commercial quotations he found in an antique looking scrapbook, and three incautious little mice, venturing too hastily into Colbert's Astronomy,[3] fell into the Dipper and couldn't get out, until an old rat helped them with the North Pole and a line dropped from the plane of the ecliptic, through the parallax of the sun, whatever that is. In another room, the cockroaches had a carnival in the Night Editor's coffee-pot. It was one of the most touching sights

1. This commentary refers to popular writers and works of the period.
2. These were typical newspaper headlines of the era.
3. Elias Colbert, the commercial editor of the *Tribune*, was an accomplished astronomer. His scientific treatises were extremely popular in the city, and he perhaps did more than anyone else to make the average Chicagoan conscious of "science."

in the world to see them enter in festive procession at the top and come out through the nose. On my own old desk, twenty-three assorted cockroaches, of a beautiful bronze color, each one of whom I have killed twenty-three times in twenty-three various ways, were dancing a can-can. A few of the odoriferous, small brown bugs stood round in various attitudes, like supernumeraries, while an old rat, against whom I once swore eternal war, as Hannibal swore against the Romans, beat time with his stump of a tail. I forgave the rat, but I shall never forget the scene. I shall miss those cockroaches in the coming days, surrounded by the inanimate splendors of the new desk.

Muscular Christianity

["Muscular Christianity," published August 17, 1869, was probably occasioned by the *Tribune*'s interest in the Chicago baseball teams, which were not doing well. The newspaper announced on September 2, 1869, that baseball "is a noble game and has a great future" but recommended that the city's teams merge to form one good team. At the same time, the column gave Upton a chance to spoof the clergy in Chicago, many of whom had become social and political leaders.]

• • •

Are you a base-ballist? If not, take my word and retire from the world.

You are a nullity, a nothing, a 0.

The cholera of 1866 is among us, but it has assumed the base-ball type. It is malignant, zymotic and infectious. Its results are not so fatal as last year, and manifest themselves in the shape of disjointed fingers, lame legs, discolored noses, and walking sticks.

The disease is prevalent among all classes. Editors, actors, aldermen, clerks, lumbermen, commission men, butchers, book-sellers, doctors and undertakers have it, and many of them have it bad.

Even the tailors tried to make up a club, but as they found it took eighty-one men to make up a nine they gave it up.

The only class not yet represented is the clerical.

More's the pity.

They would derive many advantages from the game. You see they would learn the value of the short stop. That is an important point on warm Sundays. They would also learn to hit hard. There are lots of old sinners who need to be hit that way. This continual pelting away with little theological pop-guns at old sinners whose epidermis is as thick as an elephant's, is of no consequence whatever. The shot rattle off like hailstones from a roof. They must learn to hit hard—hit so it will hurt—hit right between the eyes—fetch their man down, and rather than take such another theological bombshell, he will reconstruct.

There isn't a minister in this city who wouldn't preach better next Sunday for a square game of base ball. This Christianity of the soft, flaccid, womanish, alabaster, die-away muscle kind, is pretty, but it isn't worth a cent in a stand-up fight with the Devil.

The Devil is not only a hard hitter with the bat, but he is a quick fielder, and he will pick a soul right off the bat of one of these soft muscle men while S. M. is wasting his strength on the air. He has another advantage over our clergymen. Most of them are confined to one base. The Devil plays on all the bases at once, and he can take the hottest kind of a ball without winking. Our ministers ought to get so they can do the same thing.

Melancthon[4] was one of the soft muscle kind. He was gentle, sweet, amiable, gracious, and all that, but if he had been compelled to carry the Reformation on his shoulders, he never would have left his home base. While old Luther, a man of iron muscle, a hard hitter and a hard talker, who keeled the Devil over with his inkstand, and kicked Popes and Popes' theses, bulls and fulmina to the winds, made home runs every time, and left a clean score for the Reformation.

A great many of our ministers have bones—some, rather dry bones—nerves, sinews and muscles, just as an infant has, but they want development. They need blood which goes bounding through the veins and arteries and tingles to the finger tips. Their sinews must stiffen up, their nerves toughen and their muscles harden. This process can be obtained by base ball. It will settle their stomachs and livers, and when these are settled, their brains will be clear. They won't have to travel to cure the bronchitis, and won't be so peevish over good sister Thompson, who needs a great deal of consolation, owing to her nervous system.

Now, I would like to see two ministerial nines in the field. Robert Collyer at the bat would be a splendid hitter, and would send the Lib-

---

4. Melancthon (1497-1560), an outstanding German theologian, was an associate of Martin Luther (1483–1546).

eral ball hot to Brother Hatfield, on the short stop, and I would stake all my money that he couldn't make it so hot that Brother H. wouldn't stop it.[5] These two clergymen wouldn't need to practice much, because they represent my idea of muscular Christians. Whenever they hit, they hit hard, and I pity the soft-muscled parson that gets into a controversy with either of them. But then they would get all the rest of the nines into good trim and harden up the muscles of Dr. Ryder and Robert Laird Collier, Father Butler, Dr. Patton, and Revs. Everts and Patterson, and the rest.[6] To be sure, the clerical fingers would sting, and the clerical legs would be stiff, and the clerical backs would ache for a few days, but it would take all the headaches and dizziness, and dyspepsia and liver complaints, and heartburns out of the system. Their inner men would be refreshed, and their outer men regenerated, and they would go into their pulpits with firmer step, and their sermons would be full of blood and muscle, and they would kick the old musty tomes on one side and preach right out of their consciousness and hearts, man to man, and all would get their salaries increased and a month's vacation to go to the seaside.

I tell you, my brethren, in this city of Chicago, the Devil is getting the upper hand, and you must go in on your muscle. Get your backs up. Stiffen your muscles and then hit like a sledge-hammer. If old Crœsus, in your congregation, is a whiskey-seller, don't be afraid of him. Hit him on the head so it will hurt. If Free-on-Board is a professional grain gambler, hit him on the head. If old Skinflint acts dirtily with his tenants, tell him he is a miserable old devil. Don't be afraid of him. He will like you all the better for it. If he won't get down on his

5. During the nineteenth century a certain group of local ministers became extremely popular with the business and social elites. They ranged in theology from the liberal to the conservative, but they shared a common interest in the life of the city. All of them occupied outstanding pulpits. Robert Collyer (1823–1912) was the minister of Unity Church. Robert M. Hatfield (1819–91) was the minister of the Wabash Avenue Episcopal Church from 1865 to 1867 and again during the year 1870–71.

6. Dr. W. H. Ryder (ca. 1822–83) was the pastor of the St. Paul's Universalist Church from 1860 to 1882. Robert Laird Collier (1837–90) was the pastor of the Wabash Avenue Methodist Episcopal Church from 1862 to 1865. After a break with the congregation and a shift in his own theological beliefs, he moved to the pastorate of the First Unitarian Church in 1866. Thaddeus Butler was the priest of the Church of the Immaculate Conception until 1870 when his brother, Patrick, became the pastor. Dr. W. W. Patton (1798–1879) led the First Congregational Church from 1856 to 1867; Dr. William Wallace Everts (1814–95?) was the pastor of the First Baptist Church from 1859 to 1879; Dr. Robert Paterson organized and led the wealthy Second Presbyterian Church from 1842 to 1873.

knees by fair talking, take hold of his coat-collar and put him upon his knees.

A Trip to Hell

[The didacticism of some of Pickle's essays can be annoying to modern readers; these columns, however, often carry a perceptive view of ur-ban life of the 1860s. Such is "A Trip to Hell," which appeared on Sep-tember 19, 1869, and describes a country "of vast extent" with a large population that essentially is a composite of urban types.]

• • •

If you should ask me why I went to Hell, I do not know that I could answer you. I only know that I have often wanted to go there. I have more than once envied Swedenborg, who could go in a jiffy where he pleased, and the rat who lived in a well, and when he died went——— you know where. If you do not know, I can tell you that the place rhymes with well.

I only know that I went there and came back safe and unsinged, and with no smell of fire in my garments, although I saw and talked with him who is never mentioned in polite company, strange to say, considering that he is the politest person that I ever met.

. . . .

I went down the hill-side, and came to the river, and there I found an old ferryman and his boat waiting to convey me over the dark flood. He asked me for the obolus with which to pay toll across the river, but, unfortunately, I hadn't a cent with me. He then asked, rather impa-tiently, if my friends were so poor when I died that they couldn't afford to put an obolus in the coffin with me. I smilingly replied that I wasn't aware I had ever died, whereat he answered, very seriously, that he had carried a great many dead men across, but never any dead-heads. I tried to coax the old man into giving me a ride gratis, but he obsti-nately refused, saying that only the disembodied were allowed to cross, and that if he took me over he would catch the———

"Just the man I want to see," said I. "If I cannot go to him, except as a blessed defunct, will you have the goodness to hand my card to him, and say that I come from Chicago?"

The old man took the card, and, after taking on board two or three people whom I used to know, and supposed were saints, he paddled across and soon returned, saying that the Devil had sent his compliments and was willing to see me. He also sent word that he was desirous of sending back by me his thanks to Chicago, which was just now conferring a great favor upon him in the way of business.

I accordingly jumped into the boat. The old man had to work very hard in getting me over. The spirits which he was accustomed to carry weigh nothing and pack close, but I was quite substantial.

In my passage across the river I observed that it was full of robes, mitres, crosiers, censers, creeds, canons, and other articles floating along, and I asked the old man the cause of it. He simply replied that he didn't know what they were. He believed they were some sort of stuff which some people brought along with them and had to throw away because nobody used them here or in the other place. When we had reached the other shore I landed, and the old man informed me I was in Hell, and would find the Devil a short distance away. I found him without difficulty. As soon as he had settled a little dispute between some Board of Trade men who had been getting up a corner,—which he declared was too disgraceful even for *his* country,—he turned to me and bade me welcome.

I must acknowledge that I was disappointed in his appearance. He was a very polite, affable person, and, apparently, a perfect gentleman. There were certainly no claws upon his fingers. His feet were not cloven. There were no horns upon his head. Neither did I, after a rather secret and anxious scrutiny, discover any indications of a tail. He greeted me as if he knew me well, and at once put me at ease with himself. I made bold to congratulate him upon his personal appearance, whereat he smiled and said: "Yes, the old story—horns, hoofs and tail, I suppose. I know it is the custom for you people on that little planet, which is called, I think, the Earth, when you wish to represent anything infamous or abominable, to paint the Devil, and you generally paint him very black. Now we know a thing or two here, and we always return the compliment, for when we wish to represent anything infamous or abominable we paint Man in his natural colors. I assure you sir, I am not so black as they paint me. Why, sir, I have been obliged to blush more than once at the crimes which some men have committed who come here for cleansing."

I acknowledged the justness of his remarks and then, anxious to settle a suspicion which had been troubling me, I asked him where the fire was. He smiled again, and said:

"Fire? It is all round you. Hell-fire is by no means a falsehood. Look at these people. They have brought all their passions with them. We cannot manufacture a fire which can burn and consume like the fires of passion in man's breast. We know of no hell so terrible as the hell in a man's bosom."

. . . .

The Devil then offered to show me about his dominions, and we trudged along together. I was surprised to find so many people there I had known on Earth and supposed were saints; men whom I had known with serene faces, and upturned eyes, and saintly expressions, who were all the time deprecating the sinfulness of Earth; who held up their hands in holy horror at pleasures and snuffed evil in every wind that blew; and among them some whose names had been blown abroad loud and long, and who had mounted upon the top of popular opinion by means of the stepladders of piety. The Devil noticed my surprise and said: "Yes! we have a good many of that sort. They are all entered on the books as hypocrites. One of our choicest vintages, which we serve on State occasions, is their tears bottled up. They are much superior in flavor to the tears of the crocodile."

. . . .

We wandered on, and found several other classes of persons, each of whom was punished in some unique manner. There were pot-house politicians by the multitude, who were chasing after offices which constantly eluded their grasp just as they thought they had them. There was an army of street-corner organ-grinders condemned to wander for a term of years and never to cease grinding "Captain Jinks," while the man who wrote "Captain Jinks" was condemned to follow them and listen to it as long as they played it. There was a large multitude of people from Cincinnati, condemned to sit for a thousand years upon a bank of a river and read the daily papers of Chicago. There was a crowd of tradesmen, who cheated with false weights, condemned to trudge for centuries with their weights hung about their necks; and others, who mixed sand with sugar, and turmeric with butter, and sold other villainous compounds for the genuine article, who were forced to eat their own abominable adulterations incessantly. And thus we went on until we came to a spot where there was a fearful chattering and screaming. The Devil stopped his ears as we approached, and I immediately discovered a crowd of able-bodied, stout-armed women chasing a piece of paper which was fluttering through the air. Every time that they were on the point of seizing it, a puff of wind would blow it away again. And on the paper was written the single word "Ballot."[7] I smiled as I recognized some of them.

Thus we went on, but it was everywhere the same story. Those who had bad passions on Earth brought their bad passions along with them, and made their own hells. . . .

We again reached the River Lethe, and I asked him what word he wished to send to Earth. He smiled, as he answered: "Nothing special. My business is doing well there, and I have no fault to find with your representation. The supply quite exceeds the demand."

. . . .

I promised the Devil I would take his message to Earth, and then said: "I have but one more question to ask."

"What is that?" he replied.

"Do editors come here often?"

"No! they have quite enough of this place where they are."

I thanked him from my heart of hearts, and bade him good-bye as one not utterly bereft of comfort and consolation.

As the old ferryman landed I noticed that his boat was full of stock speculators, and that the Devil looked utterly disgusted when they stepped into his dominions.

We passed over the river in silence. I climbed the hill and crossed the blank moors, passed through the golden sea again, and then on through the systems until I reached Earth and awaked.

It may be barely possible that a quarter section of hot mince pie had something to do with this visit.

Franc B. Wilkie

Known in journalistic circles as "Poliuto," Franc Bangs Wilkie (1832–1892) did not go to Chicago until he was thirty-one years old. Born in Charleton, New York, he served as an editor of the Dubuque (Iowa) *Daily Herald* and as a Civil War correspondent for the New York *Times*. He joined the editorial staff of the Chicago *Times* in 1863 and remained

---

7. The Western Female Suffrage Association met in Chicago during September of 1869. Such "activists" as Susan B. Anthony and Mary Livermore attended the meeting.

until 1888. During that time he spent two years as the foreign correspondent for the *Times* (1877–1878, 1880–1881) and two years (1881–1883) as a free-lance writer. Although Storey relied heavily on him and apparently respected his ability, Wilkie made it clear in his autobiography, *Personal Reminiscences of Thirty-Five Years of Journalism* (1891), that theirs was really a love-hate relationship. After Storey's death in 1884, Wilkie remained with the paper for four years and elected to move to the Chicago *Globe* in 1888. By 1890 bad health forced his retirement from active participation in the city's journalistic circles although he continued to write.

Wilkie was a prolific writer, and his publications covered a wide range of interests. His first published work was the humorous *Walks About Chicago* (1869), a collection of articles that had appeared in the *Times*.

Wilkie also wrote *Sketches Beyond the Sea* (1879), which covers some of his foreign experiences as a correspondent. In his next work, *The Great Inventions: Their History . . . Their Influence on Civilization* (1883), Wilkie tried writing history and repeated this genre in *A Life of Christopher Columbus* (1892). In addition to his well-known autobiography, which reveals as much about Wilbur Storey as it does about Wilkie, he also published *Pen and Powder* (1888), a series of Civil War sketches that are largely autobiographical. His one novel, *The Gambler*, also appeared in 1888.

The following selection, "Westside" (1869), is taken from the popular newspaper series. Wilkie knew the city and its tunnels well. His descriptions are still understandable, and his mock seriousness adds to the comic effect.

Westside

Any person who has ever traveled much, or who has studied physical geography, must have visited, or must have seen, a place known as Westside.[8] It is one of the largest places of its size, and the most singular in respect to its singularity, in the world.

---

8. Strictly speaking, the West Division is that area "on the other side" of the two branches of the Chicago River from approximately North Avenue (1600N) to Eighteenth Street (1800S). The West Side—unlike Chicago's lakefront or "front yard," which developed quickly and received a great deal of attention—is, in effect, the city's "back yard" and was virtually ignored in literature until the twentieth century. The fashionable

To get to Westside, the traveler provides himself with a waterproof suit of clothing, an umbrella, a life preserver, and a box of troches. He then enters an immense hole under ground which leads mainly westward in one direction, and eastward in another.

This subterranean entrance to Westside was constructed for a double purpose. One of these purposes was to prevent anybody who lives on Westside from leaving. The other was because there is a river which nobody can cross, owing to its exhalations. The subterranean entrance runs under this river.

Going through this hole is a work of immense difficulty and danger. The best way to get through in winter is to skate through. In summer, for a few days, in dog days, there is good boating. The innumerable cascades, cataracts, pitfalls, and the intense darkness make its navigation a work of great risk. Like the entrance to Rasselas' Happy Valley, it is constructed to keep people in, who are once in, and to discourage the coming in of those who are out.

Once in Westside the traveler finds himself on an enormous plain sparsely covered with houses. Westside extends from the river to a park somewhere on its limits to the westward. Just where this park is, nobody knows. The boundaries of Westside are as limitless and indefinite as the interval from the Gulf of Mexico to the present time.

The architecture of Westside is fine and peculiar. A residence with a marble front always has a butcher's shop on one side, and a beer saloon on the other. The people who live in Westside are as diversified as their architecture.

Westside has streetcars which are sometimes visible when a rain has laid the dust. One conductor on one of these streetcars washed his hands one spring. At least it was said he did. . . .

When ever a man in Westside builds a house and puts up a fence in

---

colony that grew up in the West Division remained small and was never as popular as its South Side counterpart where many of the well-known financiers, such as George M. Pullman and Marshall Field, lived on Prairie Avenue. Transportation across the river was not always reliable. The many bridges that spanned both branches of the Chicago River were often a matter of concern and occasionally a subject for humor. Travel to all parts of the city was highly dependent not only upon the peculiarities of the bridge operators but also upon the mechanisms of the bridges. The few existing tunnels were often flooded. As a result, the three sections of the city were far more isolated than they are today.

front of it, he immediately calls the space in front of his lot an avenue. Almost every Westsider lives on an avenue. Sometimes a Westside avenue is as much as two hundred or three hundred feet long.

Every other shop in Westside is owned by a butcher, who has always a bloody and half-skinned calf hanging up in his door for a cheerful sign. The thing is so agreeable to Westsiders, that on every pleasant afternoon, the ladies take their knitting work and go and sit in front of the butcher's shop.

Westside is the residence of a good many notable, strong-minded women. These strong-minded women all have virtuous and docile husbands, who are further characterized by their sweetness, and their retiring dispositions. Whenever a Westside woman gets to weigh 270 pounds, she immediately starts out in favor of woman's rights. In this way, she is able to afford great weight to the cause which she advocates.

Every woman in Westside once lived on The Avenue of a place known as Southside. Whenever she goes downtown, she goes to visit a friend on The Avenue. Whenever she has been downtown, she has been to call on a friend who lives on The Avenue. A good many ladies who live in Westside carry the idea, in the cars, that they live in Southside, on The Avenue, and are only in Westside for a visit. The uncle, aunt, cousin, grandmother, brother-in-law, step-sister, half-uncle, and godfather of everybody in Westside lives on The Avenue in Southside. No young lady in Westside will receive permanent attention from a young man unless he lives on The Avenue in Southside. When a Westsider of the female persuasion dies, her spirit immediately wings its way to the blissful and ecstatic realms of The Avenue on Southside.

The railway companies in Westside never water their track. They do their stock. The result, in both cases, is to throw dirt in the eyes of the public.

There are no carriages in Westside. It is so dusty there, that a vehicle which does not run on rails can never find its way from one point to another. When it is not dusty it is muddy. The dust has no top, and the mud no bottom. In either case, locomotion, except on tracks, is impossible.

Westside has no newspapers. It likewise has no opera house. . . . Its principal local amusements consist, among the men, in chewing tobacco, and among the women, in going to church. Whenever there is a corner in Westside not occupied as a drugstore, it is occupied by a church.

All the churches in Westside have something going on in them every evening, and seven afternoons in every week, and four times every Sunday. Whenever there is anything going on in any church, they toll the bell for an hour and a quarter before it commences, and at intervals during the performance. The result is, that every man in Westside hears from one to eleven bells tolling cheerfully three-fifths of his time.

A stranger in Westside would conclude that the whole town was dead, or that ten or fifteen melancholy funerals were in progress in every neighborhood. There is one church, on the corner of Washington . . . and Robey [avenues], that has been tolling its bell without cessation for two years. When there isn't a prayer meeting, or somebody dead, they toll it for somebody who is going to die. They use up a sexton there every thirteen days. When there is no prayer meeting, or anything else, or anybody dead, or anybody who is going to die, then the bell tolls for the last deceased sexton.

Westside is immensely philanthropic. It has an asylum for inebriates from Southside, and other places. The asylum has often as many as from one to two inebriates who are undergoing treatment. The treatment consists in leaning against the fence, when tight, and in stepping over the way to a saloon and getting tight, when sober. The asylum is a very cheerful building, with enormous windows of four-by-six glass. Some of the rooms are fine and airy, and would answer for dog kennels if enlarged and properly ventilated.

There are a good many other peculiar things in Westside, which can be better understood by being seen than by being heard of. Anybody who dares to face the dangers and darkness of the hole in the ground by which one reaches Westside, will be well repaid for his visit.

What Damage Hath Been Wrought by a Cow? The Chicago Fire, 1871

The Chicago Fire of 1871 began on Sunday evening, October 8; before it had run its course, much of the city had been destroyed. Although the death toll was placed at a low three hundred, there was a loss of property valued at almost $200 million. Just as the Civil War produced some local humorous incidents that were repeatedly told, so also did the Chicago fire have its share of tales and anecdotes. Many stories center on Mrs. O'Leary's cow which—according to a popular legend—kicked over a lantern in a barn, thus starting the fire. Through the years the "cow story" has diminished in importance. Other explanations are illustrative morality tales which use the fire either as an indication of God's displeasure or as a suggestion that the disaster was "for the best." In their *Chicago and the Great Conflagration*, Elias Colbert and Everett Chamberlin—two well-known journalists for the *Tribune*—included a section entitled "Humors of the Fire."

From "Humors of the Fire"

Henry Ward Beecher, whose ready sympathies doubtless entitled him to make such a remark, notwithstanding he lost nothing by the fire, declared in Plymouth Church on the Sunday following, that "we could not afford to do without the Chicago fire"—that it was revealing to us such cheering views of humanity that it was proving a blessing, rather than a calamity. Some caviled at this optimist view of the case, and likened Mr. Beecher to the oriental prince, who, discovering in the ruins of his father's house, which the fire had consumed, the carcass of a pig most exquisitely roasted, was so delighted with the discovery that he kept burning down his subjects' houses, in order that he might enjoy more roast pig.

...

Upon hearing of the burning of Chicago, [Mr. Hudson, a railroad superintendent at Macoupin, telegraphed] to all agents to transport free, all provisions for Chicago, and to receive such articles to the exclusion of freight. He then purchased a number of good hams and sent them home with a request to his wife to cook them as soon as possible, so they might be sent to Chicago. He then ordered the baker to put up fifty loaves of bread. He was kept busy during the day until five o'clock. Just as he was starting for home the baker informed him the hundred loaves of bread were ready.

"But I only ordered fifty," said Ed.

"Mrs. Hudson also ordered fifty," said the baker.

"All right," said Ed., and he inwardly blessed his wife for the generous deed.

Arriving at home he found his little boy, dressed in a fine cloth suit, carrying in wood. He told him that would not do; he must change his clothes.

"But mother sent all my clothes to Chicago," replied the boy.

Entering the house he found his wife, clad in a fine silk dress, superintending the cooking. A remark in regard to the matter elicited the information that she had sent her other dresses to Chicago.

The matter was getting serious. He sat down to a supper without butter, because all that could be purchased had been sent to Chicago. There were no pickles—the poor souls in Chicago would relish them so much.

A little "put out," but not a bit angry or disgusted, Ed. went to the wardrobe to get his overcoat, but it was not there. An interrogatory revealed the fact that it fitted in the box real well, and he needed a new overcoat any way, although he had paid $50 for the one in question only a few days before. An examination revealed the fact that all the rest of his clothes fitted the box real nicely, for not a garment did he possess except those he had on.

While he admitted the generosity of his wife, he thought the matter was getting entirely too personal, and turned to her with the characteristic inquiry:

"Do you think we can stand an *encore* on that Chicago fire?"

Benjamin Franklin Taylor

After graduating from Hamilton Literary and Theological Institute in 1838, Benjamin Taylor (1819–1887) became interested in journalism when he recognized that the life of a rural schoolteacher was not for him. His move to Chicago in 1845 carried him a long way from his hometown of Lowville, New York; however, he arrived full of the optimism that seemed to infect the city's early settlers. He became the literary editor of the Chicago *Daily Journal*, a post he held for twenty years while he also served some of the short-lived magazines of the period. After the Civil War he decided to devote himself to travel and to the writing of poetry. He was considered a poet of some talent; indeed, the London *Times* called him the "Oliver Goldsmith of America." The scope of his work can be seen in his *Complete Poetical Works*, which was issued the year before his death.

The variety of his work is illustrated by the types of publications he produced. At the time that *Attractions of Language* (1842) appeared, Taylor had plans to do scholarly writing; however, his experiences as a war correspondent led to the publication of *Missionary Ridge and Lookout Mountain* (1872), the book that assured his national reputation as an essayist. His best-known volumes of poems before the publication of his *Complete Poetical Works* include: *January and June* (1854), *Old Time Pictures and Sheaves of Rhyme* (1874), *Songs of Yesterday* (1875), and *Dulce Domum . . .* (1884). During his lifetime he wrote a single novel, the autobiographical *Theophilus Trent* (1887). But it was ultimately in the travel book that he was to make a lasting contribution as a stylist and humorist. These began with *The World on Wheels and Other Sketches* (1874) and continued with *Between the Gates* (1878) and *Summer-Savory* (1879).

The World on Wheels and Other Sketches is a "Chicago" book by virtue of its having been written by one of the city's journalists, and it was published by S. C. Griggs, one of the earliest and most successful book publishers in the city; however, many of the sketches first appeared in the New York *Examiner and Chronicle* during 1873.

What is a marvel to one generation is frequently taken for granted by another. Whereas the present age is in danger of losing its great passenger trains, it is of interest to read of an era that was just entering its period of rail travel. Taylor used a transcontinental train ride not only as a means of seeing the country but also as a device for commenting on modern American life. In the 1870s railroad travel was gaining many advocates, but the "iron horse" was still new enough to provide a fit subject for a collection of essays, some of which are didactic. For example: "The more you travel, the less you carry. The novice begins with two trunks, a valise, a hatbox, and an umbrella. He jingles with checks. He haunts the baggage-car like a 'perturbed spirit.' He ends with a knapsack, an overcoat, and a linen duster. Bosom, collar, wristbands, he does himself up in paper like a curl. He is as clean round the edges as the margins of a new book." This is followed by the observation: "We throw away a great deal of baggage on the life journey that we cannot well spare; a young heart, bright recollections of childhood, friends of the years that are gone. And so we 'fly light,' but we do not fly well" (p. 62).

For a post–Civil War world interested in unification, the railroad served an admirable purpose. In his typical way of turning a phrase, Taylor observed: "The East and the West have kissed each other across the Continent, and every body and thing between is brisk as a flea, and breathless as a king's trumpet" (p. 248). Taylor's wit ranges from the interestingly subtle phrase to the more boisterous elements of slapstick.

Vicious Animals

A great many animals get on board first-class passenger trains that should have been shipped in box-cars, with sliding doors on the sides. There is your Railway Hog—the man who takes two seats, turns them *vis-a-vis*, and makes a letter X of himself, so as to keep them all. Meanwhile, women, old enough to be his mother, pass feebly along the crowded car, vainly seeking a seat, but he gives a threatening grunt, and they timidly look the other way. He is generally rotund as to voice and person, well-fed, but not well-bred. Not always, however. I have seen a meek-faced man, as thin and pale as an ivory paper-cutter, who looked as if he had just gone with the consumption, who made an X of *him*self as if he were the displayed emblem of porcine starvation. Have you ever thought of taking up burglary for a livelihood? Be a burglar if you must, but a Railroad Hog never! Had the ancestors of this type of creature only been among the herd that ran down that "steep place into the sea," what a comfort it would have been!

Did you ever see the Bouncers? They are young, they are girls, they always go in pairs, and they bring a breeze. Like the man whose voice in secret prayer could be heard throughout the neighborhood, they discuss private affairs in a public manner. They throw scraps of loud, laughing talk at you much as if they were eating a luncheon. It is November. The wind comes out of the keen North. Be-shawled, be-cloaked, be-furred, never laying off fur or feather, they open the windows with a bounce, and there they sit snug as Russian bears, and the wind blowing full upon you seated just behind. You venture to beg, after freezing through, that they will close the windows and let you come to a thaw. What a word "supercilious" is, to be sure! Up go their two pairs of eyebrows, and down come the windows, both with a bounce. Then they grow sultry, and one whisks off "a cloud" or something square in your eyes, and the other flings back her fur cape on to the top of your head, sees what she has done, brushes the garment a little, and says nothing—to you. The train halts at some station. Up go

THE GREEN TRAVELER.

From *The World on Wheels and Other Sketches*, by Benjamin Franklin Taylor.

the windows and out the two heads, and a rattling fire of talk is exchanged with more Bouncers on the platform—all loud, talk and talkers, as a scarlet vest and a saffron neck-tie. By-and-by they fall to fixing their back-hair, smoothing their eyebrows with a licked finger, and making other preparations to leave the poor company they have managed to get into.

Lest they be forgotten, let me impound certain offending people in a few paragraphs just here, that, like that place in the Valley of Hinnom, shall be a sort of Railway Travelers' Tophet. Capital punishment should not be abolished until they have all been executed at least *once*:

The man whose salivary glands are the most active part of him, who spits on your side of the aisle when you are not looking, and spoils the lady's dress who occupies the seat after him.

The man who puts a pair of feet, guiltless of water as a dromedary's, upon the back of your seat, and wants you to beg his pardon for being so near them.

The man who eats Switzer cheese, onions and sausages from over the sea, in the night time.

The man who prowls from car to car, and leaves the doors open in the winter time.

The boy who pulls the distracted accordion by the tail, he having several mothers and six small sisters to feed, and then wishes you to pay him something for "cruelty to animals."

The boy who throws prize packages of imposition at you, and insists you shall buy the "Banditti of the Prairie," or the "Life of Ellen Jewett," or the pictorial edition of the Walworth Family, or a needle-book, or a bag of popped corn, or some vegetable ivory, and wakes you out of a pleasant doze to see if you wouldn't like a Railroad guide.

The man who, with a metallic voice, in which brass is as plain as a brass knuckle, does the wit for the car; who tells the train-boy he'll get his growth before the train gets through; who talks of stepping off to pick whortleberries, and then stepping on again; who says that orders have been issued to the engineer never to heat the water hot enough to scald anybody; who talks in the night, and makes it hideous. There is no apparent reason why this man may not be made shorter by a head immediately. Let him be guillotined. "Brevity is the soul of wit."

What shall we do with her?—the woman who sails through the crowded car, and brings to beside you like a monument, looks as if you had no business to be born without her consent, and says in a clear, incisive voice, that cuts you like a knife, "I know a gentleman when I see him!" Is there a needle or something in the cushion? You are seventy, and have the rheumatism. She is twenty-five, full of strength and health, and with a pair of supporters of her own as sturdy as the legs of a piano. But what can you do? You feel red, and draw your head into your coat-collar like a modest and retiring mud turtle, and pretend not to hear. But there she stands, and a young fellow across the way with a sky-blue necktie just lighted under his chin, laughs out loud at the situation, and you think, as pretty much all the blood you have, has gone into your head and ears, you will go and warm your feet. So you get up, with joints creaking like a gate, and hobble to the stove, where you stand and bow to the stove-pipe in an extraordinary way, and catch it around the waist now and then, and all the while she sits in your place like a fallen angel. "What shall we do with her?" Send her to the tailor to be measured, and "let her pass for a man!"

Everybody has met the man on a railway train who, as no one ever learned his name because no one ever cared to, may be designated as *"Might I?"* with a rising slide. All sorts of a man to look at, he is but one sort of a man to encounter, to-wit: an animated cork-screw, forever trying to pull the cork from the bottle of your personal identity. "Might I?" begins his acquaintance by stealing; stealing a look at you out of the tail of his eye, the meanest kind of pilfering, though the law doesn't mention it. Then he begins upon you. He says, "Might I ask how far you are traveling? Might I inquire what business you follow? Might I inquire if you are married? Might I ask your name?" His talk is as lively as a mite-y cheese, and he assaults you like the New England Catechism. This man has been growled at, snapped at, requested to go beyond the possible limit of frost, but he cuts and comes again the very first opportunity. "Might I?" has never been put to death by anybody. The remedy could be tried once, and if it failed to quiet, and only killed him, we should know better than to try it again.

The Railway Opossum is not vicious but he is amusing. He enters a car that is rapidly filling, drops into a whole seat, adjusts his blanket, chucks his soft hat under his head, swings up his feet to a horizontal—all this in two minutes—and is asleep! Objurgations fall upon him like the sweet rain. Shakes fail to disturb him, and no one ever tried Shakespeare. Tender women passing by say, "O, he's asleep—perhaps worn out with long travel"; and not till that swarm settles, and he thinks himself sure of his elbowroom, does he open an eye and "come to," and grow as lively as the opossums ever get.

They board the train—they two—he in white gloves, new clothes, and a white satin necktie; she in a lavender silk, a bridal hat, and a small blush. Seated, they incline towards each other like the slanting side-pieces of the letter A. He throws one arm around her, and she reclines on his shoulder like a lily-pad. They whisper, they giggle, they talk low, they contemplate each other like a couple of china cats on a mantlepiece. He takes a gentle pinch of her cheek as if she were maccaboy, when she is only a very verdant girl. She sits with her hand in his, like a mourner at a funeral—the funeral of propriety. They punctuate their twitter of talk with pouncing kisses. They fly at each other like a brace of humming-birds. The sun shines. The car is filled with strangers. They are the target for thirty pairs of eyes. They smell of cologne or patchouly—or musquashes! They are the sorghum of the honeymoon—saccharine lunatics, and there they are—turned loose upon the public!

The Union Pacific Company has made provision to shut such people up. They have just begun to run a lunatic asylum with every San Francisco train, but they give it an astronomical name. They call it a "honeymoon car." The Company deserves well of the public for keeping traveling idiots out of sight. In certain circumstances it *is* difficult for some people to avoid being fools.

The ? that wears clothes, and goes away from home by the cars, and afflicts the conductor and the brakeman and his traveling companions—he is of recent origin. There is no account of him in Job. The Patriarch had a great many uncomfortable things, but he didn't have *him*. Had he been let loose upon Pharaoh, that stiff-necked Egyptian would have "let the people go" before breakfast. His natural diet is conductors and brakemen, but he will not refuse anybody. He has told the man before him and the woman behind him where he wants to go, and shown his ticket and his trunk check, and asked if this is the right train, and if the check is good, and when he will get there, and how far it is, and whether he knows anybody there. His victim pronounces the check genuine, gets out his "Guide," hunts up the place, ascertains the distance, tells him the time, and *doesn't* know anybody there.

The conductor enters, collecting tickets and fare, has a heavy train, and it is only five miles to the first station. ? makes for him on sight, tries to get him by the collar or button or elbow, and tells him where he wants to go, and shows his check, and inquires if this is the right train, and when he will get there, and how far it is. The conductor answers him, nips a spiteful nick out of his ticket, and hurries on. ? returns to his seat, and watches for the brakeman. Him he catches by the coat-tail, and he asks him if he is on the right train, and if the check is good, and if he thinks his baggage is aboard, and when he will get there, and how far it is. The brakeman has seen him before, and his replies are too short for a weak stomach, but he tells him.

The last morsel finished, he turns to you, and he says, as a woman who deliberates and is therefore lost, "I think now I am on the wrong train. I thought so all the while," and then he tells you where he wants to go, and shows you his check, and asks you if you think it is good for the trunk, and how far it is, and when he will get there, and you tell him. The conductor returns, he makes a grab at him, and he wants him to tell him when he will get there, and who keeps the best house, and how far it is from the depot, and whether that is really the best house or some other, and whether he meant three o'clock in the forenoon or afternoon, and the conductor doesn't tell him.

Henry Ten Eyck White

Born in Chicago, Henry White (ca. 1853–1942) was the son of Julius White—a popular Union officer and highly respected businessman. The young boy knew the city well, a knowledge that was to aid him in his long career in journalism. He was much in demand as an editor and humorist. After a series of appointments on several newspapers, including the *Tribune*, White was hired by Melville Stone to become city editor of the *Daily News* about the time that Eugene Field was beginning his sojourn in Chicago. Later he served as managing editor for ten years.

White was nicknamed "Butch" because he "butchered" the copy of young reporters. He felt that a brief editorial with a hard-hitting humorous angle had far more value than a more-involved philosophical treatise. He himself was a master of the short sentence and terse paragraph. It appears that White "discovered" Finley Peter Dunne and hired him from the *Telegram*.

While still a journalist for the *Tribune*, White wrote a series of prose pieces and poetry which ridiculed the businessmen as well as the sham society that was developing in Chicago. He created the Mulcaheys, an Irish family from Bridgeport, through whom he often commented on the affairs of the city. This was probably the first literary use of the section that was to become immortalized by "Mr. Dooley" and Mayor Daley. He also created "the horse reporter," whose realism was the bane of the young men and women of society who sought information about the "ways" of the city. These essays and poems, which appeared in the latter part of the 1870s, appeared in book form as

Lakeside Musings (1884). An expert on horse racing, White published *Life with Trotters* in 1889.

A Modern Parable

A certain man went down from Chicago to Ohio, taking with him a return ticket, lest he fall against a Cincinnati wheat speculator and be robbed of that wherewith he would fain buy flour and gum shoes for his family, in the season of cold which cometh on those who live in Chicago from the tenth to the fourth month, and find himself amid sinners and publicans, whose mercy is strained, even so fine that it would bother you some to discover it.

And when he had reached Cincinnati he went to an inn, and gave to the landlord thereof three pieces of silver, saying, "No monkey business with me, Charlie; I am from Bitter Creek." And he who kept the inn marveled greatly, and said unto himself: "These be strange men that come from Chicago; never are they to be bilked by a hotel bill, and he who endeavoreth to outwit them is invariably headed off." But, nevertheless, he bethought himself of a Poker Game which was that night in the inn, and laughed to himself with exceeding great joy. Then arose the landlord and went unto the place called Bar, where of a certainty he should find the man from Chicago, and, approaching him, said:

"There be in this inn, even in the third story thereof, a small party of prominent citizens which do play at the game called Draw-Poker. Perchance thou might, after much travail, secure a seat among them."

And when the host of the inn had spake these words a witching smile did play around the lips of the Chicago man, and he answered, saying: "I am yet young, and of a certainty far from mine home and family, and fearful lest I fall among thieves."

But the landlord rebuked him, saying: "In this party whereof I speak are only Business Men, two being Colonels and one a Judge. Would you not think it an honor to play with these?" And the Chicago man was overcome, and said softly: "I should twitter," which being interpreted, means that he should blush to giggle.

So they went up in that which is called Elevator until three stories were below them, and the landlord knocked softly on the door of a room in which a light gleamed brightly.

And the door opened.

And when the Chicago man had seated himself and bought of chips an hundred shekels' worth, he spake not, but drank heartily. And it came to pass that after many deals one of the Colonels did bet seven shekels; whereupon bet also the Chicago man a like amount, and did vanquish the Colonel, who had that which is called two pair. And when this had occurred thrice, the Colonel said unto the Judge: "He is playing them close to his stomach."

And it was so.

But presently there came to the Colonel a hand of exceeding beauty and strength, being four aces. And he who held them was filled with glee and knew not fear, placing in the centre of the table great quantities of shekels. And when it came to that which is called the draw, the Chicago man took not of the cards, saying he was content. But the Colonel drew one with great boasting, telling, with intent to deceive the others, of how he would bet, if perchance he made a full, which is a hand of great strength, and capable of overcoming threes, or even a flush, but which can not prevail against fours. And having said these words, he wagered heavily of silver and gold, all of which the Chicago man did cover, and even betted more, whereupon put the Colonel also his watch and diamond on the table, and wagered them freely. And when all had been betted, the Chicago man said, "Straight flush," even as he spoke gathering unto himself all the treasures which the table held. And when he had placed in his pocket all the shekels, and in his shirt-front the diamond, and had adorned himself with the watch, he became suddenly sleepy and said: "I am too full to play well to-night. I will go to my bed."

And he went.

But those who were left did beat their breasts and cry out, saying: "How are we knocked around and paralyzed by this stranger who cometh from Chicago and dresseth not in fine raiment, but who has of money great store and will wager it lavishly on a hand which can not be overcome. It were better we had remained this night with our wives and children. To-morrow night, however, we will again play with him at the game called Poker, and compass him about with a cold deck, so that he shall be overthrown and cast down in spirit."

But they wist not what they said.

For in the morning the stranger departed from out their gates and came back to his wife, who fell upon his neck and kissed him. And he did kiss her on the cheek, saying: "Mary, you can order that sealskin."

And she made answer and said: "Charlie, you're a darling; kiss me again."

Obituary Gems

. . . .

Put away the wooden boot-jack
   That our parent used to shy
At the tomcats on the woodshed.
   Papa's home is in the sky.

     • • •

Mend the hole in father's trousers,
   Soon they'll fit our oldest son.
Frame the verdict for the parlor:
   "Rotten barrels in the gun."

     • • •

Mary, we shall always miss you;
   Absent is your pleasant smile.
Had the oil can been much larger
   You'd have gone about a mile.

     • • •

Tie the bull dog in the woodshed;
   Little Johnny's passed away.
Keep his checkered pants for brother,
   He will fill them up some day.

     • • •

A St. Louis maiden in love
Put some kerosene oil in the stove.
   It is thought that her toes
   Were turned out as she rose,
By the size of the hole just above.

     • • •

Give his pants to Cousin Tommy,
   And his little silver cup.
It was in the month of August
   Green corn curled our darling up.

     • • •

Get out Robert's yellow trousers,
   Fix them up for little Will;

Brother went to fish on Sunday,
   And his grave is on the hill.
         •••
Little Jim is no more with us,
   Let us not bewail his fate;
When he sank, his cousin Henry
   Was away in search of bait.
       •••
Summer days are swiftly waning,
   Autumn tints are on the leaves;
Never tackle a green melon—
   Rupert's gathering golden sheaves.
       •••
Put away dear Arthur's speller,
   Vacant is his desk at school;
Tell his comrades that it's dangerous
   Playing tag behind a mule.
       •••
Do not cry for little Georgie,
   He is in the golden camp;
Gently was he wafted upward
   By the non-explosive lamp.

"Literary Frolics" and Other Miscellanea from *America* and the Chicago *Ledger*

America (1888–1892) was a serious journal that avoided dealing too frequently with the lighter aspects of life. Committed to the notion that the nation was being "ruined" by "aliens," the magazine published articles, stories, and poems supportive of this idea. At the same time, the magazine not only used the talents of Harry B. Smith as the conductor of "Folly As It Flies," a collection of jokes and verse, but also presented as fillers the work of numerous local and national poets.

    Harry B. Smith (1860–1936), the humorist and librettist, was born in Buffalo, New York, and in the 1880s became part of the "sophisticated crowd" that had gathered in Chicago. He is perhaps best remembered for the hundreds of stage productions that have been credited to him, many of which had extensive Broadway runs. Smith was a longtime associate of the musician Reginald DeKoven (1861–1920), and the two men were extremely successful. While they were young, they tried magazine publishing in Chicago. They began *The Rambler* in 1884 and managed to maintain it for two years. In a city, however, which was being flooded constantly with new journals, Smith and DeKoven could not meet their magazine's demands; they gave up in 1886, and the magazine ceased in 1887. The following year Smith joined the staff of *America* and edited a column of humor entitled "Folly As It Flies."

Beginning with *Robin Hood* in 1890 and while still associated with the Chicago-based *America*, Smith published many plays. Among his more popular works are: *The Fencing Master* (1894), *The Wizard of the Nile* (1895), *The Mandarin* (1896), *The Fortune Teller* (1898), *Babette* (1899), *The Siren* (1911), *The Girl from Utah* (1912), *Sybil* (1912), *Angel Face* (1919), *Carolina* (1922), and his excellent autobiography *First Nights and First Editions* (1931).

Much of the following light verse appeared in his column "Folly As It Flies."

A Proverb

> There is a proverb not profound
> Which has for years been going 'round.
> 'Tis true, although 'tis somewhat old;
> It illustrates the pow'r of gold:
> > " 'Tis money makes the mare go."
>
> In politics, as all can tell,
> This scion is true as well;
> For ev'ry demagogic "boss"
> Admits the mighty pow'r of dross:
> > 'Tis money makes the Mayor go.
>
> Its pow'r is never known to fail
> When balanced in the social scale.
> Match-making mothers all look out
> For some well-funded wealthy lout.
> > 'Tis money makes the *mère* go.

The Mastodon's Memory

> The skeleton of the mastodon,
> > It stood in its wonted place
> In its corner up in the museum,
> With its calm and placid face;

From an illustration by T. E. Powers for the text in *America* magazine.

And for life in that tranquil visage one
　　Might vainly search for trace.
Way back in the paleozoic age
　　It had been a gay young thing;
It had seen this wintry world of ours
　　In its very earliest spring;
But now it seemed as if naught on earth
　　Could reanimation bring.

Two youths dropped into the museum
   And the mastodon they saw.
They were not impressed by its size; its age
   O'ercame them not with awe;
And one was telling a tale whose theme
   Was a shot at mothers-in-law.

He reached the point of that dismal yarn,
   And both with the laugh joined in,
For the mother-in-law as a theme for jest,
   It appears, will always win.
Then they both looked up at the mastodon
   Whose face wore a cheerful grin.

Oh, then it spake with an awful voice,
   Like an antediluvian roar;
And it said, "That story, boys, is one
   In my youth I heard of yore.
Now, while you're about it, tell us one
   That I never heard before."

Folly As It Flies

Angelina—Do you see that handsome, middle-aged man over there?
Belinda—Yes. Who is he?
Angelina—He lives by his pen.
Belinda—Ah! A poet?
Angelina—No; a pork-packer.

      •••

Frau Braun—Yes, mum; my husband haf had no luck for a long time
    mit his saloon, but now he haf got a splendit location and a fine
    business.
Frau Schmidt—Vere his new blace vas, anyhow?
Frau Braun—He's got a saloon under a hall vere der temperance odd
    fellers meet tree times a veek.

      •••

Theatrical Manager—Say, can't I have an hour or so of your time?
Hotel Clerk—What is it you wish me to do?
Manager—I wish you would come over to the theatre and wear your
    diamond stud. We want to photograph the audience by flash
    light.

      •••

Book Agent—I am selling a very fine work here; a book of etiquette.

Merchant—Don't want it.

Book Agent—Just cast your eye over that chapter headed "How to Give a Dinner."

Merchant—I'm too busy finding out how to get one.

• • •

Kidder—That Miss Maud Estey is the most sensitive girl I ever saw. She is shocked at the least thing.

Softmark—How do you know?

Kidder—Last time I called on her I happened to speak of a "bare possibility," and she blushed so you could hear her.

• • •

Mulligan—Me woife used to be a good Catholic, but lately she says she's an infidel.

Riley—That's bad, Pat, me bye. O'im sorry for yez. Phy don't ye git a divorce from her.

Mulligan—On phat grounds?

Riley—Infidelity.

• • •

Fond Mother—Spell and define bigotry?

Future Statesman—B-i-g-o-t-r-y. Independent assertion of views at variance with mine. For instance, the speeches of Doctors Henson and Barrows in behalf of honesty and purity in politics in the late campaign was offensive bigotry, while the sermons and appeals of the Polish Catholic priests in favor of Kiolbassa, free whisky on Sundays and race prejudice was liberal and enlightened toleration.

• • •

Hardtack—How are you getting along with your new clerk? Is he a good man?

Clambake—He works like a charm. Did you ever see a charm work?

Hardtack—I never did.

Clambake—Well, that's him.

• • •

Dashley—I can't abide these Wagner operas. They strike me as being beastly tedious.

Cashley—You will like them better after you have heard them two or three times.

Dashley—Yes, I suppose one learns then just what times it is best to go to sleep.

Old and New—An Ancient Rhyme and How It Would Be Written Now, by Pan

The Original

Jack and Jill
Went up the hill,
To fetch a pail of water;
Jack fell down
And broke his crown,
And Jill came tumbling after.

As Alfred Tennyson Would Sing It

"Forward!" said Jack to Jill,
"And toward the rugged hill"—
Not though that Jill knew
   The tin pail was rocking.
Hers not to make reply,
Hers not to reason why,
Hers but to work and sigh:
Up to the hill she walked,
   Fixing her stocking.

Up then the hill they went,
But poor Jack's strength was spent,
And though he struggled hard,
   He tripped and stumbled;
Down like a comet bright
Dives through the starry night,
Or, like a flash of light—
Plunged to the valley there,
   While the hills rumbled.

And poor Jack's head was split;
Quickly Jill followed it.
   Down from the hill she fell,
Squirming and roaring;
Tearing in wild despair
For some firm foothold there,
Grasping the very air—

She, too, like Jack, fell—
Her spirit went soaring.

When can their glory fade?
  Honor the plunge they made
Down the steep hill.
Into the grave they're laid,
Papa the bill he paid—
Poor Jack and poor Jill.

As Walt Whitman Would Have It

Jack, broad-shouldered, deep-chested, and merry,
Like the rocks prehistoric—gigantic,
Had for a sister Jill, petticoated, proud, and pedantic.
On a day they ascended a hill, cloud-kissed and craggy,
Overlooking the hut primitive of Jack and his sister.
With them went a pail—sunlight reflecting—of clear,
    translucent water,
Reflecting images of mountain, hill, and deep-wooded valley.
Adown the hill came Jack with a four-footed tramping,
And after him, making the hills reverberate with noises
    pandemoniac,
Came Jill performing feats acrobatic,
And Jack's cranium, round, polished, and empty,
Split with the sounds of thunders majestic.

Longfellow's Method

As unto the pail is water,
So unto his Jill was Jack,
Useless each without the other.
Proud and fair upon the hill-top,
Stood they watching, looking westward;
All the glory of the evening,
All the radiance of the sunset,
Played around their golden tresses;
And the birdies flying southward
Stopped and whistled to the children.
As they walked—the pail between them—
Great Nekomis, heavy-hearted,

Caused the stones beneath to roll.
And the water, Jill and Jack,
In one mass adown the hill
Rolled and rolled unto the bottom;
And the water spilling o'er them,
Made a fall like Minnehaha.
And Jack's head was split asunder,
And rolled onward all before him,
Followed then by Jill his sister,
With the pail of water with them—
Useless each without the other.

Owen Meredith's Way[9]

The time is not o'er
When devotion and brother's affection is past. There are more
People in this vast spreading world where we live
Whose examples they free to the world's vision give,
And among them was Jack. Proud, pensive, and sad,
He heard not the swallows call, no, nor the sad
Cry of the whip-poor-will as homeward it flies
When the deep golden sunset illumines the skies.
The weight of her years and the weight of the pail
Conspired to make Jill, his poor sister, so frail,
That scarce could she walk up the hill by his side.

Arrived at the top, the swift-flowing tide
Attracted both Jack and his sister. They looked
And leaned over too far. In a second earth shook
And swift as an eagle, full downward they fell,
The pail pealing paeans and sounding their knell.
Jack's head from his body was sundered.
And the storm was abroad on the mountain. It thundered
And shook like a reed in its grasp, the tall mountain:
But Jack and poor Jill, like the Fountain
Of Youth, are gone and forgotten.

9. Owen Meredith was the pseudonym under which George Bulwer-Lytton
(1831–91) published some of his early work.

Thus Would Keats Sing

'Twas Christmas Eve—ah, bitter chill was it!
    And Jack, for all his clothing, was a-cold:
Poor Jill walked, shivering, with an ague fit,
    While both their fingers on the pail did hold
As tight as misers do the yellow gold.
    Together up the hill they wend their way;
While Jack, poor boy, some harmless chestnuts told,
    And roosters sung the knell of parting day,
Proclaiming that Queen Night had now begun her sway.

And soon the top of that vast hill was gained:
    Ah! me, that I must sing you such a song!
Jack slipped—and all the ground with blood was stained.
    His head it broke, alas! and from among
The clouds was heard fierce clangings, deep and long,
    Like sheep or goats, that, on distant hill,
Fly frightened from the sound of horn or gong—
    Just so Jack's sister, frightened fit to kill,
Came rolling down, and so poor Jack was joined by Jill.

Byron Prefers This Way

It happened on a morning long ago—
'Twas winter, as I think, but I'm not sure—
That Jack and Jill, with footsteps short and slow,
Went up a hill some water to procure.
Oh, water is a cursed stuff and low,
And many does it kill and few does cure;
I like it for the whisky it does link,
For then it makes a pretty solid drink.

But Jack thought naught of whisky or of beer;
His mind reverted more to baggy pants,
While Jill, intent on "Fashions for the Year,"
Let fall a tear and thought of all her wants;
And so, wrapped half in coats and half in fear,
They gained the top, like patient, plodding ants,
And gazed below on sweetly-feeding flocks,
While winds were playing duets through their locks.

But while the winds Æolian tunes discoursed,
A sudden gust took Jack from off his feet,
And down the hill unwilling was he forced;
His head against the cruel stones did beat,
And Jill fell down as does a man unhorsed—
In wild disorder and in no ways neat—
An angel hovers over them and sings
And fans the air with soft-descending wings.

An Incident   [Anon.]

We sat within a railway car,
  A man named Jones and I,
While I fond glances sent afar
  Upon a damsel nigh.
So by this optic telegraph
  The trip was swiftly whiled,
Her glances mingled with our chaff,
  And once, I thought, she smiled.

"By Jove!" said I to Mr. Jones,
  My new conquest to air,
In most enthusiastic tones:
  "Yon maid is wondrous fair,
And ever since I sat me here
  She's wafted glances pert;
She's pretty, and it would appear
  She is inclined to flirt."

Said Mr. Jones: "Nay, think you so?"
  (I know not well the youth.)
"Well, if you say so, we will go
  And ascertain the truth."
So over to her side we sped,
  My mind with sweet words rife,
And Jones—the villain—blandly said:
  "Ah! Mr. Brown, my wife."

A Practical Lullaby, by Benjamin H. Jefferson

Mr. Eugene Field, in the Chicago *Daily News*, has set the fashion of publishing lullabies, and daintier verses could not be devised than those which he has composed. From an artistic standpoint they are perfect. But I am under the impression that the crying need of the (midnight) hour is a practical lullaby—one that is warranted to rival paregoric in soporific effect; one that will not only bring sleep, thrice blessed sleep, to the infant, but that will speedily bestow repose upon the victims of insomnia of every age. This godlike end I have striven to accomplish in the following stanzas, and lest I have been successful, I wish to caution readers to leave word at what hour they desire to be called before proceeding further.

I

Hush-a-bye, lullaby, softly we'll drift
Out of the world that has burdens to lift,
Out on a stream that is hazy and gray
That carries us bound with its sweet-scented spray,
And takes us a captive in a triumph away—
    St. Louis! St. Louis![10]
Now rising, now falling, the sleep-god is calling
    St. Louis! St. Louis!

II

Hush-a-bye, lullaby, sweet little stream,
Dimmer, and grayer, and wider you seem,
While gently, so gently, your speed you decrease
'Till we come to the haven of rest and of peace,
Where waking can't be, and action must cease—
    St. Louis! St. Louis!
Milwaukee's a roué compared with St. Louis.
    St. Louis! St. Louis!

Deft Definitions by Various Hands from Various Sources

[One of the staples of "Literary Frolics" was the column "Deft Definitions," which popularized a form perfected by Ambrose Bierce. The editor explained the frequent lack of originality by asserting: "We propose to give a weekly selection from our collection of literary curiosities made during twenty years' miscellaneous reading, and we shall be pleased to receive others of equal merit when our list is complete."]

• • •

10. Chicago's great competitor among midwestern cities was St. Louis, and any joke

Abbey: A quiet place where monks and chickens fatten each other.

Alderman: A statesman in the wrong place.

Arms: The brains of the majority.

Biographer: The rag-picker of history.

Christmas: An excuse for gluttony, the Good Friday of misers.

Congressman: An amateur legislator who has passed no apprenticeship to his business.

Democrat: A Republican who can't, though he tries.

Falsehood: Imagination, traveling *incognito*.

Fellow-Countryman: A stranger at home; a brother abroad.

Hero: A man who thinks little of his own life, and much less of the lives of others.

History: An amateur concert, in which passion and prejudice rarely allow the small voice of truth to be heard.—One side of a question.

Hospital: A workshop for repairing nature's slopwork.

I: The domestic divinity at whose shrine we all worship.

Idler: An animal who nibbles time.

Land: Almost the only property which gentlemen may steal without being transported or losing caste.

Laws: Amateur regulations made by legislators for the government of the universe.

Legitimate Drama: A drama whose authors are dead and whose copyrights have expired.

Oath: A ceremony invented to save men of honor from the necessity of telling the truth.

Ovation: A neat way of throwing stones at some people, by strewing the paths of others with flowers.

Peace: The slumber of war.

Poet: A marvellous biped, whose singular fancy is to appear insane.

Power: A mantle which we always think too large on the shoulders of others, and too small on our own.

Prodigy: Every mother's first baby.

---

against that town suited local taste. The theme in the following piece is St. Louis' supposed dullness.

Republican: The reverse of the republic—a Democrat who cants.

Senator: A legislator—two of whose qualifications are his law and his maw.

Sermons: Soothing syrup.

Statesman: A village genius on the verge of a precipice.

Taunt: A verbal weapon, strongest in the weakest hands.

Tour: A journey 'mongst thieves.

Tyrant: There is no such thing as a tyrant—there are only slaves.

Masthead, Chicago *Ledger*.

From *"Cornfield Philosophy"* by the Ledger's *Hired Hand*

[The Chicago *Ledger* (1889) was a story newspaper that appeared every Wednesday. It was designed to appeal more to the communities surrounding Chicago than to an urban readership. The *Ledger*, however, did enjoy a degree of success in the city and was read by those who enjoyed its homespun wit and romantic tales.]

• • •

Don't blame a mule for being a mule. Remember that he is an improvement on his father.

Good biscuits cause more happiness than good music.

It is the ability of the hen to lay eggs that makes her valuable.

The man who wants a seat on his plow will soon want an umbrella over the seat.

Defensive Humor ────────────────────────────────

By the time of the World's Columbian Exposition of 1893, easterners viewed Chicago as an "upstart" city that placed materialism above everything else. Filth, municipal fraud, impure water, crooks of all sorts, and an absolute lack of culture were just some of the city's attributes—according to detractors. In return, Chicago developed the "second city" syndrome, which produced an energetic defense designed to prove that it was "better" than New York or Boston or—for that matter—any other American city.

One of the earliest humorous attempts to explain the differences between the East and the West was published in Chicago in 1845. Entitled "Epistle of a Prairie Poet to His Cousin in the East," by William Asbury Kenyon, it poked gentle fun at the polyglot language of the Middle West and at the population where "a Jack was . . . just as good as a King."

Sectional conflicts between East and West became more pronounced by the end of the Civil War. Journalists in Chicago ranged from those who supported the "down-easter" to those who bitterly attacked all aspects of the East. The local-color movement did little to lessen this sectional animosity. Increasingly, Chicagoans poked fun at the pretensions of the men and women from the East, though they may have secretly admired their business acumen or their inclinations toward culture. There was a concerted effort to show Chicagoans what they should not be, which often resulted in the ridicule of anybody who appeared "to put on airs" or anything that seemed pompous. Eventually, Chicagoans—who took much of this seriously—were able to laugh at themselves, though there was continued resentment against any outsider who tried to point out the flaws in the life of the city. Truly, there developed a "defensive humor."

Zebina Eastman and *Chicago Magazine*

Perhaps indicative of some of the concerns and interests during the mid-years of the nineteenth century were the magazines and newspapers that flourished during the period. The growth of Chicago had been as phenomenal as the early historians had predicted. These early

Chicagoans seem to have been not only a people of enterprise and industry but also readers of journalistic literature. Before it was incorporated as a city in 1837, the village had two newspapers. Later newspapers and magazines appeared frequently—more than a hundred, of varying duration, before the Civil War. One such journal, whose short life belies its importance, was the *Chicago Magazine* of 1857, which lasted for seven monthly issues. Subtitled "The West As It Is," the journal was the organ of the Mechanics' Institute (an organization founded in 1843 to promote the young city's educational and cultural activities). It was edited by Zebina Eastman (1815–1883), who has been remembered more for his antislavery activities in Illinois than for his role as a lawyer, writer, and professional editor of a number of early works in the city.

Eastman, the staunch abolitionist, was born in North Amherst, Massachusetts. He was orphaned when he was six years old and spent time with various families until he became apprenticed to a series of printers. In 1837 he decided, along with other young men of the area, to try his luck in the West, lured by the stories of western fortunes that prompted many easterners to leave home. By 1842 he was in Chicago, where he soon gained a reputation as an editor. His avid support of Abraham Lincoln was rewarded when Lincoln appointed him the U.S. consul at Bristol, England, in 1861. Eastman held the position for eight years, after which he spent the remainder of his life practicing law.

Chicago Magazine was clearly designed to be a literary journal of high quality—a midwestern response to such popular eastern journals as *Harper's* and *Godey's Lady's Book*. Serious though it was in intent and committed though it was to functioning as "a go-between carrying to the men of the East a true picture of the West," it eschewed the humor of the frontier so closely associated with the prairie midlands; when humor appeared—as it did on many occasions—it tended to be the sophisticated, urbane humor later associated with the city.

Generally some humorous tales, jokes, and witty poems appeared in the most serious newspapers and magazines. But perhaps of even greater distinction—given the course of later developments in journalism—was the extensive use of satire.

One of the practical goals of *Chicago Magazine* was to show the distinct advantages of the West over the East. Noggs, apparently a creation of Zebina Eastman, is an observer. Although Noggs is a commentator

on affairs in the West, it is significant to remember that he is an easterner who has cast his fortunes in the West because he views Chicago
as an inevitable result of urban progress. He is an example of the philosopher who, speaking of a multitude of subjects, in his down-to-
earth approach utters some significant truths.

From "The Editor's Table"

There is sometimes a great swell of pretension, which has more of
amusement in it than disgust, from the eccentricity of the pretense itself. Noggs, the other day, was talking to a down-east friend, who had
not been here quite so long as Noggs had, and therefore the circum-
ference of this new city looked to him more like the surface of the
changeable-hued soap bubble. He intimated to Noggs that there were
other places somewhat in advance of Chicago—as Boston, New York,
and certainly London or Paris. "Yes," said Noggs, "but you must remember we *are young yet*." And intimated as much in point, the cir-
cumstance of a satelite of the late Emperor Nicholas, who once upon a
time was boasting to a Yankee of the wonderful qualities of his august
highness, and affirmed that he was the greatest statesman, civilian,
warrior, christian, philosopher, &c. But the Yankee was a sort of sly
wag, and modestly, and perhaps impiously suggested that the Creator
of the world might be greater even than his highness, the Czar of all
the Russias. "Ah! yes!" replied the admiring Russian, not to be taken
aback in that way—"but the Emperor is young yet!"

Noggs on Progress

Noggs is a character. While he lived "away down east," we thought him
one of the institutions of that part of the land. But Noggs being a progressive being, he thought he must follow the star of destiny, and
therefore, not long ago, he made tracks for the West. We heard of his
oscillations in Wisconsin, but having strong faith in natural equilib-
rium, we concluded of course that he would in time find his level, and
therefore we were not surprised the other day to meet Noggs in Chicago. Noggs had floated to Chicago as naturally as the duck floats on
water. We could not do otherwise than ask Noggs for an article for the
Chicago Magazine. As he had advanced considerably in his journey of
life, on coming to Chicago, it was very natural that he should give us
his views on PROGRESS.

"Change is written on the face of everything; first the seed, then the blossom, and anon the ripe fruit; all beautiful, and yet how different. Nothing Nature so abhors as vacuums, stagnation and sameness. No two things alike, no two persons see alike,—jostle, jostle, jostle,—advance, march on, *re*-form, presto—change.

To-day we're here, to-morrow we're where? Why all this constant transformation and newness of things? I answer, to display the goodness of Him "who doeth all things well," for He knew how miserable man would be without it.

Just imagine a live Yankee, where everything was in one eternal *fix*; with no shadow of turning or changing; no rise or fall of stocks; no ups and downs of trade; no new inventions to be even thought of; no whittling out any new device; no new jackknives; no new minister; no change of season, weather or political dynasty; and how long do you think he would live? Not long, I ween; and wouldn't want to if he could, though in the garden of Eden itself. If some old fogies could have their way, I know they would have mighty little variety. Their motto is, "let well enough alone"; but, thank the Lord, they have not the control of things, else, I fear me, the very air we breathe would be kept from circulating, so fearful of change are they.

Aye! PROGRESS and ONWARD! these are the two great words, especially of this, the latter half of the nineteenth century. It is laughable to see the vain efforts of the selfish slow-coaches that disfigure every age, to stop the tide of human progress, and stem the current of a world's reform.

In olden times, long, long ago, the only means of vehicular locomotion in London, was to get into a wherry, or small boat, and be rowed by a pair of oars up and down the Thames, and landed wherever the passenger might desire on its banks. But as this, of course, was troublesome, exceedingly, to those who lived far from the river, necessity, the mother of supply, brought about the invention of hackney coaches; and then such an hue and cry as the boatmen raised, you never heard before, and terrible was the warfare between the watermen and coachmen. It was carried on even to bloodshed; but the coachees triumphed, for coaches became at once a necessity, its mother's own child—of course it could be nothing else—and folks will have the necessities of life anyhow. Time wag'd, and it was soon found to be rather expensive, to poor folks at least, to hire a coach every time it rained, which is as often in London as every now and then. And, again, necessity being married to economy, conceived, and lo! there sprang into existence an umbrella, a sort of portable coach that a man could carry in his hand, and that was cheap withal. And now the owners of the coaches began to fret and fume, but umbrellas have ever since been made and sold—and now and then one borrowed and stolen—in spite of all circumstances, and will be. Just think of a man, or the mass of men, now-a-days standing under awnings and porches, till a two hour's shower was over, as common folks used to have to do, and they with notes to pay in less than an hour, and the money not yet raised! Then came the omnibusses, and the anathemas were loud and deep against their inventors. But the public liked them, and taking a buss is now one of the commonest and most indispensible thing out of doors; whereas, in days of yore, it was confined to a meeting of the sexes, and was mere lip service at best.

But time, as well as carriages, kept rolling on, and the first thing the world knew, steamboats and railroad cars were invented, and the way they have made packets and stages stay at home is known to everybody. But they are still in use, in spite of all the old folks at home. Before the advent of steam it took three or four weeks to go from Chicago to Boston; now you can go quicker than you can stay at home.

But steam, even, is not quick enough for all purposes; the spirit of go-ahead-a-tiveness demanded a telegraph. And he who made the universe, "and all that is in it," and pronounced them good, made even the lurid lightning to become subservient to the wants of man, his master-piece. And now messages, which it took weeks to carry, during which the news thereof became literally "stale, flat and unprofitable," can be sent a great deal quicker than can be let alone, especially if important. Just imagine a Chicago house sending a man on horseback to New York city to find out the price of wheat! He would just as soon think of wheeling himself there on a hand-barrow.

No, no, Neighbor Slow-coach, the world does move, and old things are constantly being done away, and new things coming to pass; and all the things which seem so new and strange to you, and which you think bad, or of no use, because your father didn't know of 'em, you'll find are all useful and necessary in their day and generation. First the grub, then the chrysalis, both here and hereafter.

Time was when the world got along well enough with such cities as

London, Paris, Liverpool, New York, &c. But Convenience, the hand-maid of Progress, said we must have something faster, freer, more central; a place where the beauties of all these cities shall be combined in one, with a position in the world that all of them combined cannot vie or compare with; and hence Chicago sprang up. And now all those cities, so mighty in their day, are of consequence only in proportion to their distance from the North-Western Metropolis, and the inhabitants thereof are commisserated as being so unfortunate as to be obliged to live so far from Chicago.

In olden times, 'way back in the dark ages, there was scarcely any such thing recognized as Nature! but now she is considered to be quite an institution; and is allowed to be adequate to the task of doing very many things much better than anybody else can do them for her.

But, to bring the matter right down to our own times, it was but a few short years ago when the present Post Office in Chicago was pronounced a monster concern, and altogether too large for the necessity of the city. And now it will hardly afford a box a piece for each nation here represented, let alone the individuals who in countless thousands daily mourn the want of such a convenience. As there are no limits to learning, so also are there none to progress. What is well enough to-day, will be intirely inadequate, it may be, to-morrow; for the same reason that "dogs delight to bark and bite," 'tis the law of nature; and is therefore inevitable, and to the inevitable, we must all in humble submission bow."

Character Sketches

The character sketch became one effective means of presenting the differences between easterners and westerners. George P. Upton—an original Bostonian—willingly admitted that he could see in his native city all of the stereotypical restrictions that Boston had been accused of producing. In a Peregrine Pickle letter (September 7, 1867), Upton presented the following.

The Boston Girl

The Boston girl, necessarily, was born in Boston. Necessarily, also, her ancestors, and she can trace back her lineage to that Thankful Osgood, who came over in 1640, and owned the cow that laid out the streets of

Boston. The wolf that suckled Romulus was held in no more respect by the Latins than is the bronzed image of that cow, cast by Mr. Ball, the sculptor, upon a commission from her father, a solid man, who lives on Beacon street, in a brown stone front with two "bow" windows and a brass knocker.

The ambition of every Boston girl is to live in a brown stone front with two "bow" windows and a brass knocker, before she dies. Having accomplished that, and attended a course of medical lectures, she is ready to depart in peace, for after that, all is vanity.

There are three episodes in the life of every Boston girl, viz., the Frog Pond, the Natural History Rooms, and the Fraternity Lectures. In her infancy, if so majestic a creature ever had an infancy, she sailed small boats on the Frog Pond, and was several times rescued from drowning in its depths, by the same policeman, who to-day wanders along its stone coping, watching the reflection of his star in the water, as he did a quarter of a century ago. She visits the pond daily on her way to the Natural History Rooms, where she inspects with diurnal increase of solicitude the bones of the megatherium and the non-descript fœti of human and animal births, preserved in Boston bottles, filled with Boston spirits.

But the series of Fraternity Lectures is the great fact of the Boston girl's life. She dotes on Phillips, idolizes Weiss' social problems, goes into a fine frenzy over Emerson's transcendentalism, and worships Gail Hamilton and her airy nothings.

The Boston girl is of medium height, with a pale, intellectual face, light hair, blue eyes, wears eye-glasses, squints a little, rather *deshabille* in dress, slight traces of ink on her second finger, blue as to her hose and large as to her feet. Of physical beauty she is no boaster, but of intellectual she is the paragon of animals. Gather a dandelion by the roadside, she will only recognize it as *Leontodon taraxacum*, and discourse to you learnedly of fructification by winged seeds. She will describe to you the relative voicings of the organs of Boston and the size of the stops in the Big one. She will analyze the difference in Beethoven's and Mendelssohn's treatment of an *allegro con moto*. She will learnedly point out to you the theological differences in the conservative and radical schools of Unitarianism, and she has her views on the rights of woman, including her sphere and mission. But I doubt whether the beauty of the flower, the essence of music, the sublimity of Beethoven and Mendelssohn, or the inspiration of theology, ever find their way into her science-laden skull, or whether her spectacled eyes ever see the way to the core of nature and art.

The Boston girl is a shell. She never ripens into a matured flesh and blood woman. She is cold, hard, dry and juiceless. Gail Hamilton is a type of the Boston girl at maturity. Abby Kelly Foster was a type of the Boston girl gone to seed. If Gail Hamilton lives as long as did Abby, she will carry a blue cotton umbrella, wear a Lowell calico, and make speeches on the wrongs of woman and the abuses of the Tyrant Man. If the Boston girl ever marries, she gives birth to a dictionary, or to a melancholy young intellect, who is fed exclusively on vegetables, at the age of six has mastered logarithms and zoology, is well up in the carboniferous and fossiliferous periods, falls into the Frog Pond a few times, dies when he is eight years of age, and sleeps beneath a learned epitaph and the *Leontodon taraxacum*.

The Boston Matron

[In Harry B. Smith's poem the Boston girl has become the Boston matron.]

...

> She speaks in calm sarcastic tone;
>   She frowns on all that's naughty;
> She is a Boston chaperone
>   And eke supremely haughty.

> A youth who vainly tried to win
>   This Boston matron's favor,
> To flatter thought he would begin:
>   A little rose he gave her.

> A sneer passed o'er her phiz high bred,
>   Her profile like a vulture;
> "I little care for flowers," she said,
>   "But much for haughty-culture."

From The Idle Born

[By the turn of the century there had developed in Chicago a coterie of sophisticated wits who entertained each other as well as the general public. Composed of such sometime journalists as Harry B. Smith, Reginald DeKoven, Henry B. Fuller, and Hobart Chatfield Chatfield-Taylor, this group took comfort—as the Pharisee—in declaring that they "were not like other men." Theirs was not the intellectual and social camaraderie of the Saints and Sinners Corner of McClurg's Bookstore or the productive literary Bohemia of the Chicago Renaissance. Consequently, the effects of this group (which lacked a cohesive force) have not been studied.

One of the products, however, was the publication of *The Idle Born* by Hobart Chatfield Chatfield-Taylor in collaboration with Reginald DeKoven. The following excerpt from "A Homily," the introduction to the work, published in 1900, was written by Chatfield-Taylor.]

• • •

Perhaps we are no better—let us hope we are no worse—than the idle born of other days; but what do we amount to after all? The world moves on without us, while good men like Isaac Watts silently pray for our betterment.

The story of The Idle Born which follows is a satire of this little world of fashion. The canvas is small because the people are small. If the talk is fatuous, and the actions at times contemptible, it is because to be straight-forward and outspoken is to be serious, and that is fatal in society.

Perhaps Lord Chesterfield was right when he said to his son: "Throw away some of your time upon those trivial futile books published by idle, necessitous authors, for the amusement of idle and ignorant readers." However, the life of the idle exists; it is shallow and petty, no doubt, but in its present form it is a product of the times. If Beau Nash no longer rides Godiva-like upon a cow his prototype does some equally foolish thing; if there is no longer a King of Bath, to decree that the music of the Pump-Room shall stop at eleven, there are kings and queens of other places to keep it going until dawn, and "Satan finds some mischief still for idle hands to do."

• • •

[One aspect of the character sketch and a variation of the comedy of manners is the "put down," which often relies heavily on understatement. Although the "put down" as a comic type was not an innovation of the Chicago humorists, it became a frequent means of defense against real or imagined attacks from outsiders. The following two tales, which present recognizable urban types, are commonly told with many deviations.]

The Boston Lady and the Chicago Matron on "A Matter of Breeding"

A lady from Boston, eager to see the newest metropolis of the Middle West, journeyed to Chicago. She could not, however, forget her up-bringing and eastern background, nor was she going to let anybody else overlook these fine points.

At a Chicago tea in her honor, she took great delight in regaling the guests with tales of her Boston forebears. At first her audience tried to match her tales. Eventually they were subdued into silence.

The Boston lady brought her recitation to a close by saying with appropriate condescension: "You know, my dears, in Boston we place all our emphasis upon breeding."

One of the Chicago matrons, determined that this easterner's smugness should not go unchallenged, answered softly: "Well, we think it's loads of fun, but we manage to keep up a few outside interests."

The Speediest of Them All?

It seems that a fellow from New York was visiting a friend in Chicago, and the two friends were walking down Michigan Avenue in the latter part of the nineteenth century. The Chicagoan, aware that his city was known for the speed with which it had been built, was proudly pointing out sites of importance. Like others of his city, he was not at a loss when it came to boasting.

Finally, his eastern friend asked as he pointed to the Auditorium, one of Chicago's big hotels: "How long did it take to put that up?"

"Oh, about two years," replied the Chicagoan.

"Not bad," said the New Yorker, "but in our city we could have built it in half the time."

The two men walked on silently for a while. The New Yorker then asked: "How long did it take to put *that* up?" He was pointing to a gigantic structure which looked for all the world like it had come from the Italian Renaissance.

"That? You mean the Art Institute? Less than four months," said the Chicagoan trying to outboast the New Yorker.

"Four months? We could have done it in two." A few seconds later the New Yorker asked: "And what about this one?" Now he was pointing to the public library.

"I dunno," said the Chicagoan hesitantly. "It wasn't there last night."

Chicagoans Laugh At Themselves

Much of what amused nineteenth-century Chicagoans was related in some way to proof that the West was indeed better than the East; however, these loyal citizens were not beyond poking fun at themselves, though they resented having "outsiders" do it. Customarily the journals of the period included some humorous anecdotes relating the foibles of the nouveaux riches.

Elias Colbert and Everett Chamberlain: From Chicago and the Great Conflagration

[The 1860s] was the epoch of uneven sidewalks, about which the eastern papers used to be as facetious as they were subsequently over the odors of the Chicago River. It used to be reported that when the genuine Chicagoan visited New York he found himself unable to walk on a level surface; he was obliged to turn into the adjacent buildings, every half block or so, and run up and down a stairway, for the sake of variety.

From the Chicago Ledger

While Chicago business men have the reputation the world over of rushing in where angels fear to put up a margin, her literary men are distinguished by a retiring and modest opinion of their own abilities, that might be copied to advantage in Boston. An illustration of this was given the other day when one of Chicago's classical scholars was invited by the Literary Association of Kalamazoo to read a paper before it on Ibsen. He declined, pleading as his excuse that he did not read Ibsen in the original. Who but a Chicago literateur would have been deterred by such an insignificant consideration?

From America

Mrs. Startup: Isn't that acquaintance of yourn a Spaniard gentleman? He's so dark-complected, he must be.

Mr. Startup: No, my dear, he's a Portuguese.

Mrs. Startup: I wish, my love, that you would be more particular about punctuating your grammar. How can one man be Portuguese? You mean Portugoose for the singular gender.

         • • •

Mrs. Startup: Several of the wealthy parishioners have had memorial windows placed in our church, and I really must order one or be out of fashion. I think I will order one in memory of Mr. Startup.

Mrs. Newrich: Why, I thought your husband was living. Isn't——

Mrs. Startup: Oh, yes; but he is in as delicate health as any of my relations.

         • • •

Mr. Newrich: Yes, old man, I seen some wonderful things in Egypt. There was the Sphinx. Say, that's a wonder. I wanted to write and tell you all about that.

Mr. Wheatpit: Why didn't you?

Mr. Newrich: 'Cause I'll be goll durned if I could spell the name o' the thing, and there wasn't a dictionary to be had in the place.

         • • •

Mrs. Newrich: Did you hear much music while you was abroad?

Mrs. Mushroom: Yes, indeed. Slathers of it.

Mrs. Newrich: Did you hear "Tristan and Isolde"?

Mrs. Mushroom: No; I heard "Tristan," but I left just a few days before they done "Isolde."

         • • •

Mabel: You say Alice has musical tastes?

Annabel: Decidedly.

Mabel: What makes you think so?

Annabel: Why, she even wears "accordeon [*sic*] pleats" on all her street costumes.

         • • •

Miss McFlimsey: They tell me that you are quite a musician, Mr. Bigorders.

Mr. B. (*commercial traveler*): Yes, I do a little that way.

Miss McF.: What is your favorite instrument?

Mr. B.: Well, I'm pretty good as a drummer, and I'm something of a 'cellist, too.

         • • •

At a dinner party:

Mr. Hodgkins (*aside to Mrs. Hodgkins*): Gosh, Maria, I got no less than six forks by my plate.

CHICAGO.—Brace up, old boy! Perhaps there'll be another anniversary in four hundred years to which you can come via the Crow-Flight Balloon Line—if you're still on earth.

From *America*, August 27, 1891.

Mrs. Hodgkins: Hush! You must not notice it.

Mr. Hodgkins: But, thunder! there must be some mistake. I don't want to corner the fork market.

Mrs. Hodgkins: No, it's all right, Jeff, I tell you.

Mr. Hodgkins: Well, of course it's all well enough to have plenty of forks; but I ain't never goin' to drop that many on the floor at one meal.

• • •

Mrs. Goldust: John, I wish you would send the office-boy up this morning with $25. I want to send it to the fresh-air fund. I see that $25 will keep a poor child in the country for a week.

Mr. Goldust: Can't do it. The office-boy has a holiday to day.

Mrs. Goldust: Drat the little imp. Why can't poor people stick to their work.

· · ·

Teacher (*in a Chicago school*): We hear a great deal of talk about a World's Fair in 1892. Now, can any boy tell what there is to commemorate?

Chicago Boy (*promptly*): The discovery of Chicago.

· · ·

Caller: What will you give me if I will put you onto a scheme for the extending of your business to an extent that you have never dreamed of?

President of an Accident Insurance Company: My dear sir, you astound me. Give me some idea of what your plan is.

Caller: What do you think of establishing branch offices at the entrance of LaSalle street tunnel. You could reap a harvest from the passengers on the North Side cable cars.

The Rise of Ethnic Humor and Disturbing Laughter ___

It is ironic that in a land of immigrants there should have been such a concerted effort to seal the door of welcome to the "land of opportunity." As men and women scrambled for the spoils of urban life, and as various cultures were thrust close to each other, problems increased. Given Chicago's emphasis upon "democracy" and upon accepting people on the basis of worth rather than some predetermined traditional standard, it is significant that paralleling the comic spirit in the city was a strong anti-immigrant strain. It is further ironic that Chicago, long noted as a "place where anything goes," should have become so early in its history willing to look upon the foreign immigrant as a cause for alarm and ultimately as a butt of humor.

There has been an outstanding literature dealing with the foreign immigrant's adjustment to the American experience. The theme was to be treated realistically and sympathetically by such writers as Willa Cather and Ole Rölvaag, but early Chicago literature seldom included the more noble aspects of the painful adjustments many immigrants were forced to make not only in a new land but also in the city. The urban experience was—and still is—often traumatic for people who have spent all of their lives in rural communities. It was no less so for those of foreign birth.

Early Chicagoans frequently overlooked the fact that ethnic groups had considerably enhanced, and deepened, the American experience. Even Chicago—as reluctant as some were to acknowledge the reality—was a product of these many groups coming together in a single locale for the express purpose of "making it" in the new world. The literature of the region, especially that of Chicago, has been enriched by the rough and tumble antics of various ethnic characters who have become integral parts of the nation's literature. Who can forget the gentle laughter of Carl Pretzel, the German immigrant created by Charles Harris, or the cogent observations of a Martin Dooley as he moved his attention from Bridgeport to the national scene? Remembering these two characters can sometimes obliterate the memory of the cruel and vicious streak displayed in the city's early humor. It was humor clearly indicating that the fine lines between sarcasm, cleverness, and vitriolic attacks are often nonexistent.

In Chicago the initial reaction against the foreign-born came in the political arena and partially reflected some national concerns. In the presidential campaign of 1840 it was the Irish vote that succeeded in putting Martin Van Buren in the White House, even though as early as 1836 the Whigs had objected to giving the vote to foreign immigrants. Whether the vote was abused is a moot point; what is significant is that the foreign immigrant was an integral part of the life of the nation as well as of Chicago.

These new Americans soon saw the ambiguity of their position in American life. The egalitarianism of the Declaration of Independence seemed to assure foreign immigrants a "place in the sun." Yet they were constantly being attacked by those who equated their differences with inferiority or lack of moral principles. In Chicago the Irish and the Germans were the groups most frequently lambasted.

Prior to the Civil War adverse criticism was essentially based upon religious rather than national differences. Since both the Irish and the Germans had strong Roman Catholic ties, "native Americans" feared for the safety of their religious institutions. The publication of "The Holy Coat" in the *Watchman of the Prairies* (July 9, 1850) is an early example of a religious satire illustrating the insecurity of Protestant groups as they attempted to "protect" a territory they considered to be theirs. The story pokes fun at the "Romanists" who believe in relics and repeats the prejudicial comments about the corruption of the leaders of the Roman Catholic church.

Anti-immigrant humor—for reasons that are not hard to discover— subsided slightly during the Civil War and during the period of the Chicago fire. Foreign groups made up many of the volunteer regiments, such as the Irish and German battalions. Furthermore, the rebuilding of the city after the devastating Fire of 1871 needed a sense of commitment from every citizen and the cooperation of all groups. By the late 1870s, however, Chicagoans had forgotten the sacrificial contributions, and the attacks began again.

During the postwar period, industrialization made the competition for urban jobs even more pronounced. Although this was important in Chicago, the competition for control of the municipal government was of greater significance. With the antipathy toward the Germans in the city, the organized efforts "to put them in their place" often succeeded. Much of this negativism culminated in the Haymarket Affair (1886), but extreme concern about the Germans had surfaced before the 1880s; and of all the foreign groups in the city, the attitude toward Germans suffered the most radical change. At first they were excluded from the type of animosity that was directed toward the Irish; eventually, however, they became associated with all types of political upheavals. During the period of a renewed interest in temperance immediately after the Civil War, the beer "gartens" were constantly being attacked by the moralists as "dens of iniquity." The right to drink beer, however, was strongly defended. Fortunately, Charles Harris' creation of "Carl Pretzel" in the 1870s did help to temper the anti-German attitude; still, the events of 1886 created widespread hysteria.

By the 1880s, the contributions of foreign immigrants were minimized, as magazines—such as *America* (1888–1892)—gained widespread acceptance. This was not the first time in the city's history that an anti-immigrant journal had achieved such popularity. In 1854 W. W. Danenhower, editor of the successful *Literary Budget*, had stopped his literary magazine to publish a rabidly anti-immigrant journal the following year. *America* was initially edited by Hobart Chatfield Chatfield-Taylor, whose fortune initially financed the project, and by Slason Thompson, who is perhaps best known as a confidant of Eugene Field.

As Chicago prepared for the World's Columbian Exposition of 1893, the city eagerly awaited the approval of international visitors. *America* had folded, and the anti-immigrant spirit appeared to have run its course; however, one of the popular jokes of the day underscored the continued existence of this negative attitude.

> Trueblue: I don't see the use of all this talk about a World's Fair in 1892.
> Oldflag: Why? Don't you believe in celebrating the 400th anniversary of the discovery of America by Columbus?
> Trueblue: No I don't. Columbus was only an alien intruder anyway.

The selections that follow are representative of the 1870s and 1880s. They reflect the shift in attitude from the gentle and homespun wit of Carl Pretzel to the diatribes that appeared in *America* magazine.

Charles H. Harris

Little is known of the life of Charles Harris (1841–1892), who early discovered that some materials and opinions that would not be tolerated if presented in standard English were acceptable when written in the dialect of the foreign immigrant. Had Harris lived longer and been able to settle on a decisive form for his journal, he would now perhaps be considered a major contributor to the development of ethnic humor rather than a regional curiosity. He was one of the first writers in Chicago to discover the appeal of material written totally in dialect. Although the use of speech aberrations in writing was not new in the city, Harris used dialect as a means of gentle humor rather than ridicule.

For nearly twenty years Chicago and the rest of the nation had an opportunity to follow the antics of Carl Pretzel. Created by Harris in a city with a heavy German population, Carl was a popular figure who commented on everything—from the doings of the city council to the actions of small-time wardheelers, from local to national politics. In addition to politics, his observations covered religion, love, race relations, history, *ad infinitum*. Especially interesting is his survival through the 1880s, one of the strongest anti-immigrant periods in Chicago's history and an era that saw many attacks directed toward German immigrants and their descendants. Clearly Chicago had ambivalent attitudes. The city could recognize the cultural contributions of some

German-Americans, but it could also highly resent the presence of the German element in the city.

First introduced before the Fire of 1871 in *Der Leedle Vanderer*, Carl Pretzel became popular the following year through *Carl Pretzel's Magasine Pook*. Subsequently Harris issued *Carl Pretzel's Weekly*, *Carl Pretzel's Illustrated Weekly*, and *National Weekly: Illustrated Political Journal*. Each successive name change took Harris further from his original style until the *National Weekly* became truly a weekly of "social, political, and miscellaneous matters" in a city that had too many of these ephemeral journals. Much of the material written in standard English was no longer a clear appeal to the German reader, but the *National Weekly* remained politically a Republican journal.

For those who had risen above the restrictions of ethnicity, Carl Pretzel undoubtedly had a peculiar charm. It was the success of Carl that made Harris expand into a national weekly, which folded the year after Harris' death. When the magazine, which was advertised as "the most popular, humorous, interesting, witty publication in the West," became a weekly, Pretzel remained the central figure but increasingly became simply a means by which Harris discussed general political issues of a national nature.

Unlike Martin Dooley, who generally remains in character, Carl Pretzel often drops his German-American lingo—especially in the weeklies—to speak in standard English. Sometimes Harris used an aphoristic style when presenting Pretzel's homespun wit in standard English as well as dialect. Ultimately, it is significant that the first journal devoted exclusively to humor in the city came out of the ethnic humor tradition. The following selections are taken from the various journals ascribed to Carl Pretzel.

Carl Pretzel. Der Author of der "Self-Made Misers," Mine Boughtoffogravy.

Der underlyin feadures vas more dhrue as der ubberlyin feadures. Shtil as it vas mit egwalidy divided, it could make notting tifference, bote ways togedder. Der pedikree of der hero of dis shkedge could been more easily oxtingwinished as hunted ub. Suffice it to said, I vas porn vhen ogstremely young. Mine fodder vas a dutchman, und mine mudder vas a Dutchess. Dey kepbt a sassidge foundry in der old coun-

Carl Pretzel's Magasine Pook

Of Reffleations, from Shenerations to Reffalootions.

Reffle 3.	OONITED STATES.	No. 3.

Carl Pretzel introduces himself in an early issue of the *Magasine Pook*, 1872.

dry, und ofer your head be of goot shapes, you know who dot vas, no matter vat your name vas. Vhen on der skoolhouse, I thought dot der "rule of three" times vas proverbially trying to der conshtidootion, but in mine more madurer years I did found mineself out dot der rule *one* vas about so much I vished to dackle. Dhere vas no umbrageous elm, oak, nut tree, mit its o'er shaddowing bowers growin round der shpot of mine childhood. Notting but der shweed shmellum cabbage broke der stillness of der scene, consekerwend'y vas mitout der influences of an oxberienced nurse, und I got to trink der milk from a bottle out mit few times pleasant surroundings, vhich sometimes vas charachteristic of der odder little girls vat vas growing ubward about der same times. I vas porn mitout mine knowledge or consents, und on dot ackound vas unackoundable for mine ignorance of certain tings vhich gone to make ub a comblete masterbeices of der shkiences, shtill, in my mine infantile days I saw at once mine shkidurvation, und mit a goot determination shdruck out to fulfill der decrees of fate. I vas lifin today oxulting ofer der success of tings, dhankful of mine outside in dot nadure vas keeb of me heldy enuff, und dhankful dot I could shallow a whole row set of teeths mitout getting a gnawing on mine shtomach. Life vas a great succeed. It vas human to lif, und so vhile dot vas a complimented cases, dots besser we dond make him fool. Und in der language of Bayrum we did said "Dhere vas notting like life," mitout it we would go pooty qwick died. Bayrum vas dead now. Vhen I shook me dot mordal coil off, I vant to been dead, you aind more worth as lefen cent peices, vhen dot vas shook, und I vant me to been ready vhen dot time vas comed. I hafe been a long time here. I yoost vant to dook mine frow und go to dot Borneo, vhere der cold freezy Shack frost coodn'd got in, efen ofer he gif two tollars, und vhere dot vas summer all der year. I vas done.

Bollydicks

[Carl Pretzel reflects on "Politics," 1872.]
...
I yoost dells you der bresent bolidickal shampain vas der most humerous und funny like notting at all, vhich hafe efer dook some blaces. Der imbartial opserfer can sthand on one leck aloof, und look on in wonder at der fackceetiously redickilous vay in vhich der bartizan bress und pooblick condukt it. New pabers und efery kind of lideradures hafe been shtarted all ofer der coundry by enderbrising roosters, who vill reab ub a wealthy harvest out of dis oxtradinary bolidickal var. Dot dhere is blendy shkope for a goot much gridicism on der bote sides, dhere vas no doubt. But dhere vas shtill much fun to saw der racecourse pursood by der bote bardies in dheir endeavors to make der odder feller bite indo mudder earthy. Ofer bote sides would oney confine dhemselfs to der simple shtaderoom of facts mitout oxagerations, dhey could told mit one eye out, dot vhich would damage der odder one harder as sefenteen tollars und a half worth. Ofer you can traw a conclusion here, dot besser you do it, or pooty gwick you dond got a chance.

General Grant und Horace hafe done a goot much to commend dhem to der peobles public, dot is so mitout a doubt. Der foorst one, dis coundry owes some salvations, und he hafe suckcessfully conduckted der Gofernment dooring his term of office as Bresident. We efery body know dot he relingwished der most lucratif und lasting bosition mitin der gift of der beople's representatif to took hold of der reins und drife der Gofernment out riding on der shores of Long

Switch, vhich vas done at der inshdance of some of dose fery mens vat now so bidderly oppose him.

On der odder left hand, Mr. Horace Greeley vas one of our ablest bolidickal economists, who hafe wielded a great influenza in der goot conduct of der Gofernment, und whose ideas of shoostice und equal-idy hafe been, as a sheneral ting, bully. He hafe, no doubt, ackted mit good faithfullness, on efery solemn ockasion, but like all human peobles, vas liable to make some err, und dherefore vas mitout a blem-ishments, so far he could see sometings.

But look vonce how der bardy pabers shnab at der odder ones.

Bending der nominations at Zinzinnati, Oheeo, der suggestion of Mr. Greeley's name vas laffed about it, but he made em broof it, und der laff dears vas soon emblazoned und got hot on der faces of some of der boys, und on a leedle vhile, dhem tings dried ub on der feadures vhen dhey found out der realidy of der shoke. Dhen his goot gwalidies vas comed ub mit bredickting his shkalping on a leedle vhile. It hafe been said dot H. G. vas a South sympadizer, und vent bailments for Sheff Davis, und all dot sort of ting, und hafe been occused of being an en-emy to der Demockracy efer since Mr. und Mrs. Noah comed der ark out, und now he has gone und done it by flopping right indo der lofing arms of his enemies. Vell he beliefs in der goot pook Pible, "Lofe your bad friends." Der rebresentatif mens dot subbort him do not escabe der ire of dheir obbonents. Dhey vas denounced as draidors, rene-gates, hirelingouts. Dheir visits to "Chap a shgwaw" vas faceetiously ridiguled und beshmalled, und promised a lamboosting at der pox of-fice next November. It is asserted dot ofer Mr. Greely vould been eglected, he vill oxercise disputed und dangerous bowers, dot he is radical und agressif, und dot he vas der worst sort of a broteckionist. Yoost der man der Democrats dond did vant.

Der Liberals are accused of a bolidickal crimes in going ofer to der Democrats, und "wice or wersa."

Dot vas said der Democrats vill gobble ub all der fleshy offices, on der evention of Mr. Greely's ecklection, und dot der old time enemies of der Republicans vill yoost inaugurate a sysdem of gofernment dot vill shwamp dis habby nation. Yoost eglect Greely, say der obbonents, und you eglect a man mitout brains or execkutif apilidy, nor shtam-pede enuff to conduct der affairs of der nation.

Der dear peobles public are varned dot der coundry could oney been safed by eglecting Sheneral Grant. Yoost eglect him und dhere shall been no more tariff; he vill pay der whole national debt from his pocket out. He vould been willing to been the Rothschilds of America.

Dook der Greely pardy, und in equally pidder und denunciadory tone of woice, dhey cry "Down mit Grant." Der Bresident is charged mit bad conduct generally. Der Liperal und Democratic pabers did said he byed "Long Switch" coddages mit a fleshy abbointments. Dhen a contradicktion vas ensue, und dhen dhey took it all back. Grant vas urged as unfit for der Bresidency, because he dond vas shtatesmenshib, oney a lucky soldier. He vas occused of many bad tings during his derm of office, und der peoble vas told dot dhey need look for no goot Gofernment vhile he vas in der chair. Cendralization vas perhabs der greatest cry out of der Grant obbonents. Eglect him, und he vill gif you a taste und shmell of one-man bower, by centralizing der Gofernment so dot all der Shtates would been bereft of any rights vhich dhey now bossess. Yoost put him in annodder four years und der coundry vas hopelessly lost und gone to der deuce.

Der addacks of der Liperals on der publick officers vas also severitude. It vas freely und repeadidly said dot der convention by Philadelphia vas composed of office-holders und Gofernment laborers, who, mit a subsidized bress, backed by a milidary dicktator, vat all vas comed to nominate him in der most unanimous vay about it.

Korubtion in all der offices of der authoridies is charged indisshkriminadely by der Liperal press, vhich daily teems mit all sorts of ardickcals on der failure of der administration of Sheneral Grant. Efery peddy postmaster is besed by der local pabers, und vhen der Grantides hold vat dhey call a grand mass out meeting, der obbosition dwindles him down like der deuce, und dhen "wice a wersa." Dhus it vill go on, und vhen der time comed along in der Novemper mondth, der publics vill saw who vas der man, und vill also saw mit dhere eyes out vat pabers will took a back seat mit dhere eyebrows between dhere feetshteps.

Yoost eglect me to der office of der Bresident of der Oonited States, und I will agreed to dook all der presents vat shall comed. Und so vill efery man dots got sense.

Eglect me to der Bresidential sead und to der man vat shall got ub a

Mayor Medill und his leedle Hatchet.

Chicago
BoliceS

1873
LET US HAVE
REFORM

From *Carl Pretzel's Magasine Pook*.

moneyed subscribtion of 105 tousand tollars, by mine hand paid out to me in my house, und vhen I got it in my safe lockt out, I vill gif him der fleshiest office in der gift of der people, so help me gracious.

Ruth und Naomi

[Carl Pretzel retells the Old Testament story of Ruth and Naomi.]

...

I dink dhere vas notting so supremely, so douchingly beaudifull, so ex-bressive of good affection und devotion as Ruth's langwages to her mudder-in-law, Naomi. Dhey vas about to leaf der home vhere dhey had passed der summer of life, der home vhere dhey refelled in all der delights of tomestic bliss. Dhey had trank from der same foundains of vasser oud, of home und lofe. Der leedle lambs vas shkipped und blayed around der homes, in der kreen bastures und on moundain side. Der fhlowers dhey had tended plossomed yoost so beaudifull as efer, und threw dheir rich berfumes ubon der morning air. Der dew klittered und trempled on efery plade of grass, trinkin der sunpeams ub dot rested ubon em. Der prite Heafens dot pent ofer dheir once habby homes mit soft tints und golten-crested clouds, all dot vas klorious in ouder vorldt vas hid from dheir tear-dimmed eyeses—for der crushing plow of afflicktion had balsied dheir imachinations like der tree vat got shtruck mit lightnin in dwo blaces.

Alone, childless, und vidowed, sad und sick at heart, dhey knew not vhere to vhent. Naomi she say:

Go each to der mudder's house, und may been der Lord vould deal out kindly mit you as you hafe dealed kindly oud mit me.

Dhen der shendle Orpha keesed her mudder und vhent mit her people und her gods oud.

Dhey lifded dheir voices ub und cryed like dheir hearts vas break. How eloquendt vas dhem tears! how lonely like der deuce, und how beaudifull dhey vas in dot loneliness.

But her goot-lookin Ruth clung unto her, for she had nursed him from his Maker's hands. She had yoost vatched ofer him und guided his feetshtebs droo der shlibbery valks of yooth to manhoot. His head vas been billowed ubon her preast! How ofden, too, in her feadures she could drace his linesments so fair, ubon whom she had lafished all her youthfull affektions! Dhey vas like gushin floods of sunlight to her choyous heart! By her voice his voice vas der same kind dot fell in witching kadence ubon her charmed ear, und filled her soul shuck full mit melody, und shtirred der foundain of her lofe dot now vas lay burried from her sight in der cruel grafe-yard oud.

> Dond told me, mudder, mine angel mudder,
> To gone avay und leaf you now,
> Alone togedder by yourself to vhent,
> Mit sorrow und trouble on your brow.

> Efery vhere, no matter vhere I vhent,
> You, too, shall go, und I vill share
> Der burden of all dot suffering,
> Of all dot sorrow und dot care.

> Mine house dot shall been your house,
> Und your God shall too been mine,
> We'll valk togedder efermore
> Und mine heart vill shduck to dhine.

> I dond vill leaf you, nefer, nefer,
> Dill der chilly Death did said,
> Gif me your mudder dot you lofe;
> Und he dooks you from me dead.

> Und, mudder darling, vhen you vas dooken,
> No matter vhere der grafeyard be,
> In der vasser or vhere der fhlowers grow,
> Der same shall kover me.

From The Wit and Wisdom of Carl Pretzel

A man who apparently was more of a wit than a madman, but who, notwithstanding was confined in an insane asylum, being asked how he came there, answered: "Merely by a dispute of words. I said that all men were mad, and all men said that I was mad, and the *majority carried the point.*"

...

> Man is a strange mixture. He can
>   war like a lion,
>   bellow like a bull,
>   grunt like a hog,
>   bray like a jackass,

coo like a dove,
sing like a nightingale,
crow like a rooster,
cackle like a hen,
howl like a fiend.
    He can be
cunning as a fox,
slimy as a snake,
harmless as a lamb;
he can love today and hate tomorrow.
    Poor devil, he may, within forty-eight hours, be afflicted with
        gripes,
        lumbago,
        piles,
        vomit and yellow fever.
But he is plucky; he never dies before his time comes.
We refer to man as developed in Chicago.
In the insignificant outside world he is, of course, an
    insignificant nothing.

• • •

Two gentlemen, Mr. D. and Mr. L. stood candidates for a seat in the legislature. They were violently opposed to each other; by some artifice, Mr. D. gained the election. When he was returning home, much elated with success, he met a gentleman, an acquaintance of his.

"Well," says D. "I've got the election; L. was no match for me; I'll tell you how I flung him; if there happened [to be] any Dutch votes, I could talk Dutch with them, *and there I had the advantage of him*. If there were any Frenchmen, I could talk French with them, *and there I had the advantage of him*. But as to L., he was a clever, honest, sensible little fellow."

"Yes sir," replied the gentleman, "*and there he had the advantage of you*."

• • •

A Frenchman, having repeatedly heard the word *press*, used to imply *persuade* one evening when in company exclaimed: "Pray squeeze that lady to sing."

• • •

A Chicago woman recently married a Chinese laundryman, and in three days thereafter the unhappy Celestial appeared at a barber's shop and ordered his pigtail cut off, saying, in explanation, "Too muchee Yank!"

[The anti-immigrant attitude in Chicago reached its zenith during the 1880s when Slason Thompson (1849–1935) and Hobart C. Chatfield-Taylor (1865–1945) began *America: A Journal for Americans*, a weekly that existed from 1888 to 1892. Initially the magazine was strongly "literary" (perhaps as a reflection of young Chatfield-Taylor's interests); however, it soon became a sociopolitical publication. Its emphasis upon the possible threats to the "American way of life" was documented by material that appeared in a section called "Americanisms," a report of the number of foreign immigrants who had arrived in the United States through the various ports of entry during a given week. Clearly designed to instill fear, "Americanisms" ostensibly was thought to be protective of American institutions. Of further concern was the status of the public school system, which the editors considered to be jeopardized by the Irish and German Catholics as well as by instruction in foreign languages. Much space was devoted to the "alien" and "parochial" aspects of public education.

America was against anything or anybody who did not fit into its plan of "America for Americans." It was also against such philanthropists as Andrew Carnegie because it believed that their gifts made people "lazier." It was in favor of restrictions on foreign immigration and considered itself a watch dog "to preserve the native stock." In many ways *America* was an incarnation of W. W. Danenhower's *Weekly Native Citizen* of 1855, which maintained that "America shall and must be governed by Americans." The earlier journal failed in the 1850s for much the same reason that *America* failed in the 1890s; something in the American spirit is inimical to this type of journalism in spite of its momentary popularity. Clearly the editors played upon the trepidations of readers who believed that somehow the integrity of churches, schools, as well as the English language, would be compromised with the arrival of each group of immigrants.

The "humor" of the selections is indeed grim, but any survey of the comic spirit must include a record of what made people laugh, at a given moment in history.]

An American

I Wish I Was a Foreigner

I wish I was a foreigner. I really, really do,
A right down foreign foreigner, pure foreigner through and
    through;
Because I find Americans, with all of native worth,
Don't stand one-half the chances here with men of foreign
    birth.

It seems to be unpopular for us to hold a place,
For we are made to give it up to men of foreign race.
The question of necessity and fitness we possess
Must never be considered—who cares for our distress?

Perhaps it is not wicked to be of foreign birth,
Or to mutter a mild protest when an alien wants the earth;
But the latest importation is sure to strike a job,
And be the sooner qualified to strike and lead a mob.

A Dutchman or an Irishman, a Frenchman or a Turk,
Comes here to be a voter, and is always given work;
A native-born American is here, and here must stay;
So it matters little how he lives, he cannot get away.

The Spaniard and Bohemian, the Russian and the Pole,
Are looking toward America with longings in the soul,
Because the politicians will receive with open arms,
And the goddess of our freedom bid them welcome to her
    charms.

But the law-abiding Chinaman from the celestial shore,
Because he has no franchise, is driven from our door;
Americans and Chinamen are not in much demand,
The one remains neglected while the other's barred the land.

So I wish I was a Dutchman, or some other foreign cuss,
I'd lord it o'er the natives—who don't dare make a fuss.
But my blushes tell the story, I am native to the soil;
So the aliens hold the places—visitors must never toil.

J. William Pope

Don't Neglect the Bars

John, don't neglect the bars, but keep them up
    For fear of cattle straying, coming here,
And givin' ours some horrible disease;
    'Tis not so much our pasturage, I fear,
For we have lots, and can afford to give
    To hungry brutes, but I cannot forget
My Uncle Sam, and what a time he had
    With lousy cattle, and his feel it yet.

'Twas at a time when pasturage was short—
    Excepting with a few who kept high breeds—
But uncle did not keep a single hoof
    More than a farm well kept and farmer needs.
But he was good, nor would he turn away
    A hungry beast, and that proved his mistake,
For 'twas not long until such herds was there
    That 'neath their tread the very hills would quake.

His cattle got disease of hoof and horn;
    They also got the wolf in tail, and grew
More lanky than the cattle which had come;
    Then uncle pondered what was best to do.
His fences could not keep the stranger beasts,
    They tossed the riders quicker than a wink;
They pulled down stacks, and trampled fields of grain,
    And pushed his cattle from their feed and drink.

At last he said: "I'll drive them from my farm,"
    And went to do it, but they pawed the ground,
And tossed their heads, and set up such a roar,
    He said: "I thought all hell had been unbound."
He called the dogs, they came; all good dogs, too;
    Then one fat bull, the leader of the herd,
Came out to meet his pack. It makes me laugh
    To think how uncle underlined each word.

The Pope's American Footstool.

How long will this cushion resting on beer glasses afford comfort and repose
to the Pope's ten toes?

From *America*, June 25, 1891.

My uncle was a strange old man; he gave
  Such funny names to all his dogs—he cried:
"Maine! bounce that bull; Penn.! take that crossed horned
    steer;
  There, Ohio! don't you see that heifer, pied
About the rump, and bloody red before?
  Attack her front! Mass.! Vt.! Ill.! N. Y.?
On to the rest now! whoop her up! Good dogs;
  Down to the stream, and over make them fly!"
And fly they did, but many, ere they reached
  The stream, gave out and died; the crossed horned steer,
The bull, and heifer fed a thousand crows.
  Ha! ha! ha! their owners came, next year,
Demanding pay for what were lost, but he,
  Uncle Sam, just called the dogs and said: "Thar's
My answer; now just you git." They got. John!
  Remember this, and don't forget the bars.

Nineteenth-Century Ethnic Jokes: A Sampler

It is perhaps in ethnic humor that one can see the limitations and the callousness of much of this wit. It is self-centered and selfish. As the humorist rails against a particular group, the fact that people laugh says as much about the audience as about the subject. These jokes, which are seldom clever, illustrate the true meaning of the theory of the scapegoat and are often tasteless. At the same time, they reflect the concerns of various national groups.

Ethnic jokes—an integral part of the oral tradition, produced by fear—when printed appeared in anti-immigrant journals such as *America*; however, many of them are a part of the folklore of the region. What is ultimately of significance is their unchanging quality as one moves from the nineteenth century to the twentieth. The last joke, for example, clearly marks a move from the specific to the general as its relevance transcends the nineteenth-century Chicago that produced it.

In 1889

[The nineteenth-century attacks on the teaching of German in the public schools are similar to the present concern for bilingual education with emphasis upon the teaching of Spanish in public schools and the conducting of some courses in Spanish for the benefit of Puerto Rican and Cuban students.]

•••

Mr. Donnervetter: Vot do you suppose does Yankee beebles vill vant next?

Mr. Hockheimer: Vot do dey vant now?

Mr. Donnervetter: Some of 'em had de cheeck to vant dose English language teached in der bublic schools.

In a Street Car

[While only tangentially related to ethnic humor, the many jokes about William Dean Howells and the growing popularity of the realistic method in fiction were in part a product of the notion that realism was a "foreign" ideology, brought in by the foreign immigrants.]

•••

First Passenger—For heaven's sake, what have you got in that package; is it Limburger cheese?

Second Passenger—I don't notice anything.

First Passenger—But, man alive, you can't help noticing it; it comes directly from that bundle you are carrying.

Second Passenger—Ah, it is probably this new school American novel that I am carrying home. Excuse me while I throw it out of the window.

•••

First Author—I understand you sent a story to *Harper's Magazine*, where Mr. Howells presides.

Second Author—I did.

First Author—What was its fate?

Second Author—It was declined. Curses on the luck! It had a plot.

The Jewish Merchant, the Irish Politician, and Others

Einstein—Vull, Oppenheimer, how did you find Morgenthal dis morning?

Oppenheimer—Vorse, Jakey; he was died.

Einstein—He was de silent bardner in der house, und I suppose ve ought to let dot flag down at half-mast.

Oppenheimer—Dot's a good idea. Here, Isaac, take a couple of der boys up on der roof and mark dot flag down 50 per cent.

• • •

Alderman Dooley: Oi roise to mek a move that Casey's motion be laid on the table.

Alderman Casey: An' oi roise to say that if that motion is laid on the table oi'll make a motion that will knock Dooley unther that same.

• • •

Question: What's black and blue and rolls in the gutter?

Answer: The next guy who tells a Polish joke.

Part Two
The Heyday

State Street, looking northward toward the 1892 Masonic
Temple, at the time "the world's tallest building." From an
illustration by John T. McCutcheon for *The Chicago Record's
Stories of the Streets and of the Town*.

Introduction

In the years just preceding the great fire, Chicago newspaper publication had been much dominated by the *Tribune* and the *Times*. Although the two papers poured quantities of energy into political spokesmanship, both also found increasing opportunity for the more general appeal illustrated in Part One. The *Tribune* in particular opened its ranks to an increasing number of writers of literary ambition and attainment under the editorship of Horace White during the decade just following the Civil War. The Fire of 1871 itself, virtually destroying the city's business district and its environs, had an enormous impact, and one that at first seemed to cancel out much of the material progress of thirty-eight years. In fact, however, it was to call forth so great an effort at rebuilding and improving that in the end it became a prime stimulus to renewed prosperity. As the city's growth leaped ahead, one of the consequences was a parallel expansion in journalism marked by the advent of new publishers, editors, and writers.

Founded in 1872, J. Y. Scammon's *Inter-Ocean* attempted an even more rigidly Republican appeal than that of the *Tribune* but found space as well for lively feature writing, and 1883 saw the establishment of the *Morning Herald*. In 1875 another publishing force appeared in the person of Melville Stone, who founded the *Daily News* as a politically independent journal; this policy of independence would prove to be the largest single impetus to the furtherance of Chicago's public wit. Stone's aim was to create a paper that could be sold cheaply (its price was one cent) and would seek the broadest possible readership by lively and accurate reporting, informed editorial opinion, and literate entertainment features, all without political or commercial side-taking. As time passed, it developed strong public service interests. Its advertising was clearly separated from its news and editorial writing, and the two from each other. Advertisers themselves were not catered to in either general policy or detailed content. In effect, Stone put the success of his enterprise very much into the keeping of its staff's ability to inform and interest the general reader.

He was fortunate in finding able editors and writers quickly and, after a difficult early period, in consolidating the paper's business management in the hands of a new partner and longtime friend, Victor F. Lawson, who after 1888 became not only full owner but editor also as Stone moved on to other interests. In the early eighties, Lawson and Stone decided to expand their enterprise by adding a morning edition, the *Morning News*, which in 1893 was renamed the *Record*; by the mid-nineties the two papers combined were circulating over three hundred thousand copies each day. Stone had briefly secured the services of Finley Peter Dunne as a reporter for the *News* at an early stage in Dunne's career, but the inventor of "Mr. Dooley" was shortly to join with friends who were turning the *Morning Herald* into the channel of independent and appealing journalism marked out by the *News*. In 1890 the *Herald* launched an evening affiliate called the *Evening Post*. The *Herald* and *Post* combination made much use of entertainment and other feature material, and it was in the *Post* in 1893 that Dunne inaugurated his "Mr. Dooley" pieces. In 1909, the *Post* also began publication of "The Friday Literary Review" as a weekly feature. Just as Mr. Dooley came into existence in order to assist the appeal of a fledgling newspaper, so Eugene Field had been brought from Denver to Chicago in 1883 to strengthen the then new *Morning News* with his "Sharps and Flats" column. In 1893, the same paper would put George Ade and his artist friend John T. McCutcheon to work on another kind of column, "Stories of the Streets and of the Town." Bright inventiveness had become a mainstay of the new publishing wave.

It seems fair to conclude, then, that the rise of the major Chicago wits occurred above all because of their contribution to innovative journalism in the city. By 1901 the *Tribune* also had moved some distance in the same direction. In that year it added the sophisticated column of Bert Leston Taylor, "A Line O' Type or Two," and in 1913 it hired Ring Lardner to conduct an established column of sporting and more general humor, "In the Wake of the News." It made another change in the direction of enlightened feature writing when, in 1918, Burton Rascoe became its chief book reviewer. Field died in 1895, and both Dunne and Ade had left Chicago by 1900, but the *News*, passing to the highly literate editorship of Henry Justin Smith, developed a group of feature writers that included Keith Preston, Carl Sandburg, and Ben Hecht, that extended to our own days, and the final period of its history, in the person of Mike Royko.

Although all this represented most immediately a phenomenon of changing publishing strategies, there was much also in the general history of Chicago that was at least congruent in spirit with it. Figures evaluating the city's chief economic enterprises soared in the two decades between the Fire of 1871 and the opening of the Columbian Exposition of 1893. This world's fair was in itself a handsome and opulent success and did much to stir the mind and imagination of the city in regard to itself and its place in the world. The expansion and liberalization of newspaper publishing thus came as a direct response to the city's waxing prosperity and urbanity, and the world's fair of 1893 stood as a striking emblem of the new era.

The post-fire decades also witnessed cultural uplift within the city, which gave Eugene Field much occasion for joking but in fact betokened the rise of the kind of intelligence to which he and the other wits appealed. Extending the concern of such earlier periodicals as the *Chicago Magazine* and the *Literary Budget*, Francis Fisher Browne originated the *Lakeside Monthly* in 1876 and followed it with the *Dial* in 1880. The latter made Chicago the home of a conservative but knowledgeable literary review largely written by Chicagoans and midwesterners. After the destruction of earlier library efforts in the Fire of 1871, the Chicago Public Library opened its doors in 1873. In 1887 the Newberry Library appointed its first librarian and began its service to humanistic study, to be followed in 1897 by the Crerar Library with its appeal to scientific and technological learning. The Chicago Historical Society had been active since the city's early years, and in 1892 it began construction of its own headquarters and library building. The seventies and eighties saw the organization of such cultural associations as the Philosophical Society of Chicago, the Polytechnic Society, the Athenaeum, and the Chicago Literary Club; and with the advent of Henry B. Fuller's, Hamlin Garland's, and Robert Herrick's fiction at the turn of the century and after, the city saw itself supporting highly visible literary production. Northwestern University in suburban Evanston experienced substantial growth after 1870. In 1892 the University of Chicago began its rise toward national and international prominence, and in 1893 the Armour Institute (now the Illinois Institute of Technology) began its attention to useful learning.

Finally, the physical aspect of the city underwent great alteration during the period. Rebuilding after the fire took much more substantial and ambitious forms than those prevailing before 1871 and included, as time went on, numerous structures like the library buildings, the Fine Arts building, the Auditorium, Orchestra Hall, and the Art Institute that greatly improved the city's livability and its imaginative life. Progress in Chicago architecture included inauguration of the steel-frame "skyscraper" building in 1885, which made for further dramatic change, while the work of such individual architects as Louis Sullivan and Frank Lloyd Wright marked Chicago as a center of innovative design. In 1892 work was undertaken on the Chicago Sanitary and Ship Canal, which would finally succeed in reversing the flow of the Chicago River to make it drain from the lake westward and southward and so open meaningful possibilities of lakefront development free of the heavy pollution that had oppressed the earlier town. Inauguration of the 1909 "Chicago Plan" and its eventual opening of Michigan Avenue as a continuous north-south boulevard was a dramatic result. As the city's wealth and population grew, so did its area. Pre-fire Chicago included about 35,000 square miles. By 1893 the city had annexed land to stretch to 185,000 square miles and to begin its spillover into newer suburbs that, for the time at least, fed the city and its life and constituted a leavening and relieving resource for it.

Eugene Field

Eugene Field (1850–1895) was born in St. Louis, Missouri, on September 2 or 3, the son of a successful lawyer and his wife, Roswell and Frances Field. Roswell Field (his name was carried forward by Eugene's younger brother, also a newspaperman, poet, and essayist) was notable for having initiated the original legal action in behalf of the escaped Negro slave, Dred Scott. Field's mother died in 1856, and he was raised by his paternal cousin, Miss Mary Field French of Amherst, Massachusetts. He was a lively boy, better known as a youthful prankster and adventurer than as a scholar. He graduated from a private academy and attended college for three successive years, without graduation, at Williams, Knox, and the University of Missouri. His father's death in 1872 left him a patrimony which he exhausted in European travel and residence, whereupon he returned to St. Louis to find a place as reporter on the *Evening Journal* and to marry Julia Sutherland Comstock. As his newspaper work continued he advanced to editorial posts on the St. Joseph *Gazette*, the St. Louis *Journal* and *Times-Journal*, the Kansas City *Times*, and, from 1881 to 1883, the Denver *Tribune*. He had practiced verse writing early and in Denver turned his hand to publishing his verse regularly in his paper and to a humorous column, "The Tribune Primer," the content of which was printed in pamphlet form and attracted the attention of Melville Stone, who was then organizing a morning edition of his Chicago *Daily News*. Field came to Chicago with his family in 1883 and moved quickly toward a major success with his writing of verse and prose. He was a longtime sufferer from what he called "dyspepsia," though his sudden death in his forty-fifth year seems to have followed from a heart arrest.

In the early eighties he gave his Chicago column the title "Sharps and Flats," a phrase borrowed from the title of a play written by his *News* colleague, friend, biographer, and editor, Slason Thompson, who was a cofounder and editor of *America* magazine, where numbers of Field's poems also appeared. Virtually all of his book publication was drawn from this column, from the earlier Denver column, and from his contributions to *America*. The poetry was of the humorous or sentimental kind popular in his day and was marked also by his special pleasure in imitating Horace and in a mock Middle-English kind of spelling and expression he picked up from Thompson's more scholarly interest. Similarly, from Dr. Frank Reilly, for a time managing editor of the *Record*, he formed a bookish taste for the lore of Francis Mahony's curious nineteenth-century volume *The Reliques of Father Prout* and for the *Noctes Ambrosianae* of "Christopher North," the English editor and essayist, John Wilson. He was the author also of a small amount of bawdy verse, still largely fugitive, much relished by his newspaper friends. The prose varied widely, ranging from the topical squib, which was a staple of his columns, to the developed short tale, comic, sentimental, or romantic, with which he might fill one of his daily two-thousand-word assignments. Across its breadth, his wit is perhaps best described as "Horatian" in character—genial, delighting in special and private jokes (he was an elaborate practical joker) as well as in the free use of the names of many of the city's more or less prominent persons, and expressing considerable irreverence toward the city's shibboleths while displaying a perdurable loyalty to its life and ways.

His writing was a true image of his person. Although a devoted family man, the father of five living children, Field warmed both hands at such of the colorful life of Chicago as came his way. His custom, according to Thompson, was to appear at the old *News* building about noon, perhaps with a part of that day's material already completed in his lavishly designed home study. He proceeded to lunch with friends and to spend the early afternoon in conversation, conference, joking, and general socializing. About three o'clock he would retire to the writing cubicle that was his, take off his coat, don the Turkish slippers kept there for the purpose, prop his feet on his desk, and take pad in hand. By six, the daily stint would be finished. Although he might dine at home, he often was joined by others for dinner in the city and for entertainment afterward, particularly theater or concerts, both of which he enjoyed. His friends and acquaintances included not only cronies from Chicago's extensive newspaper world but theater and other professional figures from the town's public life—anyone, in short, who enjoyed and was up to his company. His health had made him a total abstainer from drink, but despite his persistent stomach complaint he relished good food and good company. The company, in turn, might well be surprised, but often, apparently, pleased, to find their names made rather free with in Field's column, a practice, however, over which his editors kept an anxious eye. He was only a licensed entertainer and jester.

Field was not a major satirist. Indeed, he was more humorist and sentimentalist than satirist at all. He chided his friend Thompson's fierce devotion to an Anglo-American chauvinism in *America* with the remark, "Reform away. The world is good enough for me as it is." At the same time, he brought a deft urbanity to his work that made him unique in the Chicago newspaper world and marked also a distinct addition to contemporary popular humor.

Only a small part of Field's newspaper publication is collected in the twelve volumes of *The Writings in Prose and Verse of Eugene Field* (appearing with numerous imprint dates from 1901 to 1920). It is still the most complete selection. His newspaper wit is primarily concentrated in two earlier volumes: *The Tribune Primer* (1881) and *Culture's Garland* (1887). The most complete biography is Slason Thompson's *Eugene Field, a Study in Heredity and Contradiction* (1901) and Thompson's later work, *The Life of Eugene Field, the Poet of Childhood* (1927). A more recent study is Robert Conrow, *Field Days; the Life, Times, and Reputation of Eugene Field* (1974).

From "An Auto-Analysis"

[In order to meet the demand for information about himself, Field drew up and had printed in 1894 a document containing a biographical summary, a list of his publications, and a compilation suggesting something of his tastes and habits. The compilation is printed here, and though there are some errant-sounding statements in it, his testimony nevertheless offers vivid suggestions of his personality and foibles.]

• • •

I have a miscellaneous collection of books numbering 3,500, and I am fond of the quaint and curious in every line. I am very fond of dogs, birds, and all small pets—a passion not approved of by my wife.

My favorite flower is the carnation, and I adore dolls.

My favorite hymn is "Bounding Billows."

My favorites in fiction are Hawthorne's "Scarlet Letter," "Don Quixote," and "Pilgrim's Progress."

I greatly love Hans Christian Andersen's Tales, and I am deeply interested in folk-lore and fairy tales. I believe in ghosts, in witches, and in fairies.

I should like to own a big astronomical telescope, and a twenty-four-tune music box.

My heroes in history are Martin Luther, Mme. Lamballe, Abraham Lincoln; my favorite poems are Körner's "Battle Prayer," Wordsworth's "We Are Seven," Newman's "Lead, Kindly Light," Luther's Hymn, Schiller's "The Diver," Horace's "Fons Bandusiae," and Burns' "Cotter's Saturday Night." I dislike Dante and Byron. I should like to have known Jeremiah the prophet, old man Poggio, Horace, Walter

Scott, Bonaparte, Hawthorne, Mme. Sontag, Sir John Herschel, Hans Andersen.

My favorite actor is Henry Irving; actress, Mme. Modjeska.

I dislike "Politics," so called.

I should like to have the privilege of voting extended to women.

I am unalterably opposed to capital punishment.

I favor a system of pensions for noble services in literature, art, science, etc. I approve of compulsory education.

If I had my way, I should make the abuse of horses, dogs, and cattle a penal offense; I should abolish all dog laws and dog-catchers, and I would punish severely everybody who caught and caged birds.

I dislike all exercise and play all games very indifferently.

I love to read in bed.

I believe in churches and schools: I hate wars, armies, soldiers, guns, and fireworks.

I like music (limited).

I have been a great theater-goer.

I enjoy the society of doctors and clergymen.

My favorite color is red.

I do not care particularly for sculpture or for paintings; I try not to become interested in them, for the reason that if I were to cultivate a taste for them I should presently become hopelessly bankrupt.

I am extravagantly fond of perfumes.

I am a poor diner, and I drink no wine or spirits of any kind: I do not smoke tobacco.

I dislike crowds and I abominate functions.

I am six feet in height; am of spare build, weigh 160 pounds, and have shocking taste in dress.

But I like to have well-dressed people about me.

My eyes are blue, my complexion pale, my face is shaven, and I incline to baldness.

It is only when I look and see how young and fair and sweet my wife is that I have a good opinion of myself.

I am fond of the companionship of women, and I have no unconquerable prejudice against feminine beauty. I recall with pride that in twenty-two years of active journalism I have always written in reverential praise of womankind.

I favor early marriage.

I do not love all children.

I have tried to analyze my feelings toward children, and I think I discover that I love them in so far as I can make pets of them.

I believe that, if I live, I shall do my best literary work when I am a grandfather.

I give these facts, confessions, and observations for the information of those who, for one reason or another, are applying constantly to me for biographical data concerning myself.

Eugene Field

From The Complete Tribune Primer

[Field's first effort at humorous column writing occurred while he was managing editor of the Denver *Tribune*. The result was immediately popular, and in 1881 the paper issued a pamphlet entitled *The Tribune Primer*, culled from the column, which sold out quickly and was pirated by another publisher as *The Model Primer*. The first copyrighted edition of the work, illustrated by Frederick Opper, appeared as *The Complete Tribune Primer* (Boston: Mutual Book Co., 1900), and this is the edition most readily available today. To promote its sale, the publisher brought out a small sample volume called *A Little Book of Nonsense* and supplied the following comment on the composition of Field's text. "This series of skits as they were originally published in the *Denver Tribune* began with the issue of Monday, October 10, 1881. Each series consisted of from nine to twenty paragraphs, without titles, and each series numbered by itself with Roman numerals. . . . Each series bore the general heading, 'The Tribune Primer,' with subheadings varying with each issue, such as 'Tales Designed for the Information and Edification of the Nursery Brigade,' 'Nursery Exercises for the Precious Little Folks,' etc. . . . They were discontinued because the style was being adopted all over the country, some twenty papers 'having fallen into the primer line since the *Tribune* set the fashion.'"

The squibs were divided between those on newspaper life and what may be called grim domestic humor: naughty children, errant fathers, nagging mothers, politicians, bill dodgers, and the like; and across their breadth they suggested a grainier sense of fun than Field would often allow himself in Chicago. The emphasis in this selection is on the newspaper squibs, to suggest Field's comic sense of his own métier, especially its still-shadowy social and economic standing.]

Here we Have a City Editor. He is Talking with the Foreman. He is saying he will have a Full Paper in the Morning. The Foreman is Smiling Sadly. Maybe he is Thinking the Paper will have a Full City Editor before Morning.

• • •

This is the Man who has had a Notice in the Paper. How Proud he is. He is Stepping Higher than a Blind Horse. If he had Wings he would Fly. Next Week the Paper will say the Man is a Measly Old Fraud, and the Man will not Step so High.

• • •

The Dog looks sick. He has been celebrating the Fourth of July. There is a Bunch of Fire Crackers tied to his Tail, also a tin Dipper. The Dipper does not Seem to bother him as much as the Fire Crackers. He is Wishing it was Christmas. We fear he is not a Patriotic Dog.

• • •

The Dramatic critic is Asleep. The play Does not Interest him. He will give it Thunder in the Paper because it will Say they are not Artists. After the Play, the Critic will go to the Variety Show. Will he sleep there? No, he will Not. The Lady in the Short Dress and Pink Tights will Buy six Copies of the Paper in the Morning because the Critic will say she is an Artist. It is very comfortable to be an Artist when there are Critics in the Neighborhood.

• • •

Here we Have a Valise. It does not Weigh Four hundred Pounds. It is the Valise of an Editor. In the Valise are Three Socks and a Bottle and a Book. There is Something in the Bottle. Maybe it is Arnica for the Editor's Sore Finger. The Book is Baxter's Saints' Rest. The Socks got into the Valise by Mistake. Perhaps the Bottle will get into the Editor by Mistake.

• • •

Here we Have a Business Manager. He is Blowing about the Circulation of the paper. He is Saying the Paper has Entered upon an Era of Unprecedented Prosperity. In a Minute he will Go up Stairs and Chide the Editor for leaving his Gas Burning while he Went out for a Drink of Water, and he will dock a Reporter Four Dollars because a Subscriber has licked him and he cannot Work. Little Children, if we Believed Business Managers went to Heaven, we would Give up our Pew in Church.

• • •

Here is a Castle. It is the Home of an Editor. It has stained Glass windows and Mahogany stairways. In front of the Castle is a Park. Is it not Sweet? The lady in the Park is the editor's wife. She wears a Costly robe of Velvet trimmed with Gold Lace, and there are Pearls and Rubies in her Hair. The Editor sits on the front Stoop smoking an Havana Cigar. His little Children are playing with diamond Marbles on the Tesselated Floor. The Editor can afford to Live in Style. He gets Seventy-Five Dollars a month Wages.

• • •

This is an Editorial Writer. He is Writing a Thoughtful Piece about the Degeneracy of the Age. He talks about the Good Old Times when Men were Manly and Youthful Breasts were Pregnant with Chivalry. By and by he Will go Home and Lick his wife for not Cutting up enough Cord Wood for the Kitchen Fire in the Morning, and he will Spit Tobacco all over his daughter Esther's new Silk Gown.

• • •

Who is this Creature with Long Hair and a Wild Eye? He is a Poet. He writes Poems on Spring and Women's Eyes and Strange, unreal Things of that Kind. He is always Wishing he was Dead, but he wouldn't Let anybody Kill him if he could Get away. A mighty good Sausage Stuffer was Spoiled when the Man became a Poet. He would Look well Standing under a Descending Pile Driver.

• • •

[Aside from the *Primer*, Field contributed many verses to the *Tribune*. Almost all these were run separately from the column, and a number of them, like the first printed here, were jokingly ascribed to one or another of Denver's publicly known figures. Field here celebrates the building of a new theater in the city and adds his appreciation of a performer whose charms he admired.]

Tabor and Abbott

    The Opera House—a union grand
      Of capital and labor—
    Long will the stately structure stand,
      A monument to Tabor.

    And as to Emma, never will
      Our citizens cease lovin' her.
    While time lasts shall her name be linked
      With that of the ex-Governor.

Because of its grand Opera House,
  Our city's much elated,
And happy is the time that Em
  The structure dedicated.

For many a year and many a year
  Our folks will have the habit
Of lauding that illustrious pair
  Tabor and Emma Abbot.

                    [Attributed to] R. W. Woodbury

A Piazza Tragedy

The beauteous Ethel's father has a
Newly painted front piazza,
    He has a
    Piazza;
When with tobacco juice 'twas tainted,
They had the front piazza painted,
    That tainted
    Piazza painted.

Algernon called that night, perchance,
Arrayed in comely sealskin pants,
    That night, perchance,
    In gorgeous pants;
Engaging Ethel in a chat
On that piazza down he sat,
    In chat,
    They sat.

And when an hour or two had passed,
He tried to rise, but oh, stuck fast,
    At last
    Stuck fast!
Fair Ethel shrieked, "It is the paint!"
And fainted in a deadly faint,
    This saint
    Did faint.

Algernon sits there till this day,
He cannot tear himself away;

> Away?
> Nay, nay,
> His pants are firm, the paint is dry,
> He's nothing else to do but die;
> To die!
> O my!

From "Sharps and Flats"

[Field's efforts in Denver were touched with originality, but as news-paper chaff they contained no more than a start toward what he him-self hoped for from his writing. After his brief effort at a column, he seems to have withdrawn as regular humorist and fallen back on con-tributions, some solicited from Edgar W. (Bill) Nye, then publishing his own humorous paper, the Laramie, Wyoming, *Boomerang*, and so be-ginning a lifelong friendship with Nye. Melville Stone, attempting to lure Field to the Chicago *Morning News*, promised him all possible freedom of creative opportunity on that paper, and this promise as much as the heady offer of a $50 weekly salary seems to have been decisive.

Once settled in Chicago, Field spent a brief time relying on the short squib to fill his space, but it was not long before he had found his column's title and had begun to diversify the content of his work by expanding to the sophisticated and understated wit that was his spe-cific contribution to the newspaper humor of his day. What follows here is prose and verse selected from across the Chicago years and from poems appearing in *America* magazine as well as "Sharps and Flats." There was little difference in kind.

These three groups of selections from Field vary in length, but ex-cept for the first they reflect the miscellaneous character of a typical column. The first two are characteristic of his earlier Chicago empha-sis. The third reflects his growing drift toward what he called "biblio-mania" and toward in-group humor and sentiment.

It should be noted that although Field, in the prevailing newspaper practice of the time, did not sign his column, a stream of commercially and privately published volumes continued steadily across the period of his Chicago years and so made his name and writing widely known. This had begun with *The Tribune Primer* of 1881 and 1900 and *Cul-*

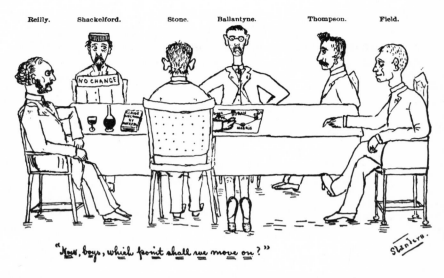

Reilly. Shackelford. Stone. Ballantyne. Thompson. Field.

"Now, boys, which point shall we move on?"

"'Daily News' Editorial Council of War." From a drawing by Eugene Field in Slason Thompson, *The Life of Eugene Field, the Poet of Childhood*. Field pictures himself with his colleagues Slason Thompson and John Ballantyne. The printer (Shackelford) is opposed to any alterations in copy received. Dr. Frank Reilly was Field's managing editor and Melville Stone his publisher.

ture's Garland, the first fruit of his Chicago writing, in 1887. Later books published in his lifetime and afterward avoided humor to concentrate on his poems and tales, with the result that Field would become most widely identified as romancer and "the poet of childhood." He did not quite succeed in turning Chicago into a national joke in *Culture's Garland*, and Chicago itself was not wholly appreciative of the effort. After its relative failure Field published no further volume that clearly identified him as a wit, although wit continued to be central in his column itself. This alteration of national appeal was in accord with his own evaluation of his work. However, it diminished perception of him as practitioner of a civilized humor that made its influence felt in the writing of such later Chicagoans as Bert Leston Taylor, Franklin P. Adams, and Keith Preston, and in others elsewhere.]

I

[As this first section suggests, Field found ample column possibilities in the awarding to George M. Pullman, the Chicago railroad car manufacturer, the honorary title of "Marchese" in return for his promotional gift of a Pullman Palace Car to the King of Italy. Pullman was a powerful businessman and a pillar of the Chicago industrial community. However, his famously single-minded devotion to building a sleeping-car empire gave point to Field's joking about more aristocratic pretensions.]

...

> "Il bianco di cazerni della graze fio bella,
> Di ternea si mazzoni quel' antista Somno della."
> > *Petrarch.*

> "He who conduces to a fellow's sleep,
> Should noble fame and goodly riches reap."
> > *Tasso.*

> "Sleep mocks at death: when weary of the earth,
> We do not die—we take an upper berth."
> > *Dante.*

Never since the great fire of 1871 has Chicago society been so profoundly agitated as it was when it became noised about that King Humbert of Italy had created our esteemed fellow-townsman, Col. George M. Pullman, a knight of the first water. At first, grave doubts as to the genuineness of the report were indulged; but when, later in the day, it became known that the rumor was credited at the headquarters of the Italian legation, the joy of the public burst all restraints, and manifested itself in every variety of ebullition.

Col. Pullman is, we believe, the first citizen of Chicago who has been honored in so distinguished a manner by royalty. It is true that the Pshaw of Persia craved the boon of investing the Hon. Frederick H. Winston with the order of the Yellow Dromedary, but the negotiations fell through as soon as the eminent American diplomate declined to advance the pshaw the ten thousand golden pistoles which his serene majesty expected as an evidence of Mr. Winston's good faith in the premises. It is true, also, that there are in the midst of us a number of royal personages—or perhaps we should say a number of persons of noble descent. Very many of our Irish citizens are of high extraction,—descendants of dukes, earls, booyars, barons, and knights, who for political offences have been exiled from the land of their nativity. To our certain knowledge, Col. John F. Finerty is a lineal descendant of Brian Boroihme; and many other fellow-townsmen of ours can boast ancestries almost as noble. Ex-Senator Millard B. Hereley is one of the Bourbons from Bourbon co., France; and we could, if we had the space wherein to tell it, specify who the Duke of Eniscarty, the Earl of Bal-lanasloe, the Duke of Cork, etc., are, and by what aliases they are known to the people of this city.

In spite of these facts which we have stated, it is true that Mr. Pull-man is the first citizen of Chicago to be recognized and honored by a crowned head of Europe. As near as we can come to it, Mr. Pullman's elevation to knighthood was brought about in this wise: Last year he made a tour through Italy; and when he reached Naples he called upon King Humbert, and made a formal complaint touching the rail-road facilities with which his Majesty's kingdom is, and always has been, cursed. His Majesty was struck at once with the learning, the elo-quence, the earnestness, the *sang froid*, and the *swaviter in modo*, of the petitioner; and he besought him to suggest an improvement, if he could, upon the system of travel then in vogue. Thereupon Mr. Pullman caused to be made by the Herculaneum and Pompeii Manufacturing Company (limited) a palace sleeping-coach, which he presented to King Humbert with his compliments, demanding no recompense for the distinguished gift further than the privilege of appointing and con-trolling the porters for said car. The grateful potentate readily granted this request; for he was charmed, positively delighted, with the lux-urious innovation introduced by the enterprising American. For the next six months King Humbert did nothing but travel around: the chances are that he would be travelling still, if he had not been com-pelled to suspend operations until after the Senate voted him another appropriation. At the end of the six months, the king found himself out of pocket about 1,500,000 lires; and about this time Mr. Pullman's porter in Naples, one Giacomo Fiozzo, began buying corner-lots, and erecting ten-story apartment-buildings on the principal Neapolitan thoroughfares. Kings, however, are liberal folk; and well can they afford to be, even when dealing with a Chicago businessman. So when King Humbert fell to thinking of all the pleasures (not to say benefits) he had derived from his six months' experience in Mr. Pullman's coach, he paid not even the tribute of a passing thought to the financial out-lay involved, but rather set his wits to work at inventing some means whereby he might further distinguish the gentleman, whom he viewed in the light of a benefactor. The result is this elevation of Mr. Pullman from the ranks of the hoi polloi to the dignity and the title of a marchese, which, in the Italian tongue, corresponds to the knighthood of Great Britain, the booyars of Roosha, and the flambustules of Siam.

Sig. Pietro Casa del Comma, secretary of the Italian legation in this city, tells us that when the official communication from his Majesty reaches Chicago, it will become the duty of the consul at this point to proceed at once to Mr. Pullman's palatial residence on Prairie Avenue, and there, in the presence of the Italian legation, and in the name of his Catholic majesty, to dub Mr. Pullman a marchese or (as Mr. Pullman may prefer to be called) a chevalier. Sig. del Comma says that "marchese" is pronounced "mar-kee-sy," and that "chevalier" is pronounced "shee-val-ya": we are inclined to think that markeesy sounds just a trifle more bong tong than sheevalya, and we hope that Mr. Pullman will choose that title.

After he has been invested with this honor, Mr. Pullman—or, we should say, the Markeesy Pullman—will be visited by the gardener of the legation (for this is an old custom), who will present him with a bouquet, saying, "Io ho l'onore, onorevole signor, di presentarvi le queste fiori e di gratularvi." Upon receiving this bouquet, the markeesy will be expected to hand the simple gardener fifty francs (or ten dollars), and this is all the money the markeesy will have to pay out for the honor. By a singular coincidence, the gardener of the Italian legation in Chicago at this time is one Patrick Murphy, a kinsman of the late Markeesy di Potata (*née* Murphy) of San Francisco, who was elevated from obscurity by the late Pope Pius IX.

Sig. del Comma tells us furthermore that one of the first things the Markeesy Pullman will have to do will be to choose a coat-of-arms, for a markeesy without a coat-of-arms would be an anomaly which the Italian potentate could not well endure. With a view to relieving the markeesy of much anxiety and labor, the signor has compiled a coat-of-arms, which he will submit for the markeesy's approval and adoption.

This chaste design represents a shield engrailed, bordured, and vert, with a supporting figure at each side; the figures are what in the vernacular of heraldry is called expectant and demandant; the shield dexter is quartured—that is to say, divided into four berths, or compartments, which are left blank for posterity to fill; the shield sinister is decorated with the portraiture of a small feather pillow issuant, this being the heraldic symbol of luxury and ease; upon this pillow appears the personification of indefatigable industry and ceaseless vigilance, rampant, illustrating not only the means by which the markeesy has achieved his noble ends, but also the still nobler teaching of the most wise Solomon, who said, "Go to the ant, you sluggard, or you will go to the dogs."

Above the shield appears a motto, "Pro Patria Caveliere," which is the Latin for "For His Country, a Knight"; but the particular beauty of this motto is, that it can be abridged to P. P. C.,[1] and thus be made to serve a business purpose. . . .

The Italian population of Chicago is highly gratified with the distinguished tribute paid by their monarch to our popular fellow-townsman. At a meeting of the Societa d'Italia in Poggio's restaurant last evening, several speeches were made in eulogy of the Markeesy di Pullman's many virtues, his enterprise, his munificence, his philanthropy, etc. An address to his Majesty King Humbert, congratulating him upon having recemented the ties which bind Italy and the United States, was read by Giovanni Bianco, the banana-merchant, and approved by the meeting: it was ordered that the address be cabled to his Majesty, provided that the Markeesy di Pullman would pay the toll.

The effect of the Italian boom has already become apparent in our literary circles. The leading book-sellers say that incessant have been the calls for Dante, for Petrarch, and for Tasso, since the news of the Pullman affair reached Chicago. The markeesy's portrait in the rooms of the dancing-class was draped with Italian flags last evening; and already the caterer at Caveroe's on Wabash Avenue has invented a new dish of macaroni, which is entitled macaroni di Pullman. We mention these trifling details merely to indicate how generally and how deeply this compliment of royalty to our amiable and gifted townsman is appreciated by his fellow-citizens.

Within the last two days we have received a large number of communications touching the handsome coat-of-arms which the secretary of the Italian legation has designed for the marchese di Pullman. Several of the communications contain comment upon the picture of the industrious insect represented as sprawling rampant on the feather pillow in the sinister half of the so-called Pullman shield. One correspondent says that the insect is not an ant, but a potato-bug; another

1. The initials of Pullman's firm, the Pullman Palace Car Company.

declares that it is a busy bee; and still a third maintains that it is neither a chinch-bug, nor a busy bee, nor yet an ant, but one of those predatory vampires known (by name only) in polite society as "the flat-backed militia."[2]

"THE CHICAGO TRIBUNE" is rather late in the day: still, we are glad to find it lumbering to the front with the venerable information that the Markeesy Giorgio di Pullman is not entitled to the title of sir. This is what we said last week. The title which our cultured and opulent fellow-townsman has, in recognition of his philanthropies, been honored with, is the Italian title of markeesy, which corresponds with the English title of sir; but the bearer cannot Anglicize the title: he must remain a markeesy all the days of his natural life, or until, at least, he is promoted to some higher dignity. The Markeesy di Pullman understands this perfectly, and he would not exchange his markeesyship for the cream and flower of English knighthood. In connection with this subject, we beg to say that we deeply deplore the existence of a bitter malice against, and a rancorous envy of, the Markeesy di Pullman in certain local society circles. The existence of this insidious hostility was first brought to our knowledge by means of a song composed by a Chicago poet, and set to music by one of our amateur musicians. The chorus to this ribald song runs as follows:—

> "When the party is breezy and wheezy,
> And palpably greasy, it's easy
>   To coax or to wring,
>   From a weak-minded king,
> The titular prize of markeesy."

II

[In regard to the opening squibs here it may be noted, in the first, that Felicia Hemans was a popular poetess noted for her ardent sentiment and, in the second, that the theatrical performers named were no doubt as amazed as the newspaper reader to hear of their supposed antecedents and connections. It was, perhaps, Field's way of encouraging a lively if misinformed audience for each of them.]

• • •

Capt. Ben Wingate has named his new barge the Felicia Hemans, and the same departed for Saginaw last evening with a cargo of shingles.

• • •

2. Contemporary slang for bedbugs.

The election of Mr. Stuart Robson as an honorary member of the Cook County Democratic Club will serve to remind the public that this popular comedian is one of the bitterest of partisans. His father was one of the most extensive slave-owners in Maryland. Naturally, therefore, Robson has always been a Democrat, and he glories in the fact that his first vote was cast for Andrew Jackson. Mr. William H. Crane, on the other hand, is a rabid Republican, and it is a wonderful coincidence that it should have been his father, the Rev. Moses Dickinson, who, as far back as 1826, harbored and protected in his home at Penobscot, Maine, three of the slaves who had fled from bondage on the Robson terrapin plantation near Baltimore.

. . .

The Bernhardt engagement[3] has brought out all the French scholars in Chicago. Never before had we suspected that there were so many able linguists in the midst of us. General Stiles, we have just discovered, speaks French like a native of Paris (Vermilion County). He attended the "Froufrou" performance last evening with his friend Judge Prendergast. The judge is a proficient Greek and Latin scholar, but he knows little of French, his vocabulary being limited to such phrases as "fo par," "liaison," "kelky shoze," and "olly bonnur"; so General Stiles had to explain the play to him as it progressed last evening.

"Now what is she saying?" the judge would ask.

"She said 'Good evening,'" the general would answer.

"Does 'bung swor' mean 'good evening'?" the judge would inquire. "Yes."

"Oh, what rot!" the judge would exclaim, and then a dude usher in one of Willoughby & Hill's nineteen-dollar dress-suits would teeter down the aisle and warn the gentlemen not to whisper so loud.

Presently Colonel William Penn Nixon, the gifted editor of the *Inter-Ocean*, came along and slipped into the seat next to General Stiles. He had an opera-glass, and he levelled it at once at Bernhardt's red red hair.

"Do you speak French?" asked General Stiles, in the confidential tone of a member of the Citizens' Committee.

---

3. Sarah Bernhardt made repeated American tours during the eighties and afterward, attracting large and fashionable audiences even though she performed in French. She was reportedly described by George Bernard Shaw as having a good enough sense of self-advertising to be an American.

"Oony poo," said Colonel Nixon, guardedly.

"Vooley-voo donny moy voter ver de lopera?" asked the general, motioning toward the opera-glass.

"See nay perzoon ver de lopera," protested the colonel. "Say lay zhoomels."

"Mong doo! What do I want of zhoomels?" cried General Stiles. "Zhoomels is twins."

"Parbloo!" said Colonel Nixon, "it is not twins; it is opera-glasses."

"You're all wrong, William," urged the general. "The French idiom is 'the glass of the opera.' *Ver* is 'glass,' and *de lopéra* is 'of the opera.'"

"I have heard them called lornyets," suggested Judge Prendergast, in the deferential tone of a young barrister seeking a change of venue.

"Well, I don't know what the general's opera-glass is," said Colonel Nixon, "but this one of mine is a lay zhoomels."

"Call it what you please," replied the judge; "it is der tro, as far as I am concerned, until the corpse de bally makes its ontray."

"I thought you didn't speak French," said General Stiles, turning fiercely upon the judge.

"Oh, well," the judge explained apologetically, "I'm not what you and the colonel would call oh fay,—I'm a june primmer at the business,—but when the wind is southerly I reckon I can tell a grizet from a garsong."[4]

Chicago society is still in considerable doubt as to where Bernhardt should be located in the artistic scale. A good many of the élite think that her Fédora is second to Fanny Davenport's, and there are very many others who prefer Clara Morris's Camille. We notice that the popular inquiry in cultured circles is, "Have you been to see Bernhardt?" not, "Have you been to hear Bernhardt?"

"Oh, you don't know how I enjoyed Bayernhayerdt the other evening!" exclaimed one of our most beautiful and accomplished belles. "Her dresses are beautiful, and they do say she is dreadfully naughty!"

[Edmund Clarence Stedman, featured in the following squib, com-

---

4. General Israel Stiles was a Chicago lawyer, a disciple of Robert Ingersoll's free thought, and a founder of the Chicago Liberal League. Judge Richard Prendergast was a county court judge, a public supporter of early efforts at labor union organization, chairman of the Chicago Sanitary Commission, and an astute if shifty politician. Their association with each other and with the conservative Republican, Nixon, was plainly an anomaly, for the fun of it.

bined a career as a New York stockbroker with that of a champion of the literary genteel. He was a friend of Field's, though one who lamented what he saw as the "journeyman" vulgarity of Field's humor. He himself was the author of comic as well as serious verses, but he had declined Field's request to write an introduction to *Culture's Garland*. According to Slason Thompson, the humorist's motive in the following squib was largely that of a practical joke to alarm Stedman about his reception at a scheduled Chicago appearance. Field was aware that the item would be reprinted in the New York papers. The supposed components of the supposed procession are largely fictional, but references to William Morton Payne, an editor of the *Dial*; the Twentieth Century Club; the Chicago Literary Club; and the Reverend Messrs. Gunsaulus, Brobst, and Bristol were to real Chicago institutions and personalities. The Reverend Frank Gunsaulus, author of blank-verse romances and an immensely popular preacher, was a particular friend of Field's, often turned up in his column, and, at the end, composed and preached the humorist's funeral elegy.]

• • •

Chicago literary circles are all agog over the prospective visit of Mr. Edmund Clarence Stedman, the eminent poet-critic. At the regular monthly conclave of the Robert Browning Benevolent and Patriotical Association of Cook County, night before last, it was resolved to invite Mr. Stedman to a grand complimentary banquet at the Kinsley's on Wednesday evening, the 29th. Prof. William Morton Payne, grand marshal of the parade which is to conduct the famous guest from the railway station the morning he arrives, tells us that the procession will be in this order:

> Twenty police officers afoot.
> The grand marshal, horseback, accompanied by ten
> male members of the Twentieth Century Club,
> also horseback.
> Mr. Stedman in a landau drawn by four horses,
> two black and two white.
> The Twentieth Century Club in carriages.
> A brass band afoot.
> The Robert Browning Club in Frank Parmelee's
> 'buses.
> The Homer Clubs afoot, preceded by a fife-and-drum

corps and a real Greek philosopher
attired in a tunic.
Another brass band.
A beautiful young woman playing the guitar, sym-
bolizing Apollo and his lute in a car drawn
by nine milk-white stallions, imper-
sonating the muses.
Two Hundred Chicago poets afoot.
The Chicago Literary Club in carriages.
A splendid gilded chariot bearing Gunther's Shake-
speare autograph and Mr. Ellsworth's first
printed book.
Another brass band.
Magnificent advertising car of Armour and Co.,
illustrating the progress of civilization.
The Fishbladder Brigade and the Blue Island
Avenue Shelley Club.
The fire department.
Another brass band.
Citizens in carriages, afoot and horseback.
Advertising cars and wagons.

The line of march will be an extensive one, taking in the packing-houses and other notable points. At Mr. Armour's interesting professional establishment the process of slaughtering will be illustrated for the delectation of the honored guest, after which an appropriate poem will be read by Decatur Jones, President of the Lake View Élite Club. Then Mr. Armour will entertain a select few at a champagne luncheon in the scalding-room.

In high literary circles it is rumored that the Rev. F. M. Bristol has got an option on all autographs that Mr. Stedman may write during his stay in Chicago. Much excitement has been caused by this, and there is talk of an indignation meeting in Battery D, to be addressed by the Rev. Flavius Gunsaulus, the Rev. Frank W. Brobst, and other eminent speakers.

A Chaucerian Paraphrase of Horace
[In the following verse Field combined his admiration for Horace

(*Odes* I, 23) with his pleasure in the mock Middle-English dialect he used with some frequency in his poems.]

•••

> Syn that you, Chloe, to your moder sticken,
> Maketh all ye yonge bacheloures full sicken;
> Like as a lyttel deere you ben y-hiding
> Whenas come lovers with theyre pityse chiding;
> Sothly it ben faire to give up your moder
> For to beare swete company with some oder;
> Your moder ben well enow so farre shee goeth,
> But that ben not farre enow, God knoweth;
> Wherefore it ben sayed that foolysh ladyes
> That marrye not shall leade an aype in Hadys;
> But all that do with gode men wed full quickylye
> When that they be on dead go to ye seints full sickerly.

[Among its many special events, the world's fair, the Columbian Exposition of 1893, had scheduled a "Congress of Authors," in which a number of writers spoke on literary issues of the day. A chief feature was the debate between Hamlin Garland, who, in 1891, had published his collection of realistic tales of the Middle West, *Main Travelled Roads*, and Mary Hartwell Catherwood, whose novels included highly romantic and melodramatic stories of early days in Illinois and Indiana.]

•••

The chances are that to the end of our earthly career we shall keep on regretting that we were not present at that session of the Congress of Authors when Mr. Hamlin Garland and Mrs. Mary Hartwell Catherwood had their famous intellectual wrestling-match. Garland is one of the apostles of realism. Mrs. Catherwood has chosen the better part: she loves the fanciful in fiction; she believes, with us, in fairy godmothers and valorous knights and beautiful princesses who have fallen victims to wicked old witches.

Mr. Garland's heroes sweat and do not wear socks; his heroines eat cold huckleberry pie and are so unfeminine as not to call a cow "he."

Mrs. Catherwood's heroes—and they are the heroes we like—are aggressive, courtly, dashing, picturesque fellows, and her heroines are timid, stanch, beautiful women, and they, too, are our kind of people.

Mr. Garland's *in hoc signo* is a dung-fork or a butter-paddle; Mrs.

Catherwood's is a lance or an embroidery-needle. Give us the lance and its companion every time.

Having said this much, it is proper that we should add that we have for Mr. Garland personally the warmest affection, and we admire his work, too, very, very much; it is wonderful photography. Garland is young and impressionable; in an evil hour he fell under the baleful influences of William D. Howells,[5] and—there you are.

If we could contrive to keep Garland away from Howells long enough we'd make a big man of him, for there is a heap of good stuff in him. Several times we have had him here in Chicago for eight or ten days at a stretch, and when he has associated with us that length of time he really becomes quite civilized and gets imbued with orthodoxy; and then he, too, begins to see fairies and flubduds, and believes in the maidens who have long golden hair and cannot pail the cow; and his heroes are content to perspire instead of sweat, and they exchange their cowhide peg boots for silk hose and mediæval shoon.

But no sooner does Garland reach this point in the way of reform than he gallivants off again down East, and falls into Howells's clutches, and gets pumped full of heresies, and the last condition of that man is worse than the first.

We can well understand how so young and so impressionable a person as Garland is should fall an easy prey to Howells, for we have met Howells, and he is indeed a charming, a most charming gentleman. So conscious were we of the superhuman power of his fascinations that all the time we were with him we kept repeating paternosters lest we, too, should fall victim to his sugared and persuasive heterodoxy; and even then, after being with them an hour or two, we felt strangely tempted to throw away our collar and necktie and let our victuals drop all over our shirt-front.

The fascination of realism is all the more dangerous because it is so subtle. It is a bacillus undoubtedly, and when you once get it into your system it is liable to break out at any time in a new spot. But Garland is not yet so far gone with the malady but that we can save him if he will only keep away from Howells. In all solemnity we declare it to be our opinion that Howells is the only bad habit Garland has.

5. By the 1890s this controversial novelist was established as a leader of the cause of literary realism.

So we are glad to hear that there is a prospect of Mr. Garland's making his home here in Chicago, where the ramping prairie winds and the swooping lake breezes contribute to the development of the humane fancy. Verily there will be more joy in Chicago over the one Garland that repenteth than over ninety-and-nine Catherwoods that need no repentance.

III

[Field regularly interspersed poems and prose materials in compiling his columns. Our first verse here is an early one, from 1883. The other material is from the column's later years.]

• • •

Col. James Russell Lowell tells the story that one of the gentlemen he met in Chicago had a great deal to say of his travels in Europe. Col. Lowell remarked that he greatly enjoyed the French literature, and that George Sand was one of his favorite authors.

"Oh, yes!" exclaimed the Chicago gentleman: "I have had many a happy hour with Sand."

"You knew George Sand, then?" asked Col. Lowell, with an expression of surprise.

"Knew him? Well, I should rather say I did," cried the Chicago man; and then he added as a clincher, "I roomed with him when I was in Paris."

How Flaherty Kept The Bridge [6]

> Out spake Horatius Flaherty,—a Fenian bold was he,—
> "Lo, I will stand at thy right hand and turn the bridge with
>   thee!
> So ring the bell, O'Grady, and clear the railway track—
> Muldoon will heed the summons well and keep the street-cars
>   back.
>
> Forthwith O'Grady rang the bell, and straightway from afar
> There came a rush of humankind and over-loaded car.
> "Back, back! a schooner cometh," the brave O'Grady cried;
> "She cometh from Muskegon, packed down with horns and
>   hide."

6. The Chicago River and its two branches created a large need for movable bridges in the city, which were a frequent source of congestion as river and street traffic tangled with each other. The resulting crisis, plus memories of Macauley's "Horatius," formed the substance of Field's parody here.

And "Back!" Muldoon demanded and Flaherty declaimed,
While many a man stopped short his course and muttered,
   "I'll be blamed!"
And many a horse-car jolted, and many a driver swore,
As the tother gangway of the bridge swung off from either
   shore.
And bold Horatius Flaherty a storm of curses heard,
But pushing bravely at his key, he answered not a word;
And round and round he turned the bridge to let the
   schooner through,
And round and round and round again O'Grady turned it too;
Till now at last the way is clear, and with a sullen toot
'Twixt bridge and shore, ten rods or more, the tug and
   schooner shoot.

"Now swing her round the tother way," the brave O'Grady
   cried.
" 'Tis well!" Horatius Flaherty in thunder tones replied.
Muldoon waved high his club in air, his handkerchief waved
   high,
To see the stanch Muskegon ship go sailing calmly by;

And as the rafters of the bridge swung round to either shore,
Vast was the noise of men and boys and street-cars passing
   o'er.
And Flaherty quoth proudly, as he mopped his sweaty brow,
"Well done for you, and here's a chew, O'Grady, for us now."

[Francis Marion Crawford (1854–1909) published over forty novels in his lifetime. His theory that the novel existed solely for entertainment, was a commitment Field heartily approved.]

      •••

The new national library will have space for four million books. We mention this merely to encourage Mr. F. Marion Crawford to keep right on.

My Sabine Farm[7]
    At last I have a Sabine farm
      Abloom with shrubs and flowers;

---

7. This verse, a broadly comic refashioning of Horace (*Odes* I, 20) is characteristic of

And garlands gay I weave by day
  Amid those fragrant bowers;
And yet, O fortune hideous,
  I have no blooming Lydias;
And what, ah, what's a Sabine farm to us without its Lydias?

Within my cottage is a room
  Where I would fain be merry;
Come one and all unto that hall,
  Where you'll be welcome, very!
I've a butler who's Hibernian—
But no, I've no Falernian!
And what, ah, what's a Sabine farm to you without Falernian?

Upon this cosey Sabine farm
  What breeds my melancholy?
Why is my Muse down with the blues
  Instead of up and jolly?
A secret this between us:
I'm shy of a Maecenas!
And what's, oh, what's a Sabine farm to me without Maecenas!

[Field's friend, the Reverend Frank Gunsaulus, had (in fact or fiction) invested in Arizona land, an act that Field, at least for column purposes, interpreted as great folly. In the next two squibs, this joke is repeated in a fashion common in "Sharps and Flats," along with a reference to Field's and Gunsaulus' passion for book collecting, a predilection Field turned into frequent fiction for the column. The "Phil Armour" referred to in the second item is Philip D. Armour, the notable Chicago meat packing magnate.]

* * *

The Rev. F. W. Gunsaulus of this city bought a quarter-section of cactus meadowland in Arizona last spring, and had it surveyed into town lots, each on a corner. Last week Mr. Gunsaulus inaugurated another public boom in Arizona by organizing the Arctic Universal Ice Company (Limited). This close corporation will henceforth ship ice from Arizona to Minnesota, and sell it to the consumers there at seven cents a pound. Mr. Gunsaulus is president of the company, and the other

---

Field's use of the Latin poet. The columnist's Sabine farm was a suburban house only, but he nevertheless enjoyed striking the role of host.

principal stockholders are a Mexican herdsman named Salvator Mar-
quesda and the rich Modoc chief Ginger-Ale Charles.

• • •

It seems that, like many other bibliomaniacs, the Right Hon. William E.
Gladstone has attacks of madness about once in so often. He had one
of these "spells" on the day before I left London, and the way he ram-
paged around the book-shops in Oxford Street was simply delicious.
The first place he entered was Westall's. I happened to be there, and I
watched him closely, for I wanted to see whether, while under the vile
influence, he was like other bibliomaniacs I knew. He planted himself
in the middle of the shop and cast his eyes slowly around the shelves
of books that lined the walls. Of course all other buyers paused when it
became known that Gladstone was present. It was a superb picture—
that Grand Old Man, erect and quivering with excitement, rolling his
splendid eyes upon those musty treasures. Suddenly he raised his majestic left arm and described, as it were, to the left of him a parabola.
"Send me those," he said. Then he raised his equally majestic right
arm, and made an equally graceful curving sweep in the other direction, saying: "Send me those, too." Then he hurried out of Westall's and
plunged into another book-shop hard by. The whole business was
done in three minutes. Westall knew what the old gentleman meant. At
any rate, he began taking down books and volumes and tomes by the
score, while a clerk went out to hire a dray.

"That's the way he always buys," said Westall. "It's as good as fifty
pounds every time he comes into a book-shop."

The scene quite astounded me. Only once before had I seen any
like it. That was in at McClurg's[8] one day. I had just asked George Millard whether Dr. Gunsaulus was buying many books, and Millard had
told me, with a sigh that bespoke poignant regret, that the reverend
gentleman had sworn off.

"Moreover," added Millard, "he assures me that he has sworn off for
keeps."

At that very moment who should enter but Dr. Gunsaulus himself,
his step as light and bounding as a gazelle's, his face as glowing as an
August moon's, and his voice as resonant as a B-flat cornet's.

And the way he did buy books! Why, it would have discounted
Gladstone, even. It took Millard and Chandler and Bell three solid

8. A noted Chicago bookstore and publishing house.

hours to make a bill of them. There must have been ten thousand of them—books of all kinds, from books of balladry up to tomes of theology, and from volumes of history down to garlands of border songs.

"You will perhaps pardon me, doctor," said I, "but I really do not understand how a meek and lowly clergyman can afford to invest so largely in books."

"Fortunately," replied Dr. Gunsaulus, "I am momentarily a Crœsus, having just sold a quarter-section of my Arizona alkali farm to Brother Phil Armour."

Dutch Lullaby

> Wynken, Blynken, and Nod one night
>   Sailed off in a wooden shoe,—
> Sailed on a river of misty light
>   Into a sea of dew.
> "Where are you going, and what do you wish?"
>   The old moon asked the three.
> "We have come to fish for the herring-fish
>   That live in this beautiful sea;
>   Nets of silver and gold have we,"
>   Said Wynken,
>   Blynken,
>   And Nod.
>
> The old moon laughed and sung a song,
>   As they rocked in the wooden shoe;
> And the wind that sped them all night long
>   Ruffled the waves of dew;
> The little stars were the herring-fish
>   That lived in the beautiful sea.
> "Now cast your nets wherever you wish,
>   But never afeard are we!"
> So cried the stars to the fishermen three,
>   Wynken,
>   Blynken,
>   And Nod.
>
> All night long their nets they threw
>   For the fish in the twinkling foam,

Then down from the sky came the wooden shoe,
    Bringing the fishermen home;
'T was all so pretty a sail, it seemed
    As if it could not be;
And some folk thought 't was a dream they'd dreamed
    Of sailing that beautiful sea;
    But I shall name you the fishermen three:
        Wynken,
        Blynken,
        And Nod.

Wynken and Blynken are two little eyes,
    And Nod is a little head,
And the wooden shoe that sailed the skies
    Is a wee one's trundle-bed;
So shut your eyes while Mother sings
    Of wonderful sights that be,
And you shall see the beautiful things
    As you rock on the misty sea
    Where the old shoe rocked the fishermen three,—
        Wynken,
        Blynken,
        And Nod.

Teresa Dean

The Chicago world's fair of 1893, more formally known as the World's Columbian Exposition, had been scheduled to commemorate the four hundredth anniversary of Columbus' discovery of the Americas. It was delayed a year, but at its opening on May 1 it began a highly successful season, lasting through the following October and attracting throngs of visitors from all corners of the nation. Toward the end of its term, on October 10, the fair drew its largest crowd as it observed "Chicago Day," marking the twenty-second anniversary of the great fire. Among other things, the fair itself was intended as powerful testimony to the dramatic recovery the city had made from that disaster, and, in turn, it marked the beginning of still greater advances, including most notably the later evolution of the "Chicago Plan" by its own chief architect,

Daniel H. Burnham. This was a detailed concept of the city's physical development which, in its topographical features, has in fact been generally adhered to through all the changes that have been made from that time to the present. The fair also served as a stimulus to Chicago journalism. Field had established the tenor of his column without its impetus, but both George Ade and Finley Peter Dunne were to be launched on their careers as authors of "World's Fair" feature writing. They were far from alone in this concern. The following pages give samples of another and similar effort, this one by Teresa Dean (d. 1935), journalist, author, and, later, an editor of her own magazine, *The Widow*, and of New York's *Town Topics*. She undertook a series of columns extending day by day across the life of the fair for the *Inter-Ocean*, and in 1895 she published a selection of these in the volume *White City Chips*, issued in Chicago by the Warren Publishing Company.

From White City Chips

September 5; 1893

At the Persian theater business was rushing. The crier was saying:

"Come right in. This is the theater that was closed because the girls were all arrested. This is the Persian theater where the dancing was stopped. Come right in and see it. The dancing is prettier than ever."

And the crowd could not get in fast enough. Every individual member of it acted as if he or she were afraid the Director General or somebody else would come by and stop it again before they had an opportunity to see.

• • •

At the Eiffel tower the "jayhawker" was laboring hard to defend himself. Some one had made his exit from the "theater," which has been added to attract people to the tower, and said that the whole thing was a fraud. The boomer was white with excitement, and when he could get his tongue unfastened from the roof of his mouth he was trying to tell how much his brother knew about genuine dancing. He said:

"I know what I'm saying. And I knows what dancing is, and my brother he knows. He is in there dancing now, as he dances before all the royalty in Europe. He has danced for kings and queens for six years. It is in here that you see the real French girls in their native dances. Come right in, and learn something about the real French dances. It is genuine and no humbug, and it makes no difference what anybody tells you. I knows, and I tells you."

Just then some one out in the crowd said:

"I knows and I tells you to come right in and see the greatest fake on the Midway. Nothing like it and nothing where you'll throw your money away so quick."

The crowd increased and the rivalry between the crier at the entrance and the wag in the crowd waxed warmer. By the scarcity of the numbers who passed into the theater it was safe to conclude the cries of "fake" in the crowd won the contest.

• • •

In the Street in Cairo is a mind-reader. He is really quite an adept in his profession. He reads your mind in his own language, and an interpreter translates it. Scientists declare him to be a wonder. Lately, however, he has dropped the mind-reading and is giving a humbug spiritualistic performance. A gentleman just ahead of me in coming out said to the cashier:

"Doesn't he do any more mind-reading?"

She shrugged her shoulders and said: "Mind-reading no pay. Thees pay big money."

There's nothing like the Midway to discover how dearly the public loves to be humbugged.

The fraudulent shows are patronized the best. The genuine shows are many times considered the fraud, while the real humbug gets the patronage.

• • •

September 14, 1893

Here's a World's Fair story that happened away from the grounds. It is an old story that Dr. Gunsaulus' church is always crowded and overflowing. Everybody expects that. But last Sunday night the crowd was greater than ever.

People were turned away by the hundreds. As a gentleman was turning back from the door he made the remark to whoever might hear: "It's no use. You cannot get in."

A man in the crowd said to his friend:

"I don't care what he says; I must get in. I'm going in any way. There are three things I said that I was to see when I came to the World's Fair, Buffalo Bill, 'America,' and Dr. Gunsaulus, and I'm going to do it."

Sunday night or not, the crowd laughed at the sifted combination of Chicago's wonders.

The man persevered until he was successful in getting into the church.

• • •

Yesterday in the Woman's Building a man stood in the "court" looking around. It was very evident that he had just stopped "tilling the land" to come in to the Fair. His hands were brown, his face was brown, and his hair was cut square and even for convenience sake, and by some kind woman in the family instead of a barber.

His eyes roamed around the walls where hang the beautiful paintings. Then they wandered on to the skylit top and the panels and delicate decorations.

I watched him a few minutes. I wondered where in his wearisome toil of farm life he had found the time to study and learn to so admire the "frills and furbelows" of the world.

He finally walked on, and said to his wife:

"By gol! You could get a pile of hay in here."

• • •

September 16, 1893

Near the Horticultural Building yesterday I heard a woman say to a guard:

"In which building is the pope?"

"The pope is not here, madam," answered the guard.

"Where is he?"

"In Italy, Europe, madam."

"Which way is that?" asked the woman, in a perplexed manner.

The guard looked at her to see if she were joking, and evidently decided that she was, so he said jocosely:

"Three blocks under the lagoon."

"How do I get there?"

I passed on. I don't know how the guard extricated himself from the tangle of his joke.

• • •

What under the sun is Eugene Field up to?

Yesterday I sat down in the Manufactures Building to watch for a few minutes the passing crowd. Two girls met each other just in front of me. One said:

"Oh, did you bring it?"

"Yes, I did and let's sit down here and look at it—did you bring yours?" replied the other.

"Yes," was the answer, and they took a seat by my side.

They dived into the recesses of some silk bags, and each brought out a carefully wrapped photograph. Their heads came together over them, and the first girl said:

"There! Didn't I tell you yours was not his picture?"

"I can't understand it. They are not alike, and yet the signature is the same, 'Sincerely yours, Eugene Field.' I wonder which one is the correct one. What do you suppose it means? I wrote to him for his photograph, because I do so love his poems—"

I looked over their shoulders, for which I hope to be forgiven. One photograph was the picture of a long-haired, sad-eyed, Raphael-like looking fellow, and the other was a handsome, prosperous looking man, and neither was the photograph of the famous journalist and poet.

The signature was genuine.

•••

September 17, 1893

In the Art Palace, or Fine Arts Building, an old man and his wife stood before a painting of Circe. She stands there in her beauty and is looking down on the companions of Ulysses, whom she has just turned into a repulsive herd of swine.

The gray-haired couple stood there long and thoughtfully. They could not make anything out of the picture. Finally the husband turned to a gentleman who stood near and asked him if he would please tell him what that picture meant.

"Certainly," said the stranger, kindly. "It expresses the companions of Ulysses."

The man looked at his wife, and then again at the painting. His face was more puzzled than before. "The companions of Ulysses?" he muttered to himself. He finally turned to his wife with a pained and indignant expression and said:

"Well, I vow! Harriet, that's the worst slap at General Grant yet."

She thought so, too.

•••

October 19, 1893

It is just about possible to get through or by the crowds in some places along the Midway, particularly the theaters that have been talked about and visited by Anthony Comstock, and declared by him to be in keeping with the "low morals of Chicago."

On the outside, on a raised platform, will be some of the stage performers who dance a little, sing a little, dress a little, and do their best to inspire the crowd with a ten or twenty-five cent interest.

The crowd grows steadily larger. They stare at the "sample" and at the building, and seem to wait patiently—pathetically so—for the badness to come out to them through the roof or walls of the building, but they never go in, and never move on, until a sprinkling cart or an ambulance comes along and scatters them to make room for another crowd that will congregate the next minute.

If Anthony had not discovered or recognized so much wickedness along the jolly Midway I'm sure we would not have the trouble and the crushing we do to get along in some places.

Something naughty or something that is expected to be naughty does so chain the attention.

George Ade

George Ade (1866–1944) was born February 9 in Kentland, Indiana, where his parents had settled on a westward trek from Cincinnati and where his father became the moderately prosperous cashier of a small bank. Since the son showed no promise for banking and little propensity for the farm work that was Kentland's chief occupation, he was sent off to seek a profession at fledgling Purdue University. After graduating there, he found his way into newspaper work and, briefly, advertising writing for a patent medicine company in Lafayette. His gifted college friend, John T. McCutcheon, had found work on the Chicago *Morning News* as an artist, the same paper for which Eugene Field was then writing, and urged Ade to join him in Chicago. In 1890 he moved to the city and indeed got a place as cub reporter on the *News*. He possessed a fresh eye and ear for the city's life—an attribute that propelled him quickly into success as a news writer—and in the fall of 1893, after successful work on the bustle of the world's fair, parallel to that of Finley Peter Dunne for the *Post*, he along with McCutcheon was assigned to a daily column, "Stories of the Streets and of the Town." His task was to look at and listen to Chicago's life and write of it. McCutcheon accompanied him on his city rambles to make quick, deft sketches of the activity before them.

The column was immediately successful. The *Morning News*, by now renamed the *Record*, began issuing it in pamphlet collections in 1893, and in 1896 Ade published a first book over his own name with Herbert Stone, a venturesome young Chicago publisher and son of the *News*'s founder. That volume, *Artie*, was centered in the talk and activity of a good-hearted but brash young clerk of the city whom Ade had first invented for column purposes. Its success was followed in 1897 by a second book, *Pink Marsh*, which focused on the witty presence of mind of a Negro bootblack, by *Doc' Horne* in 1899, occupied with the winding and unreliable garrulousness of an old gentleman modestly retired to one of the city's cheaper hotels, and, in 1899, by *Fables in Slang*, a third column feature and one that propelled Ade to fortune and to national fame. These mock moral tales, making jokes of the common ambitions, attitudes, and ways of the day were written only slightly in "slang" as such, but like all of Ade's work they were rooted in the common vernacular.

In 1900 Ade left the *Record* to become an independent writer. He had long been fond of light theater and acquainted with its workings, and much of his productivity for the next two decades was divided between the fables and the writing of comic pieces for the operetta and legitimate stage, most notably, *The College Widow*.

Ade never married, but he maintained a close family relationship with his parents and brothers. He had begun early to hand his earnings over to his brother, Will, for investment in Indiana farmland, and out of the considerable wealth thus accumulated he built a substantial country house, called Hazeldon, on a farm he owned at Brook, Indiana, near his hometown. There he eventually retired to enjoy fame as a nationally known wit, a devoted Purdue alumnus, a prominent member of Sigma Chi fraternity, and a loyal if sometimes maverick Republican.

Ade's column writing was unparalleled for the breadth of its awareness of the city's many faces. His central talent was always that of an active attentiveness to the life around him; indeed, his early work met with enthusiasm from Howells and others among the realistic writers of the day. In the fables, particularly, he added the wit generated by an amused eye for human pretense, self-protectiveness, and narrow ambition. Ade had little of the scoffer or brooder in his makeup. He enjoyed his world, happily made his own choices within it, and, as happily, observed others making theirs. The success of the fables turned too quickly toward formula, but it was a formula whose appeal was difficult to ignore. Ade never lost hold of an eye-on-the-object perceptivity. Like his fellow wits of the heyday of Chicago humor, he too was an innovator redirecting a comic sense to the urban life of the day. Lacking Field's lively fancy and Dunne's more sympathetic imagination, he nonetheless mirrored a world to itself, whether faithfully or more mockingly, and nudged it on toward the fun of seeing itself so reflected.

Ade was the author of over twenty-five books including humor, travel, and plays. The fables began their book appearance in 1899 with *Fables in Slang* and proceeded through eight later and variously titled volumes, the last appearing in 1914. Fred C. Kelly published a biography of Ade, *George Ade, Warmhearted Satirist*, and a selection of his writings, *The Permanent Ade*, in 1947. A second selection has been made by Jean C. Shepherd in *The America of George Ade* (1961).

From The Chicago Record's Stories of the Streets and of the Town

[The selections that follow are typical of the writing that made George Ade's reputation, first in Chicago and then, with the advent of the fables in slang, in the nation. They begin with squibs from his daily "Stories" column of 1894. The Chicago locations mentioned in the item on the word *gent* suggest variously characterized neighborhoods of the day: Archer Avenue was the heart of Bridgeport, the predominantly Irish section already given its first fame by Finley Peter Dunne's "Dooley" pieces newly launched in the *Post*; Michigan Avenue was a fashionable resort street, in its southerly stretches still largely residential; State Street was the center of the hotel and shopping district, declining in its southerly downtown stretch to the "levee," a red light and saloon area, the heart of Chicago's notorious "first ward."

These column items are followed by selections from Ade's other early books. All the more specialized performances, however, were first developed for column purposes, as is suggested by the appearance of the humorous and perceptive black citizen, Pinckney Johnson (anticipating Pink Marsh) in the 1894 column.]

• • •

Inasmuch as the day had dawned bright and two furniture vans had

passed toward State street since morning, Uncle Zig said to himself
that the season had opened.

He looked over his effects in the shed and found them just as they
had been when he put them away in the fall, except that the brushes
were rather stiff and dusty. He borrowed a marking pot at Alexander's
grocery, and for the next half-hour there might have been heard coming through the woodshed door a low, moaning song, as of one in
thoughtful occupation. At the end of that time Uncle Zig came out
with a short handled hatchet in one hand. In the other he carried a
pine board newly lettered. He had two nails in his mouth. They inter-
fered with his song, but he kept up the tune.

He was nailing the sign against one corner of his red and black cottage when Pinckney Johnson happened along. Mr. Johnson leaned
against the picket fence and began to chuckle at the sign:

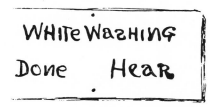

"Does yo' mean, Uncle Zig," he asked, "'at folks got to bring fences
and baid-rooms and cellins 'round heah to git 'em whitewashed?"

"Who say so?"

"Yo' does. Yo' sign it say, 'Whitewashin' done heah.' Ah s'pose yo'
woud'nt da' to go ovah to Dea'born street and take no job."

Uncle Zig began to see the point. He put the claw under the board
and loosened it; then he carried it back to the shed. In ten minutes he
returned. Pinckney Johnson was still waiting, and this was submitted
for his approval:

Mr. Johnson laughed boisterously. "Now, now, jes' yo' stop and pondah for a minute. Ah yo' raidy to go to New O'leans on a dollah job? It say, 'Whitewashin' Any Wheah.' Does yo' mean it?"

Uncle Zig was again puzzled, and he was beginning to be indignant. He pottered back to the shed and Mr. Pinckney Johnson, the critic, heard the sound of a saw. The third time Uncle Zig came out he had a sign which read:

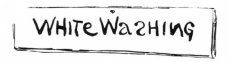

He defiantly nailed it up and Mr. Johnson quietly nodded his approval.

...

Long observation leads to the conclusion that the "gent" is not restricted to any particular part of the town. In Archer avenue he wears a blue coat, fawn-colored "pants" and a white vest. His shaggy forelock stands above the front brim of his hat and he carries a slim cane with a white-metal handle. He is seen at his best when doing a jig dance. The "gent" in Michigan avenue and the parallel fastnesses of wealth and culture may be distinguished by an excess of jewelry, a limited vocabulary and a desire to order expensive drinks in a loud tone of voice. The State street "gents" are of two kinds. One kind may be found in front of the large hotels in checked garments and with the backs of their heads shaved. They frequently look down at their shoes and then they cast oily glances at the women passing by. The other kind is the levee "gent," who wears a short coat and hisses his words. He is a "gent" because he "never smashed no woman" and eats porterhouse steaks. The inoffensive "gents" who wear low vests showing three studs, who appear in bicycle suits at all hours of the day and night, who lose their minds studying up masquerade costumes or who try to get married through a matrimonial bureau, are scattered all over the wards.

A "gent" is a man who doesn't resent the insult when someone calls him a "gent."

Not long ago two new restaurants were opened side by side in a well-known street. One put out a sign to the effect that the restaurant was for ladies and gentlemen. The other restaurant was for "ladies and gents." After six weeks the first one went into the hands of the sheriff, but the "gents" place is still making money. This is probably the meanest thing ever said about that well-known street.

* * *

On this night in the "owl" car the passengers were sitting on their shoulder-blades, with their legs sprawled out across the aisle. The conductor, when he came through, had to step high to get over the assortment of feet. The four men who had come aboard at Clinton street were breathing heavily in their slumber. The car bounced over a switch and aroused one of them. He opened his eyes dreamily and bestowed a friendly smile. Then, moved by one of those strange impulses for which there is no accounting, he began to sing with a hoarse drawl:

"There wer-her three cro-hows sat o-hon a tre-hee.
And they-hey were bla-hack as cro-hows could be.
Said wu-hun old cro-how unto-hoo his ma-hate,
'What shal-hall we do-hoo for gru-hub to ate'"?

Another of the four came out of his slumber and joined in the second verse, which was in all respects similar to the first. A third man in the party, without opening his eyes or giving other warning, suddenly joined in the song and then the fourth came with an unfinished tenor. The remaining passengers shifted in their seats and began to grumble.

"Don't sing, boys," said the conductor as he stepped in from the back platform.

"—they-hey were bla-hack as cro-hows could be."
That was the only response.

"Stop that noise."

"Said wu-hun old cro-how—"

The conductor gave to the leader a violent "yank" which caused him to sit on the floor. The other three members of the quartet arose shakily and started at the conductor, who backed on to the platform. Then as they came out, one at a time, he simply threw each of them into the street, the leader being the last to go. As the car kept on its way, the passengers could see in the dim light from the corner arc lamp four men gather themselves up from along the track and, having got together, start for a place from which the light shone out above the curtain tops.

From Artie

[Beginning in 1893, selections from Ade's "Stories" column were published annually by the Chicago *Record* for eight years without the appearance of his name. His first signed work to see print was *Artie* (1896), a series of sketches worked up from a character developed for the column and centered on the lively talk and doings of a typical downtown office clerk in the days when such figures were more often male than female. Artie is a brash, city-wise youth, but possessed of a good heart and inclinations.]

• • •

After a hurried luncheon at one of the places where patrons help themselves and compute their own checks, Miller and Artie took a walk on the sunny side of the street.

Artie was not as talkative as usual, and, as Miller seldom did more than encourage a conversation once started, the two sauntered for several minutes in silence.

Then Artie spoke abruptly. "Miller," said he, "I got a hen on."

"What is it?"

"It's like this. Would you dally with politics if you thought you stood to win out a good thing?"

"That depends. *You're* not going into politics, are you?"

"They've got me entered, but I don't know whether I'll start or not. I'm leary of it; I don't mind tellin' you those."

"What do you mean?"

"Well, mebbe you won't understand. I don't like to feature myself, but in that precinct where I hang out I'm purty strong. I'm a good mixer and I've kind o' got next to the live ones, and if I do say it myself I think there's a lot of the boys that'd vote my way if I went after 'em hard. Do you know Jim Landon?"

"Who is he?"

"He's the main squeeze in our ward, or any way he used to be. He's one o' the aldermen, and he's out for it again, but good and scared that he can't win out. He come to me last night at Hoover's cigar store and give me a big talk. What he wants is for me to come to the front for him strong. He knows I've got a drag in the precinct, and he says if I'll jump in and do what I can for him he'll see that I got a good job in the town offices, where I can cop out about twice what I'm gettin' now. Of course I'm out for the long green—but I don't know about this deal."

"Does he stand a good chance of being elected?"

"That's what keeps me guessin'. Two years ago he win in a walk, but this spring he had to do all kinds o' funny work to get the nomination. There's a lot o' people in the ward that's got their hammers out and they're knockin' him all they can. They'll put a crimp in him if things come their way."

"What's the matter with him, anyway?"

"Oh, they kind o' think he's done too well. Two years ago he was on his uppers and now he's got money to burn. There's some o' them guys out in our ward can't make out how it is that Jimmy can afford to buy wine at four bucks a throw when he's only gettin' three a week out o' the job. They say they can't stand for that kind o' work, and so there's a lot o' them church people that boosted him two years ago that's out now to skin him. They've put up a new guy against him and he's makin' a nasty fight."

"I don't understand yet what they've got against your man."

"W'y, they're crazy at him. You see two years ago he made the play that if they put him in he was goin' down to the city hall and change the whole works. He was goin' to clean the streets and jack up the coppers and build some more schoolhouses. Jimmy says to 'em: 'Throw things my way and I'll be the Johnny-on-the-spot to see that every-thing's on the level.' The talk was so good it went. Well, you know what happened to Jimmy when he got down there with them Indians and begin to see easy money. He hadn't been in on the whack-up six weeks till he was wearing one o' them bicycle lamps in his neck-tie and put-tin' in all his time at the city hall waitin' for the easy marks to come along and throw up their hands."

"I see. He turned out to be a boodler, eh?"[1]

"I don't see no way o' gettin' past it. I like Jimmy. He's one o' them boys that never has cold feet and there's nothin' too good for a friend, but, by gee, I guess when it comes to doin' the nice, genteel dip he belongs with the smoothest of 'em. And he learned it so quick, too. Ooh!"

1. Slang for a bribe-taking politician.

"Artie, that kind of a man is a thief and that's all you can make out of it," said Miller, with presbyterian severity.

"Mebbe that ain't no lie, neither. He wouldn't go out with a piece o' lead pipe or do any o' that strong-arm work, but if Jimmy saw a guy puttin' dough into his pocket he wouldn't let on. You wouldn't have to feed him no knock-out drops to make him take the coin, I guess. But the nerve o' the boy! He won't never let on that he's handled any crooked money. When he was staked to the office he didn't have a sou markee except what was tied up in a bum little grocery store. Now he's got too strong to tend store and his brother-in-law's runnin' it. He don't do a thing in the world except travel around with some more o' them handy boys and lay for jack-pots. And the talk he gives you! Mamma! He's better 'n any o' them shell-workers that used to graft out at the gover'ment pier. W'y, he can set down and show you dead easy that he done all that funny votin' because it was a good thing for the workin' boys. Sure! That's why he wants to stay in, too—so as the tax-payers won't get the short end of it. On the square, if I had his face I'd start out sellin' them gold bricks to Jaspers."

"You don't mean to say that he has any chance of being elected again?"

"Oh, he's got a chance all right. He's gone right down into his kick and dug up the long green and he's puttin' it out at the booze joints. Some o' the saloons he's overlooked for a year or two, and he's got to make good with 'em to keep 'em from knockin'. But he'll have the whole push rootin' for him, and, then, of course, there's a lot more o' people say: 'Oh, well, Jim's a good fellow and he's been white with me, and even if he does sand-bag a few o' them rich blokies what's the diff?' I think he's got a chance, all right. I wouldn't like to start in and plug his game and then find myself on a dead one."

"Artie, if you take my advice you'll keep out of it. What do you want with a political job?"

"Well, for one thing I want to get a bank-roll as soon as I can and this place he's holdin' out pays good money."

"Yes, and even if you got it you'd be out again in a year or two and worse off than ever. Besides, I wouldn't help elect a man who sold his influence." Miller spoke with considerable feeling.

"As for that," resumed Artie, "you needn't think I like Jim Landon's way o' gettin' stuff. It's just like this, though. He's gone out of his way two or three times to do things for me and fixed me for a pass to Milwaukee once, and, of course, them things count. Everybody's shakin' him down this spring, and if he gets the gaff he'll be flat on his back. If I didn't know him I'd be against him hard. But you don't like to throw down a man that's treated you right, do you?"

"I've never been in politics, but I should say that no young man could have any excuse for voting for a boodler."

"Say, now listen. It comes election day, see? I go in the place and get in one o' them little private rooms and I vote for this stranger. Then I come out and meet Jimmy. He puts out the hand and I go and get a cigar with him and do the friendship act. Wouldn't that be purty coarse work?"

"It wouldn't be any worse than his promising to be honest and then turning out a boodler" said Miller.

"Well, I guess I'll pass up the whole thing. Come to size it up, that ward's goin' to be floatin' in beer the next two weeks, and I'm not stuck on standin' around with them boys that smoke them hay-fever torches. For a man that don't want to be a rounder, it's too much like sportin' life. I didn't think you'd O. K. the scheme. I'll just tell Jimmy that I'm out of it. That's an awful wise move, too. I guess an easier way to get that roll'd be to borrow a nice kit o' tools and go 'round blowin' safes."

From **Fables in Slang** *and* **More Fables**

[Like all else in his early and most popular work, Ade's fables originated as material for his "Stories" column. The following selections are from the first two books of fables to appear, published in 1899 and 1900, before Ade's leavetaking from Chicago. Ade designated "The Fable of the Two Mandolin Players" as his personal favorite. It remains the most-often cited of the group, though its humor seems in fact more typical of the fables in general than distinct among them. "The Fable of What Happened the Night the Men Came to the Women's Club" suggests a play of wit on Chicago's bluestocking Fortnightly Club.]

• • •

The Fable of the Two Mandolin Players and the Willing Performer

A very attractive Debutante knew two Young Men who called on her every Thursday Evening, and brought their Mandolins along.

They were Conventional Young Men, of the Kind that you see wearing Spring Overcoats in the Clothing Advertisements. One was named Fred, and the other was Eustace.

The Mothers of the Neighborhood often remarked, "What Perfect Manners Fred and Eustace have!" Merely as an aside it may be added that Fred and Eustace were more Popular with the Mothers than they were with the Younger Set, although no one could say a Word against either of them. Only it was rumored in Keen Society that they didn't Belong. The Fact that they went Calling in a Crowd, and took their Mandolins along, may give the Acute Reader some Idea of the Life that Fred and Eustace held out to the Young Women of their Acquaintance.

The Debutante's name was Myrtle. Her Parents were very Watchful, and did not encourage her to receive Callers, except such as were known to be Exemplary Young Men. Fred and Eustace were a few of those who escaped the Black List. Myrtle always appeared to be glad to see them, and they regarded her as a Darned Swell Girl.

Fred's Cousin came from St. Paul on a Visit; and one Day, in the Street, he saw Myrtle, and noticed that Fred tipped his Hat, and gave her a Stage Smile.

"Oh, Queen of Sheba!" exclaimed the Cousin from St. Paul, whose name was Gus, as he stood stock still, and watched Myrtle's Reversible Plaid disappear around a Corner. "She's a Bird. Do you know her well?"

"I know her Quite Well," replied Fred, coldly. "She is a Charming Girl."

"She is all of that. You're a great Describer. And now what Night are you going to take me around to Call on her?"

Fred very naturally Hemmed and Hawed. It must be remembered that Myrtle was a member of an Excellent Family, and had been schooled in the Proprieties, and it was not to be supposed that she would crave the Society of slangy old Gus, who had an abounding Nerve, and furthermore was as Fresh as the Mountain Air.

He was the Kind of Fellow who would see a Girl twice, and then, upon meeting her the Third Time, he would go up and straighten her Cravat for her, and call her by her First Name.

Put him into a Strange Company—en route to a Picnic—and by the time the Baskets were unpacked he would have a Blonde all to himself, and she would have traded her Fan for his College Pin.

If a Fair-Looker on the Street happened to glance at him Hard he would run up and seize her by the Hand, and convince her that they had Met. And he always Got Away with it, too.

In a Department Store, while waiting for the Cash Boy to come back with the Change, he would find out the Girl's Name, her Favorite Flower, and where a Letter would reach her.

Upon entering a Parlor Car at St. Paul he would select a Chair next to the Most Promising One in Sight, and ask her if she cared to have the Shade lowered.

Before the Train cleared the Yards he would have the Porter bringing a Foot-Stool for the Lady.

At Hastings he would be asking her if she wanted Something to Read.

At Red Wing he would be telling her that she resembled Maxine Elliott,[2] and showing her his Watch, left to him by his Grandfather, a Prominent Virginian.

At La Crosse he would be reading the Menu Card to her, and telling her how different it is when you have Some One to join you in a Bite.

At Milwaukee he would go out and buy a Bouquet for her, and when they rode into Chicago they would be looking out of the same Window, and he would be arranging for her Baggage with the Transfer Man. After that they would be Old Friends.

Now, Fred and Eustace had been at School with Gus, and they had seen his Work, and they were not disposed to Introduce him into One of the most Exclusive Homes in the City.

They had known Myrtle for many Years; but they did not dare to Address her by her First Name, and they were Positive that if Gus attempted any of his usual Tactics with her she would be Offended; and, naturally enough, they would be Blamed for bringing him to the House.

But Gus insisted. He said he had seen Myrtle, and she Suited him from the Ground up, and he proposed to have Friendly Doings with her. At last they told him they would take him if he promised to Behave. Fred warned him that Myrtle would frown down any Attempt to be Familiar on Short Acquaintance, and Eustace said that as long as he had known Myrtle he had never Presumed to be Free and Forward

2. Maxine Elliott, born Jessie Dermott, was a notable American stage beauty.

with her. He had simply played the Mandolin. That was as Far Along as he had ever got.

Gus told them not to Worry about him. All he asked was a Start. He said he was a Willing Performer, but as yet he never had been Disqualified for Crowding. Fred and Eustace took this to mean that he would not Overplay his Attentions, so they escorted him to the House.

As soon as he had been Presented, Gus showed her where to sit on the Sofa, then he placed himself about Six Inches away and began to Buzz, looking her straight in the Eye. He said that when he first saw her he Mistook her for Miss Prentice, who was said to be the Most Beautiful Girl in St. Paul, only, when he came closer, he saw that it couldn't be Miss Prentice, because Miss Prentice didn't have such Lovely Hair. Then he asked her the Month of her Birth and told her Fortune, thereby coming nearer to Holding her Hand within Eight Minutes than Eustace had come in a Lifetime.

"Play something, Boys," he Ordered, just as if he had paid them Money to come along and make Music for him.

They unlimbered their Mandolins and began to play a Sousa March. He asked Myrtle if she had seen the New Moon. She replied that she had not, so they went Outside.

When Fred and Eustace finished the first Piece, Gus appeared at the open Window, and asked them to play "The Georgia Camp-Meeting," which had always been one of his Favorites.

So they played that, and when they had Concluded there came a Voice from the Outer Darkness, and it was the Voice of Myrtle. She said: "I'll tell you what to Play; play the Intermezzo."

Fred and Eustace exchanged Glances. They began to Perceive that they had been backed into a Siding. With a few Potted Palms in front of them, and two Cards from the Union, they would have been just the same as a Hired Orchestra.

But they played the Intermezzo and felt Peevish. Then they went to the Window and looked out. Gus and Myrtle were sitting in the Hammock, which had quite a Pitch toward the Center. Gus had braced himself by Holding to the back of the Hammock. He did not have his Arm around Myrtle, but he had it Extended in a Line parallel with her Back. What he had done wouldn't Justify a Girl in saying, "Sir!" but it started a Real Scandal with Fred and Eustace. They saw that the only Way to Get Even with her was to go Home without saying "Good Night." So they slipped out the Side Door, shivering with Indignation.

After that, for several Weeks, Gus kept Myrtle so Busy that she had no Time to think of considering other Candidates. He sent Books to her Mother, and allowed the Old Gentleman to take Chips away from him at Poker.

They were Married in the Autumn, and Father-in-Law took Gus into the Firm, saying that he had needed a good Pusher for a Long Time.

At the Wedding the two Mandolin Players were permitted to act as Ushers.

MORAL: *To get a fair Trial of Speed, use a Pace-Maker.*

The Fable of What Happened the Night the Men Came to the Women's Club

In a Progressive Little City claiming about twice the Population that the Census Enumerators could uncover, there was a Literary Club. It was one of these Clubs guaranteed to fix you out with Culture while you wait. Two or three Matrons, who were too Heavy for Light Amusements, but not old enough to remain at Home and Knit, organized the Club. Nearly every Woman in town rushed to get in, for fear somebody would say she hadn't been Asked.

The Club used to Round Up once a week at the Homes of Members. There would be a Paper, followed by a Discussion, after which somebody would Pour.

The Organization seemed to be a Winner. One Thing the Lady Clubbers were Dead Set On. They were going to have Harmony with an Upper Case H. They were out to cut a seven-foot Swath through English Literature from Beowulf to Bangs,[3] inclusive, and no petty Jealousies or Bickerings would stand in the Way.

So while they were at the Club they would pull Kittenish Smiles at each other, and Applaud so as not to split the Gloves. Some times they would Kiss, too, but they always kept their Fingers crossed.

Of course, when they got off in Twos and Threes they would pull

3. John Kendrick Bangs, a New York humorist, best known as author of *A Houseboat on the Styx.*

the little Meat-Axes out of the Reticules and hack a few Monograms, but that was to have been expected.

Everything considered, the Club was a Tremendous Go. At each Session the Lady President would announce the Subject for the next Meeting. For instance, she would say that Next Week they would take up Wyclif. Then every one would romp home to look in the Encyclopedia of Authors and find out who in the world Wyclif was. On the following Thursday they would have Wyclif down Pat, and be primed for a Discussion. They would talk about Wyclif as if he had been down to the House for Tea every evening that Week.

After the Club had been running for Six Months it was beginning to be Strong on Quotations and Dates. The Members knew that Mrs. Browning was the wife of Mr. Browning, that Milton had Trouble with his Eyes, and that Lord Byron wasn't all that he should have been, to say the Least. They began to feel their Intellectual Oats. In the meantime the Jeweler's Wife had designed a Club Badge.

The Club was doing such Notable Work that some of the Members thought they ought to have a Special Meeting and invite the Men. They wanted to put the Cap-Sheaf on a Profitable Season, and at the same time hand the Merited Rebuke to some of the Husbands and Brothers who had been making Funny Cracks.

It was decided to give the Star Programme at the Beadle Home, and after the Papers had been read then all the Men and Five Women who did not hold Office could file through the Front Room and shake Hands with the President, the Vice-President, the Recording Secretary, the Corresponding Secretary, the Treasurer, and the members of the various Committees, all of whom were to line up and Receive.

The reason the Club decided to have the Brain Barbecue at the Beadle Home was that the Beadles had such beautiful big Rooms and Double Doors. There was more or less quiet Harpoon Work when the Announcement was made. Several of the Elderly Ones said that Josephine Beadle was not a Representative Member of the Club. She was Fair to look upon, but she was not pulling very hard for the Uplifting of the Sex. It was suspected that she came to the Meetings just to Kill Time and see what the Others were Wearing. She refused to buckle down to Literary Work, for she was a good deal more interested in the Bachelors who filled the Windows of the new Men's Club than she was in the Butler who wrote "Hudibras." So why should she have the Honor of entertaining the Club at the Annual Meeting? Unfortunately, the Members who had the most Doing under their Bonnets were not the ones who could come to the Front with large Rooms that could be Thrown together, so the Beadle Home got the Great Event.

Every one in Town who carried a Pound of Social Influence showed up in his or her Other Clothes. Extra Chairs had to be brought in, and what with the Smilax and Club Colors it was very Swell, and the Maiden in the Lace Mitts who was going to write about it for the Weekly threw a couple of Spasms.

The Men were led in pulling at the Halters and with their Ears laid back. After they got into the Dressing Room they Stuck there until they had to be Shooed out. They did not know what they were going against, but they had their Suspicions. They managed to get Rear Seats or stand along the Wall so that they could execute the Quiet Sneak if Things got too Literary. The Women were too Flushed and Proud to Notice.

At 8:30 P. M. the Lady President stood out and began to read a few Pink Thoughts on "Woman's Destiny—Why Not?" Along toward 9:15, about the time the Lady President was beginning to show up Good and Earnest, Josephine Beadle, who was Circulating around on the Outskirts of the Throng to make sure that everybody was Happy, made a Discovery. She noticed that the Men standing along the Wall and in the Doorways were not more than sixty per cent En Rapport with the Long Piece about Woman's Destiny. Now Josephine was right there to see that Everybody had a Nice Time, and she did not like to see the Prominent Business Men of the Town dying of Thirst or Leg Cramp or anything like that, so she gave two or three of them the Quiet Wink, and they tiptoed after her out to the Dining Room, where she offered Refreshments, and said they could slip out on the Side Porch and Smoke if they wanted to.

Probably they preferred to go back in the Front Room and hear some more about Woman's Destiny not.

As soon as they could master their Emotions and get control of their Voices, they told Josephine what they thought of her. They said she made the Good Samaritan look like a Cheap Criminal, and if she would only say the Word they would begin to put Ground Glass into the Food at Home. Then Josephine called them "Boys," which probably does not make a Hit with one who is on the sloping side of 48. More of the Men seemed to awake to the Fact that they were Overlooking something, so they came on the Velvet Foot back to the Dining Room and declared themselves In, and flocked around Josephine and called her "Josie" and "Joe." They didn't care. They were having a Pleasant Visit.

Josephine gave them Allopathic Slugs of the Size that they feed you in the Navy and then lower you into the Dingey and send you Ashore. Then she let them go out on the Porch to smoke. By the time the Lady President came to the last Page there were only two Men left in the Front Room. One was Asleep and the other was Penned In.

The Women were Huffy. They went out to make the Men come in, and found them Bunched on the Porch listening to a Story that a Traveling Man had just brought to Town that Day.

Now the Plan was that during the Reception the Company would stand about in little Groups, and ask each other what Books they liked, and make it something on the order of a Salon. This Plan miscarried, because all the Men wanted to hear Rag Time played by Josephine, the Life-Saver. Josephine had to yield, and the Men all clustered around her to give their Moral Support. After one or two Selections, they felt sufficiently Keyed to begin to hit up those low-down Songs about Baby and Chickens and Razors. No one paid any Attention to the Lady President, who was off in a Corner holding an Indignation Meeting with the Secretary and the Vice-President.

When the Women began to sort out the Men and order them to start Home and all the Officers of the Club were giving Josephine the frosty Good Night, any one could see that there was Trouble ahead.

Next Day the Club held a Special Session and expelled Josephine for Conduct Unbecoming a Member, and Josephine sent Word to them as follows: "Rats."

Then the Men quietly got together and bought Josephine about a Thousand Dollars' Worth of American Beauty Roses to show that they were With her, and then Homes began to break up, and somebody started the Report that anyway it was the Lady President's Fault for having such a long and pokey Essay that wasn't hers at all, but had been Copied out of a Club Paper published in Detroit.

Before the next Meeting there were two Factions. The Lady Presi-

"The Men," from an illustration for George Ade's *More Fables*.

dent had gone to a Rest Cure, and the Meeting resolved itself into a Good Cry and a general Smash-Up.

MORAL: *The only Literary Men are those who have to Work at it.*

The Fable of the Regular Customer and the Copper-Lined Entertainer
One day the Main Works of a Wholesale House was Jacking Up the Private Secretary and getting ready to close his desk for the Day, when in blew a Country Customer. The Head of the Concern would have given Seven Dollars if he could have got out and caught the Elevated before the Country Customer showed up. However, he was Politic, and he knew he must not throw down a Buyer who discounted his Bills and was good as Old Wheat. So he gave a Correct Imitation of a Man who is tickled nearly to Death. After calling the Country Customer "Jim," he made him sit down and tell him about the Family, and the Crops, and Collections, and the Prospects for Duck-Shooting. Then, selecting an opportune moment, he threw up Both Hands. He said he had almost forgotten the Vestry Meeting at Five O'clock, and going out to Dinner at Six-Thirty. He was about to Call Off the Vestry Meeting, the Dinner, and all other Engagements for a Week to come, but Jim would not Listen to it. As a Compromise the Head of the Concern said he would ask their Mr. Byrd to take charge of the Country Customer. They could surely find some Way of putting in the Evening. He said the Oratorio Club was going to sing at Music Hall, and also there was a Stereopticon Lecture on India. Jim said he would prefer the Stereopticon Show, because he loved to look at Pictures.

The Head of the Concern said that the Country Customer would be sure to like their Mr. Byrd. Everybody liked Byrd. His Full Name was Mr. Knight Byrd.

He pushed on a few Buttons and blew into several snaky Tubes and put the whole Shop on the Jump to find Mr. Byrd. The latter happened to be in a Rathskeller not far away. When he heard that there was Work to be done in his Department he brushed away the Crumbs and Hot-Footed up to see the Boss.

In presenting Mr. Byrd to the Country Customer the Head of the Concern laid it on with a Shovel. He said that Jim Here was his Friend, and the House considered it an Honor to Entertain him. The Country Customer sat there feeling Sheepish and Unworthy but a good deal

Puffed Up just the same. Then the Head of the Firm made his Escape and the Country Customer was in the Hands of Mr. Byrd.

Mr. Byrd was known in the Establishment as the Human Expense Account. No one had ever accused him of being a Quitter. He was supposed to be Hollow inside. Whenever any Friend of the Firm showed up, Mr. Byrd was called upon to take charge of him and Entertain him to a Stand-Still. The Boss was troubled with Dyspepsia, and Conscientious Scruples, and a Growing Family, and a few other Items that prevented him from going out at Night with the Visiting Trade. He had it arranged to give each one of them a choice Mess of Beautiful Language and then pass him along to Mr. Byrd.

Mr. Byrd was a Rosy and Red-Headed Gentleman, with a slight Overhang below the Shirt Front. He breathed like a Rusty Valve every time he had to go up a Stairway, but he had plenty of Endurance of another Kind. For Years he had been playing his Thirst against his Capacity, and it was still a Safe Bet, whichever Way you wanted to place your Money. His Batting Average was about Seven Nights to the Week. He discovered that Alcohol was a Food long before the Medical Journals got onto it.

Mr. Byrd's chief value to the Wholesale House lay in the Fact that he could Meet all Comers and close up half the Places in Town, and then show up next Morning with a Clean Collar and a White Carnation, and send in word to lead out another Country Customer.

Mr. Byrd's first Move was to take Jim to a Retreat that was full of Statuary and Paintings. It was owned by a gray-haired Beau named Bob, who was a Ringer for a United States Senator, all except the White Coat. Bob wanted to show them a new Tall One called the Mamie Taylor, and after they had Sampled a Couple Jim said it was all right and he believed he would take one. Then he told Bob how much he had taken in the Year before and what his Fixtures cost him, and if anybody didn't think he was Good they could look him up in Bradstreet or Dun, that was all. He said he was a Gentleman, and that no Cheap Skate in a Plug Hat could tell him where to Get Off. This last Remark was intended for an inoffensive Person who had slipped in to get a Rhine Wine and Seltzer, and was pronging about Forty Cents' Worth of Lunch.

They got around Jim and Quieted him, and Mr. Byrd suggested that they go and Eat something before they got too Busy. The Country Customer would not leave the Art Buffet until Bob had promised to come down and Visit him sometime. When they got into the Street again the Country Customer noticed that all the Office Buildings were set on the Bias, and they were introducing a new style of spiral Lamp-Post.

They dined at a Palm-Garden that had Padding under the Table-Cloth and a Hungarian Orchestra in the Corner. Mr. Byrd ordered Eleven Courses, and then asked Jim what Kind he usually had with his Dinner. This is an Awful Question to pop at a Man who has been on Rain Water and Buttermilk all his Life. Jim was not to be Fazed. He said that he never ordered any Particular Label for fear People might think he was an Agent. That was the Best Thing that Jim said all Evening.

Mr. Byrd told the Waiter to stand behind Jim and keep Busy. When Jim began to Make Signs that he could not Stand any more, the Entertainer told him to Inhale it and rub it in his Hair.

Along toward Dessert Jim was talking in the Tone used by Muggsy McGraw when he is Coaching the Man who is Playing Off from Second. He was telling how much he Loved his Wife. She would have been Pleased to hear it.

Mr. Byrd paid a Check that represented One Month's Board down where Jim lived. They fell into a Horseless Hansom and went to see the Hity-Tity Variety and Burlesque Aggregation in a new Piece entitled "Hooray! Hooray!" Jim sat in a Box for the First Time, and wanted to throw Money on the Stage. The Head Usher had to come around once in a while to ask him not to let his Feet hang over, and to remember that the Company could do all the Singing without any Help from him. Mr. Byrd sat back slightly Flushed and watched the Country Customer make a Show of himself. It was an Old Story to him. He knew that the quiet School Trustee kind of a Man who goes Home at Sundown for 364 Days in the Year, with the Morning Steak and a Roll of Reading Matter under his Arm, is the worst Indian in the World when he does find himself among the Tall Houses and gets it Up his Nose.

He allowed Jim to stand and Yell when the Chorus struck the Grand Finale, and a little later on, when they had chartered a low-necked Carriage and Jim wanted to get up and Drive, he Stood for it, although he had to make a Pretty Talk to a couple of Policemen before he landed Jim at the Hotel.

If this were a Novel, there would be a Row of Stars inserted right here.

The Sun was high in the Heavens when the Country Customer opened his Eyes and tried to Remember and then tried to Forget. Some one was sitting at his Bedside. It was Mr. Byrd, the Long-Distance Entertainer, looking as Sweet and Cool as a Daisy.

"Before I give you the Photograph of Myself which you requested last Night, would you care for anything in the way of Ice Water?" he asked.

Jim did a sincere Groan, and said he could use a Barrel of it.

"Did I request a Photograph?" he asked, as he felt for the Boundaries of his Head.

"You did," replied the Entertainer. "And you gave me your Watch as a Keepsake. I have brought the Watch and all the Money you had left after you bought the Dog."

"What Dog?"

"The Dog that you gave to Bob."

"Did we go back there again? I remember the First Time."

"Yes, it was In There that you wanted to Run a Hundred Yards with any Man Present for Chalk, Money, or Marbles."

"Where are we now—at the Hotel?"

"Yes, and Everything is Smoothed Over. The Night Clerk has agreed not to swear out a Warrant."

Jim did not Comprehend, but he was afraid to Ask.

"It may be that I was a mite Polluted," he suggested.

"You were a teeny bit Pickled about Two, when you tried to upset the Lunch Wagon, but I don't think any one Noticed it," said Mr. Byrd.

"Take me to the Noon Train," requested the Country Customer. "Tell the Conductor where I live, and send me the Bills for all that I have Broken."

"Everything is Settled," responded the Entertainer. "But why Tear yourself away?"

"I am Through," replied Jim, "So why Tarry?"

Mr. Byrd took him to the Train and arranged with the Porter of the Parlor Car for a Pillow.

When the Country Customer arrived at Home he accounted for the Eyes by saying that the Night Traffic makes so much Noise on these

Hard Stone Pavements, it is almost impossible to get the usual amount of Sleep.

The Head of the Concern put his O. K. on a Voucher for $43.60, and it occurred to him that Stereopticon Lectures seemed to be Advancing, but he asked no Questions.

Ever after that Jim bought all his Goods of this one House. He had to.

MORAL: *Scatter Seeds of Kindness.*

Finley Peter Dunne

Born on July 10 in the original "west side" Irish district of Chicago, even then dispersing, Dunne (1867–1936) was christened Peter after his father. In his later years he added Finley, his mother's family name, to his own. Ellen Finley was a woman of education and literary interest who stimulated his reading and saw that he and a sister (who became a notable Chicago schoolteacher) attended the West Division High School, where Dunne graduated in 1884. His father felt that his success at school did not warrant college study, and thus the young graduate found a job as office boy and cub reporter on a struggling Chicago newspaper, the *Telegraph*. During the next seven years he held jobs of increasing importance on virtually all of the chief Chicago newspapers and was a notable luminary of the Whitechapel Club, a boisterous and bohemian association of newspapermen. In 1892 he became an editorial writer on the *Evening Post*, and it was here, growing out of a world's fair feature, that Mr. Dooley made his appearance.

Dunne had taken on the writing of a Sunday column for the *Post*, to be occupied with the activity of the fair. In that connection he hit upon the idea of using the recognizable image of a well-known Chicago wit and saloon keeper, James McGarry, as his spokesman. By the fall of the year, however, McGarry objected to the public comment his fame was creating for him. Dunne, consequently, altered his now popular personage into the imaginary Martin Dooley, proprietor of a small saloon on Archer Avenue in a predominantly Irish section of the South Side known as Bridgeport. This area, just north of the stockyards and east of the rolling mills, had been originally settled by laborers on the Illinois and Michigan Canal and the railroads that almost immediately followed. Dooley, in turn, advanced himself as self-elected commentator at first on the affairs of Bridgeport and Chicago but soon on those of the nation and the great world. With the advent of the Spanish-American War in 1898, he largely abandoned his interest in local matters to make his author the proprietor of a nationally read and syndicated column.

The first collected volume of Dooley pieces appeared in 1898. It was followed by seven others stretching up to 1919, to be followed in turn by syndicated publication continuing intermittently to 1926. Dunne moved from Chicago in 1900 to make New York his center and to continue the syndicated Dooley. In 1902 he joined the editorial staff of *Collier's* magazine, acting as chief editor from 1917 to 1919. In addition, he contributed regular editorial features to the *American* magazine from 1906 to 1915, all in addition to the Dooley writing. These years were marked by his love of club life in New York and Long Island and by a wide circle of business, journalistic, and literary friends.

He had married Margaret Abbott in 1902 and became the father of four children. Encountering financial difficulties upon the sale of *Collier's* after its proprietor's death, he found his later years eased by a bequest of half a million dollars from his longtime publishing colleague, Payne Whitney, and was able to enjoy and extend his gift for wit, warmth, and sociability in relative comfort. He succumbed to lingering illness in 1936 and (against his own wish) was buried in style with a large and widely attended funeral at St. Patrick's Cathedral in New York. Once when asked if he had remained a faithful Roman Catholic, Dunne replied no, that he was a Chicago Catholic. Friends, however, overrode his heterodoxy in the final event.

Master of a witty and pungent style that led to his first journalistic success, Dunne found his primary newspaper interests to be those of an editorial writer. Mr. Dooley, however, turned out to be a good deal more than simply the "mask" for Dunne's opinions that he is sometimes declared to be. He became in fact, and across his range, a personage subject to alterations of mood and feeling about himself as well as the worlds he observed. At his best, he was the solidly imagined voice and mind of a perceptive, shrewd, skeptical citizen blessed with an uncommonly apt speech and an ever patient if not wholly subduable listener in his chief auditor, Hennessy. His neighborhood, city, and nation were never failing if seldom satisfying spectacles. His person was a projection into dramatic being of Dunne's own warmth, sharpness, and radical impatience with pretense of any kind. He never sought his own glory, though he thoroughly enjoyed his own alertness and wit. He would take no nonsense willingly, however highly placed or recommended its source might be.

One- and two-line jokes fell at pleasure throughout Dunne's columns, but a piece was seldom made to rely on gags for its principal appeal. Like his contemporaries, he paced his storytelling at leisure but always with perceived imaginative substance. Dunne set store by the attitudes Dooley expressed. Much of Dooley's success, no doubt, lay in his entertainment value, but he was a constant reminder to his reader of how the individual and the common life might be enlightened by independent mind and feeling.

Dunne selected individual pieces from the columns to make up the eight Dooley volumes appearing between 1898 and 1919. The most recent selection is that of Barbara C. Schaaf, *Mr. Dooley's Chicago* (1977), and draws in particular on uncollected material appearing in Chicago newspapers before Dunne's departure from the city in 1900. Elmer Ellis is editor of a standard selection, *Mr. Dooley at His Best* (1938), and author of a biography, *Mr. Dooley's America, a Life of Finley Peter Dunne* (1941). A recent study is Charles Fanning, *Finley Peter Dunne and Mr. Dooley, the Chicago Years* (1978).

From the Preface to Mr. Dooley in Peace and War

[From their first appearance in 1893 to their last in 1926, Dunne's Dooley pieces were originally published under a wide variety of circumstances. After Dunne left Chicago and regular newspaper writing in 1900, Dooley shifted wholly to national syndication, appearing weekly in an altering variety of magazines and newspapers. From the total of these, a fraction was selected for reprinting in the original Dooley books. Since Dunne's death, in turn, no less than four books of selections have been made by later editors. Our selection has been drawn from this variety.

For those pieces not collected by Dunne in his books and there given a title, the original newspaper heading has been used. When there was no such title, the present editors have supplied one printed in brackets. If the piece is from one of Dunne's books, the author's title has been used. The pieces here are assembled in approximate chronological order and reflect Dooley's conversion from a commentator on local affairs to national and, at the end, even timeless concerns. This initial piece is a major portion of the preface Dunne wrote for the first Dooley book.]

...

Archey Road stretches back for many miles from the heart of an ugly city to the cabbage gardens that gave the maker of the seal his opportunity to call the city "urbs in horto." Somewhere between the two— that is to say, forninst th' gas-house and beyant Healey's slough and not far from the polis station—lives Martin Dooley, doctor of philosophy.

There was a time when Archey Road was purely Irish. But the Huns,[1] turned back from the Adriatic and the stock-yards and overrunning Archey Road, have nearly exhausted the original population,— not driven them out as they drove out less vigorous races, with thick clubs and short spears, but edged them out with the more biting weapons of modern civilization,—overworked and under-eaten them into more languid surroundings remote from the tanks of the gashouse and the blast furnaces of the rolling-mill.

But Mr. Dooley remains, and enough remain with him to save the Archey Road. In this community you can hear all the various accents of Ireland, from the awkward brogue of the "far-downer" to the mild and aisy Elizabethan English of the southern Irishman, and all the exquisite variations to be heard between Armagh and Bantry Bay, with the difference that would naturally arise from substituting cinders and sulphuretted hydrogen for soft misty air and peat smoke. Here also you can see the wakes and christenings, the marriages and funerals, and the other fêtes of the ol' counthry somewhat modified and darkened by American usage. The Banshee has been heard many times in Archey Road. On the eve of All Saints' Day it is well known that here alone the pookies play thricks in cabbage gardens. In 1893 it was reported that Malachi Dempsey was called "by the other people," and disappeared west of the tracks, and never came back.

A simple people! "Simple, says ye!" remarked Mr. Dooley. "Simple like th' air or th' deep sea. Not complicated like a watch that stops whin th' shoot iv clothes ye got it with wears out. Whin Father Butler wr-rote a book he niver finished, he said simplicity was not wearin' all

---

1. Non-Irish settlers in Bridgeport.

ye had on ye'er shirt-front, like a tin-horn gambler with his di'mon' stud. An' 'tis so."

The barbarians around them are moderately but firmly governed, encouraged to passionate votings for the ruling race, but restrained from the immoral pursuit of office.

The most generous, thoughtful, honest, and chaste people in the world are these friends of Mr. Dooley,—knowing and innocent; moral, but giving no heed at all to patented political moralities.

Among them lives and prospers the traveller, archæologist, historian, social observer, saloon-keeper, economist, and philosopher, who has not been out of the ward for twenty-five years "but twict." He reads the newspapers with solemn care, heartily hates them, and accepts all they print for the sake of drowning Hennessy's rising protests against his logic. From the cool heights of life in the Archey Road, uninterrupted by the jarring noises of crickets and cows, he observes the passing show, and meditates thereon. His impressions are transferred to the desensitized plate of Mr. Hennessy's mind, where they can do no harm.

"There's no bedther place to see what's goin' on thin the Ar-rchey Road," says Mr. Dooley. "Whin th' ilicthric cars is hummin' down th' sthreet an' th' blast goin' sthrong at th' mills, th' noise is that gr-reat ye can't think."

He is opulent in good advice, as becomes a man of his station; for he has mastered most of the obstacles in a business career, and by leading a prudent and temperate life has established himself so well that he owns his own house and furniture, and is only slightly behind on his license. It would be indelicate to give statistics as to his age. Mr. Hennessy says he was a "grown man whin th' pikes was out in forty-eight, an' I was hedge-high, an' I'm near fifty-five." Mr. Dooley says Mr. Hennessy is eighty. He closes discussion on his own age with the remark, "I'm old enough to know bedther." He has served his country with distinction. His conduct of the important office of captain of his precinct (1873–75) was highly commended, and there was some talk of nominating him for alderman. At the expiration of his term he was personally thanked by the Hon. M. McGee, at one time a member of the central committee. But the activity of public life was unsuited to a man of Mr. Dooley's tastes; and, while he continues to view the political situation always with interest and sometimes with alarm, he has resolutely declined to leave the bar for the forum. His early experience gave him wisdom in discussing public affairs. "Politics," he says, "ain't bean bag. 'Tis a man's game; an' women, childher, an' prohybitionists'd do well to keep out iv it." Again he remarks, "As Shakespeare says, 'Ol' men f'r th' council, young men f'r th' ward.'"

Up in Archey Road
John McKenna Visits His Old Friend Martin Dooley
News of Bridgeport Society
The Misadventures of Mlle. Grogan and M. Riley
A German Band and Its Irish Tunes

[Here follows the first Dooley piece to appear after the dismissal of "Colonel McNeery," Dunne's name for his original column spokesman. Along with other early squibs, this one also features John McKenna, a minor political figure of Chicago's real life, as Dooley's conversation partner. Beginning from Dunne's interest in the presidential campaign of 1896 and the need to find a politically unidentified character, McKenna was made to share billing with the more malleable figure of Hennessy and in a short time was wholly dismissed from the column. Unlike the real-life McGarry, McNeery's original, McKenna was disappointed at this turn since he rather enjoyed the renown the columns had brought him. The piece reflects the prevailing theme of Chicago's world's fair, with which the earliest columns were often concerned.]

• • •

Business was dull in the liquor-shop of Mr. Martin Dooley in Archey road last Wednesday night and Mr. Dooley was sitting back in the rear of the shop holding a newspaper at arm's length before him and reading the sporting news. In came Mr. John McKenna. Mr. McKenna has been exceedingly restless since Colonel McNeery went home to Ireland and on his way out to Brighton Park for consolation he bethought himself of Martin Dooley. The lights were shining in the little tavern and the window decorations—green festoons, a single sheet poster of a Parnell meeting in McCormick's Hall, and a pyramid of bottles filled with Medford rum and flies—evoked such cheery recollections of earlier years that Mr. McKenna hopped off the car and entered briskly.

"Good evening, Martin," he said.

"Hellow, Jawnny," replied Mr. Dooley, as if they had parted only the evening before. "How's thricks? I don't mind, Jawnny, if I do. 'Tis duller here than a raypublican primary in the fourth wa-ard, th' night. Sure, ye're like a ray iv sunlight, ye are that. There's been no company in these pa-arts since Dominick Riley's big gossoon[2] was took up be th' polis. . . . What was he tuk up fur, says ye? Faith, I'll never tell ye. Th' polis had a gredge again him, like as not. I belave they do say he kilt a Chiney man, an' I'll not put it beyant him, f'r he is a wild lad no less, an' wan that'd carry th' joke to anny len'th.

"Dint know where ye've been all these days, man alive. I ain't seen ye, Jawn dear, since ye led th' gr-rand march in Finucane's Hall[3] this tin years past. D'ye mind th' Grogan girls? Aha, amusha, I see ye do, ye cute man. An' well ye might. Th' oldest wan—Birdie she called hersel' in thim days though she was christened Bridget, an' I knowed it dam well, f'r I was at th' christenin', an' got this here scar on me nut fr'm an unruly Clare man that Jawnny Shea brung over with him—th' oldest one danced with ye, an' five years afterward her husband found in her pocket book a ca-ard sayin' 'Vote f'r Jawn McKinna' an' he was f'r suin' f'r a divorce, by gar, he was. She said ye give her a lot iv thim for to take home to th' old man an' she on'y kept th' wan. An' ye haven't seen her fr'm that day to this! Oh dear, oh dear! How soon forgot we are! It's little ye think iv Bridgeport whin ye'er gallopin' aroun' to wakes an' christenin's with Potther Pammer and Hobart What th' 'ell's his name Taylor.[4]

"I thought f'r to see ye at Irish Day.[5] I dunnaw how I missed ye. Did ye iver see th' like iv it? Rain, rain, rain and dhrip, dhrip, dhrip. They used to be a sayin' at home whin it was a clear day: 'It's a fine day, plaze Gawd,' an' whin it rained cats an' dogs an' pokers: 'It's a fine day f'r th' counthry.' An' mind ye, Jawn, I won't deny it might be said last Sathedah with no ha-arm done. Ye cuddent have got three hundhred thousan' Irishmen together on a fine day without thim breakin' loose. Th' rain kipt thim fr'm gettin' enthusiastic an' by gar, f'r th' first time in th' histhry iv th' wurruld they got thim in peace an' harmony. They

2. Irish dialect for "boy."
3. Bridgeport's principal building of public resort. The hall was located at the corner of Archer Avenue and Loomis Street.
4. Two well-known Chicago figures. Potter Palmer was a wealthy developer of Loop real estate and owner of the Palmer House Hotel. Taylor, a social and literary figure, was noted for the hyphenated form of his name, Hobart Chatfield Chatfield-Taylor, which he assumed in order to secure a family inheritance.
5. Especially designated day at the world's fair.

was united in denouncin' th' diputy f'r weather an' th' gazaboy that pulled down th' flag. If they knowed it before they did that, Orangey's[6] 'd be orderin' lemonades in th' place where Orangeys go through th' mercy of Gawd."

"I suppose you spent th' day in th' Irish village," suggested Mr. McKenna.

"Well, Jawn, to tell ye no lie," said Mr. Dooley, "an' don't whisper it to Finerty if you meet him at th' nex' sore-ree, but I didn't. I got mesilf fixed in a chair at th' Dutch village, an' by gar, ne'er a fut I stirred fr'm it th' livelong day. 'Twas most comfortin' an' th' band played ivry Irish tune from 'Rambler fr'm Clare' to 'Connock's Man's Dhream,' on'y mind ye, with a slight accint. There was wan lad that played th' ol' song, 'A-ha Limerick is Beautiful' an' a sweet ol' song it is, to be sure. Gawd forgive me f'r sayin' so, that hates a 'butthermilk.'[7] He played it without an accint, an' whin he come down, thinkin' he might be wan iv us, says I: 'Cunas thantu,'[8] I says. Well, sir, what d'ye think he replies? What d'ye think th' bpoor bosthoon replies? He says: 'Wee gates.' Wee gates, he says, Jawn, or may I never stir fr'm th' spot. Well, sir, I laughed in his face. I did, I did.

"An' a-are ye gown, Jawn dear? How about thim two bowls? That's right. Twenty-five to you, Jawn. Good night an' th' Lord be between ye an' har-rm."

What Does He Care?
Dooley Discourses Again on His Friend Mr. Pullman
Doctrine of "What th' 'Ell"
Archey Road Philosopher Reviews His Amiable Fellow
Townsman's Peculiar Qualities

[Dunne's politics were never wholly predictable. However, he usually sided with the "progressive" element in the American public life of his day. Here he displays his disgust with the aloof self-interest coloring George Pullman's attitude toward the strikers at his railroad car works during 1894, a judgment said to have evoked applause from the paper's typesetters when Dunne appeared among them. Pullman's admin- istration of the "model town" he had built for those workers and re-

6. North of Ireland Protestants.
7. A Limerick County man.
8. The Gaelic greeting, "How are you?"

quired them to occupy at markedly high rents was colored by pronounced paternalism. During the heat of the great American Railway
Union strike, with the army on the scene, Pullman withdrew himself
and his family to safety. At ease on his private island in the St. Law-
rence River, he awaited his employees' capitulation.]

• • •

"Jawn," said Mr. Dooley, "I said it wanst an' I sa-ay it again, I'd liefer be
George M. Pullman thin anny man this side iv Michigan City. I would
so. Not, Jawn, d'ye mind that I invy him his job iv r-runnin' all th' push-
cart lodgin'-houses iv th' counthry or in dayvilopin' th' whiskers iv a
goat without displayin' anny other iv th' good qualities iv th' craythur
or in savin' his tax list fr'm th' assissor with th' intintion iv layin' it befure a mathrimonyal agency. Sare a bit does I care f'r thim honors. But,
Jawn, th' la-ad that can go his way with his nose in th' air an' pay no
attintion to th' sufferin' iv women an' childher—dear, oh, dear, but this
life must be as happy as th' da-ay is long.

"It seems to me, Jawn, that half th' throuble we have in this vale iv
tears, as Dohenny calls Bridgepoort, is seein' th' sufferin' iv women an'
little childhren. Th' men can take care iv thimsilves, says I. If they can't
wurruk let thim go on th' polis foorce, an' if they can't go on th' polis
foorce let thim follow th' advice big Pether Hinnissy give th' Dutchman.
'I dinnaw vat to do,' sa-ays th' Dutchman. 'I have no money an' I can
get no wurruk.' 'Foolish man,' says Hinnissy. 'D'ye know what th' good
book says? To those that has nawthin' something will be given,' he
says; 'an' those that has a lot,' he says, 'some wan'll come along with a
piece iv lead pipe,' he says, 'in a stockin',' he says, 'an' take what they
got,' he says. 'D'ye see that big man over there?' he says, pointin' to
Dorgan, th' rale estateman. 'Go over an' take him be th' neck an' make
him give up.' Well, sir, th' German, bein' like all iv th' ra-ace but Hesing,
was a foolish la-ad, an' what does he do but follow th' joker's advice.
Sare Dorgan give him a kick in th' stummick, an' whin he got out iv th'
hospital he wint to th' Bridewell, an', by dad, I'm thinkin' he was betther off there than most poor divvles out iv it, f'r they get three meals a
da-ay, av'n if there ain't no toothbrushes in th' cells.

"But as I said, Jawn, 'tis not th' min, ye mind; 'tis th' women an'
childhren. Glory be to Gawd, I can scarce go out f'r a wa-alk f'r pity at
seein' th' little wans settin' on th' stoops an' th' women with thim lines
in th' fa-ace that I seen but wanst befure, in our parish over beyant,

with th' potatoes that was all kilt be th' frost an' th' oats rotted with th' dhrivin rain. Go into wan iv th' side sthreets about supper time an' see thim, Jawn—thim women sittin' at th' windies with th' babies at their breasts an' waitin' f'r th' ol' man to come home. Thin watch thim as he comes up th' sthreet, with his hat over his eyes an' th' shoulders iv thim bint like a hoop an' dhraggin' his feet as if he carried ball an' chain. Musha, but 'tis a sound to dhrive ye'er heart cold whin a woman sobs an' th' young wans cries, an' both because there's no bread in th' house. Betther off thim that lies in Gavin's crates out in Calv'ry, with th' grass over thim an' th' stars lookin' down on thim, quite at last. An' betther f'r us that sees an' hears an' can do nawthin' but give a crust now an' thin. I seen Tim Dorsey's little woman carryin' a loaf iv bread an' a ham to th' Polack's this noon. Dorsey have been out iv wurruk f'r six months, but he made a sthrike carryin' th' hod yisther-day an' th' good woman pinched out some vittles f'r th' Polacks."

Mr. Dooley swabbed th' bar in a melancholy manner and turned again with the remark: "But what's it all to Pullman. Whin Gawd quar-ried his heart a happy man was made. He cares no more f'r thim little matthers in life an' death than I do f'r O'Connor's tab. 'Th' women an' childhren is dyin' iv hunger,' they sa-ays. 'They've done no wrong,' they sa-ays. 'Will ye not put out ye'er hand to help thim?' they sa-ays. 'Ah, what th' 'ell,' sa-ays George. 'What th' 'ell,' he sa-ays. 'James,' he sa-ays, 'a bottle iv champagne an' a piece iv crambree pie. What th' 'ell, what th' 'ell, what th' 'ell.'"

"I heard two died yesterday," said Mr. McKenna. "Two women."

"Poor things, poor things. But," said Mr. Dooley, once more swab-bing the bar, "what th' 'ell."

Chicago Newspapers

[Wilbur Storey was the fiery Chicago editor mentioned earlier in this collection. Dunne had never worked for him, but he did serve the *Times*, Storey's paper, after the editor's death in 1884 and remembered him from his own apprenticeship days. The piece reflects a living knowledge of Storey and his unsparing journalism.]

•••

"I don't think," said Mr. Dooley, "that th' pa-apers is as good now as they used to be whin I was a young man."

"I don't see much diff'rence in thim," said Mr. Hennessy. "Except they're all full iv pitchers iv th' prisidint an' secrity iv th' Milwaukee Avnoo Fife an' Dhrum E-lite Society. They give ye th' same advice to vote th' mugwump ticket between ilictions an' th' straight ticket at ilictions, an' how th' business in pig iron is slowly but surely pickin' up, an' how to make las' year's dhress look like next year's be addin' a few jet beads an' an accorjeen pleat. They're as bad now as they iver were an' I've quit readin' thim."

"Ah, but sure," said Mr. Dooley, "ye don't raymimber th' ol' days. Ye don't raymimber Storey's *Times*. That was th' paper f'r ye. What th' divvle did ol' man Storey care f'r th' thrade in pig iron? 'Twas no more in him thin th' thrade in poolchecks. He set up in his office with his whiskers thrailin' in an ink pot an' wrote venomious attacks on th' characters iv th' leaders iv high society an' good-natured jests about his esteemed contimprary havin' had to leave Ohio because he stold a cukstove.[9] He didn't have no use f'r prominint citizens except be way iv heavin' scandal at thim. He knowed what th' people wanted. They wanted crime, an' he give it to thim. If they wasn't a hangin' on th' front page some little lad iv a rayporther'd lose his job. They was murdher an' arson till ye cudden't rest, robbery an' burglary f'r page afther page, with anny quantity iv scandal f'r th' woman's page an' a fair assortmint iv larceny an' assault an' batthry f'r th' little wans. 'Twas a paper no wan took into his house—f'r th' other mimbers iv th' fam'ly—but 'twas a well r-run paper, so it was.

"Ye can hardly find anny crimes nowadays. To look at th' pa-apers ye'd think they was not wan bit iv rale spoortin' blood left in th' people iv this city. Instead iv it I have to pay to know that Mrs. Dofunny iv Englewood has induced her husband to stay away fr'm home while she gives a function—an' what a function is I dinnaw—an' among thim that'll be prisint, if they can get their laundhry out, 'll be Messers an' Mesdames What-d'ye-Call-Thim an' Messers an' Mesdames This-an'-That an' Miss-What-D'ye-Call-Her-Now, an' so on. What do I care about thim? Now, if Misther Dofunny had come home with a load on an' found his wife r-runnin' up bills f'r tea an' broke up the function with his dinner pail it'd be worth readin' about. But none iv th' papers'd say annything about it, now that Storey's gone. Why, mind ye, las' week th'

9. The reference is to an attack by Storey on Joseph Medill, a founder of the Chicago *Tribune*.

Willum J. O'Brien Lithry an' Marchin' Club give a dance, an' befure it got through th' chairman iv th' flure comity fell out with th' German man that led th' band an' ivery wan in th' place took a wallup at some wan else with a wind instrument. I looked f'r it in th' paper th' nex' day. All they had was: 'Th' Willum J. O'Brien Lithry an' Marchin' Club, includin' th' mos' prominent mimbers iv society in th' sixth ward, give a function at Finucane's Hall las' night. O'Rafferty sarved an' music was furnished be Weinstein's orchesthry. Among those prisint was so-an'-so.' Th' rayporther must've copied th' names off th' blotter at th' polis station. An' there was not wan wurrud about th' fight—not wan wurrud!

"Now, if it had been in ol' Storey's day this is th' way it'd read: 'Bill O'Brien, th' tough aldherman fr'm th' sixth ward, has a club named after him, most iv thim bein' well known to th' polis. It is a disgrace to th' decent people iv Bridgepoort. Las' night th' neighbors complained to th' polis iv th' noise an Lift'nant Murphy responded with a wagon load iv bluecoats. On entherin' th' hall th' gallant officers found a free fight in progress, wan iv th' rowdies havin' hit th' leader iv th' band, who responded be knockin' his assailant down with a b-flat cornet. Th' disturbers iv th' peace were taken to Deerin' sthreet station an'll be thried befure Judge Scully in th' mornin'.' That's th' way ol' Storey'd give it to thim. He didn't know much about functions, but he was blue blazes on polis news. . . .

The Church Fair

"Wanst I knew a man," said Mr. Dooley, laying down his newspaper, "be th' name iv Burke, that come fr'm somewhere around Derry, though he was no Presbyteryan. He was iv th' right sort. Well, he was feelin' how-come-ye-so, an' he dhrifted over to where we was holdin' a fair. They was a band outside, an' he thought it was a grand openin'. So he come in with a cigar in th' side iv his mouth an' his hat hangin' onto his ear. It was th' last night iv th' fair, an' ivrything was wide open; f'r th' priest had gone home, an' we wanted f'r to break th' record. This Burke was f'r lavin' whin he see where he was; but we run him again th' shootin' gallery, where ye got twinty-five cints, a quarther iv a dollar, f'r ivry time ye rang th' bell. Th' ol' gun we had was crooked as a ram's horn, but it must've fitted into Burke's squint; f'r he made that there bell ring as if he was a conducthor iv a grip-car[10] roundin' a curve. He had th' shootin' gallery on its last legs whin we run him again th' wheel iv fortune. He broke it. Thin we thried him on th' grab-bag. They was four goold watches an' anny quantity iv brickbats an' chunks iv coal in th' bag. He had four dives, an' got a watch each time. He took a chanst on ivrything; an' he won a foldin'-bed, a doll that cud talk like an old gate, a pianny, a lamp-shade, a Life iv St. Aloysius, a pair iv shoes, a base-ball bat, an ice-cream freezer, an' th' pomes iv Mike Scanlan.

"Th' comity was disthracted. Here was a man that'd break th' fair, an' do it with th' best iv humor; f'r he come fr'm another parish. So we held a private session. 'What'll we do?' says Dorgan, th' chairman. They was a man be th' name iv Flaherty, a good man thin an' a betther now; f'r he's dead, may he rest in peace! An' Flaherty says: 'We've got to take th' bull be th' horns,' he says. 'If ye lave him to me,' he says, 'I'll fix him,' he says.

"So he injooced this man Burke to come down back iv th' shootin' gallery, an' says he to Burke, 'Ye're lucky to-night.' 'Not so very,' says Burke. ' 'Twud be a shame to lave ye get away with all ye won,' says Flaherty. ' 'Twill be a great inconvanience,' says Burke. 'I'll have to hire two or three dhrays,' he says; 'an' 'tis late.' 'Well,' says Flaherty, 'I'm ap-pinted be th' parish to cut th' ca-ards with ye,' he says, 'whether ye're to give back what ye won or take what's left.' ' 'Tis fair,' says Burke; 'an', whoiver wins, 'tis f'r a good cause.' An' he puts th' watches an' th' money on th' table.

"'High man,' says Flaherty. 'High man,' says Burke. Flaherty cut th' king iv spades. Burke, th' robber, cut th' ace iv hearts. He was reachin' out f'r th' money, whin Flaherty put his hands over it. 'Wud ye take it?' says he. 'I wud,' says Burke. 'Wud ye rob th' church?' says Flaherty. 'I wud,' says Burke. 'Thin,' says Flaherty, scoopin' it in, 'ye're a heretic; an' they'se nawthin' comin' to ye.'

"Burke looked at him, an' he looked at th' comity; an' he says, 'Gintlemen, if iver ye come over in th' Sixth Ward, dhrop in an' see me,' he says. 'I'll thry an' make it plisint f'r ye,' he says. An' he wint away.

"Th' story got out, an' th' good man heerd iv it. He was mighty mad

10. A street railway cable car.

about it; an' th' nex' sermon he preached was on th' evils iv gamblin', but he asked Flaherty f'r to take up th' colliction."

A Book Review

[The book "reviewed" here was Theodore Roosevelt's *The Rough Riders*, an account of the regiment Roosevelt personally had raised and led in the Spanish-American War. This along with his reforming reputation as New York City police commissioner, secretary of the navy, and governor of New York drew national attention to him and led in 1900 to the old guard Republican effort to "bury" him in the vice-presidency. A year later, however, following McKinley's assassination, the presidency was his. Roosevelt took Dunne's "review" good-naturedly and made a point of cultivating its author. The two developed a high regard for each other that persisted through Roosevelt's lifetime. Dunne's spelling of Roosevelt's name was not an implication of Jewishness but of Dooley's ethnic uncertainties, the Irish apart. Perhaps this item more than any other was influential in drawing national attention to Dunne. Its concluding line became a national byword.]

• • •

"Well sir," said Mr. Dooley, "I jus' got hold iv a book, Hinnissy, that suits me up to th' handle, a gran' book, th' grandest iver seen. Ye know I'm not much throubled be lithrachoor, havin' manny worries iv me own, but I'm not prejudiced again' books. I am not. Whin a rale good book comes along I'm as quick as anny wan to say it isn't so bad, an' this here book is fine. I tell ye 'tis fine."

"What is it?" Mr. Hennessy asked languidly.

"'Tis 'Th' Biography iv a Hero be Wan who Knows.' 'Tis 'Th' Darin' Exploits iv a Brave Man be an Actual Eye Witness.' 'Tis 'Th' Account iv th' Desthruction iv Spanish Power in th' Ant Hills,' as it fell fr'm th' lips iv Tiddy Rosenfelt an' was took down be his own hands. Ye see 'twas this way, Hinnissy, as I r-read th' book. Whin Tiddy was blowed up in th' harbor iv Havana he instantly con-cluded they must be war. He debated th' question long an' earnestly an' fin'lly passed a jint resolution declarin' war. So far so good. But there was no wan to carry it on. What shud he do? I will lave th' janial author tell th' story in his own wurruds.

"'Th' sicrety iv war had offered me,' he says, 'th' command of a

From an illustration by Frederick Opper for Finley Peter Dunne's *Mr. Dooley's Philosophy*. Roosevelt's companion is the war correspondent Richard Harding Davis.

rig'mint,' he says, 'but I cud not consint to remain in Tampa while perhaps less audacious heroes was at th' front,' he says. 'Besides,' he says, 'I felt I was incompetent f'r to command a rig'mint raised be another,' he says. 'I detarmined to raise wan iv me own,' he says. 'I selected fr'm me acquaintances in th' West,' he says, 'men that had thravelled with me acrost th' desert an' th' storm-wreathed mountain,' he says, 'sharin' me burdens an' at times confrontin' perils almost as gr-reat as anny that beset me path,' he says. 'Together we had faced th' turrors iv th' large but vilent West,' he says, 'an' these brave men had seen me with me trusty rifle shootin' down th' buffalo, th' elk, th' moose, th' grizzly bear, th' mountain goat,' he says, 'th' silver man,[11] an' other ferocious beasts iv thim parts,' he says. 'An' they niver flinched,' he says. 'In a few days I had thim perfectly tamed,' he says, 'an' ready to go annywhere I led,' he says. 'On th' thransport goi'n to Cubia,' he says, 'I

11. Although Roosevelt was regarded as a "progressive," like any Republican he was opposed to the "free coinage" of silver, an issue supported by the silver-producing states of the West.

wud stand beside wan iv these r-rough men threatin' him as a akel, which he was in ivrything but birth, education, rank an' courage, an' together we wud look up at th' admirable stars iv that tolerable southern sky an' quote th' bible fr'm Walt Whitman,' he says. 'Honest, loyal, thrue-hearted la-ads, how kind I was to thim,' he says.

"'We had no sooner landed in Cubia than it become nicessry f'r me to take command iv th' ar-rmy which I did at wanst. A number of days was spint be me in reconnoitring, attinded on'y be me brave an' fluent body guard, Richard Harding Davis.[12] I discovered that th' inimy was heavily inthrenched on th' top iv San Joon hill immejiately in front iv me. At this time it become apparent that I was handicapped be th' prisence iv th' ar-rmy,' he says. 'Wan day whin I was about to charge a block house sturdily definded be an ar-rmy corps undher Gin'ral Tamale, th' brave Castile that I aftherwards killed with a small ink-eraser that I always carry, I r-ran into th' entire military force iv th' United States lying on its stomach. 'If ye won't fight,' says I, 'let me go through,' I says. 'Who ar-re ye?' says they. 'Colonel Rosenfelt,' says I. 'Oh, excuse me,' says the gin'ral in command (if me mimry serves me thrue it was Miles) r-risin' to his knees an' salutin'. This showed me 'twud be impossible f'r to carry th' war to a successful con-clusion unless I was free, so I sint th' ar-rmy home an' attackted San Joon hill. Ar-rmed on'y with a small thirty-two which I used in th' West to shoot th' fleet prairie dog, I climbed that precipitous ascent in th' face iv th' most gallin' fire I iver knew or heerd iv. But I had a few r-rounds iv gall mesilf an' what cared I? I dashed madly on cheerin' as I wint. Th' Spanish throops was dhrawn up in a long line in th' formation known among military men as a long line. I fired at th' man nearest to me an' I knew be th' expression iv his face that th' trusty bullet wint home. It passed through his frame, he fell, an' wan little home in far-off Catalonia was made happy be th' thought that their riprisintative had been kilt be th' future governor iv New York. Th' bullet sped on its mad flight an' passed through th' intire line fin'lly imbeddin' itself in th' abdomen iv th' Ar-rch-bishop iv Santiago eight miles away. This ended th' war.'

"'They has been some discussion as to who was th' first man to r-reach th' summit iv San Joon hill. I will not attempt to dispute th'

12. The dashing newspaperman, fiction writer, and playwright. He was present at the battle of San Juan Hill with Roosevelt and was offered a commission by him, which he declined.

merits iv th' manny gallant sojers, statesmen, corryspondints an' ki-netoscope men who claim th' distinction. They ar-re all brave men an' if they wish to wear my laurels they may. I have so manny annyhow that it keeps me broke havin' thim blocked an' irned. But I will say f'r th' binifit iv Posterity that I was th' on'y man I see. An' I had a tillyscope.'"

"I have thried, Hinnissy," Mr. Dooley continued, "to give you a fair idee iv th' contints iv this remarkable book, but what I've tol' ye is on'y what Hogan calls an outline iv th' principal pints. Ye'll have to r-read th' book ye'ersilf to get a thrue conciption. I haven't time f'r to tell ye th' wurruk Tiddy did in ar-rmin' an' equippin' himsilf, how he fed himsilf, how he steadied himsilf in battle an' encouraged himsilf with a few well-chosen wurruds whin th' sky was darkest. Ye'll have to take a squint into th' book ye'ersilf to l'arn thim things."

"I won't do it," said Mr. Hennessy. "I think Tiddy Rosenfelt is all r-right an' if he wants to blow his hor-rn lave him do it."

"Thrue f'r ye," said Mr. Dooley, "an' if his valliant deeds didn't get into this book 'twud be a long time befure they appeared in Shafter's [13] histhry iv th' war. No man that bears a gredge again' himsilf 'll iver be governor iv a state. An' if Tiddy done it all he ought to say so an' relieve th' suspinse. But if I was him I'd call th' book 'Alone in Cubia.'"

The Supreme Court's Decision

[The concluding line of the piece below has become a fixture of the American language. The issue before the Supreme Court giving rise to it had to do with whether or not Puerto Rican fruit growers, after American annexation of the island, had to pay a 15 percent duty on their products imported to the mainland. The extended arguments Mr. Dooley parodies involved three ambiguous 1901 decisions. He suggests that the Court, despite its extended and learned concern, in fact fudged in favor of the expansionist American mind of the day and so anticipated Justice Holmes's doctrine of the "pragmatic" nature of judicial decision by some years.]

•••

"I see," said Mr. Dooley, "Th' supreme coort has decided th' constitution don't follow th' flag."

"Who said it did?" asked Mr. Hennessy.

"Some wan," said Mr. Dooley. "It happened a long time ago an' I

---

13. General William Shafter, commander of the American army in Cuba.

don't raymimber clearly how it come up, but some fellow said that ivrywhere th' constitution wint, th' flag was sure to go. 'I don't believe wan wurrud iv it,' says th' other fellow. 'Ye can't make me think th' constitution is goin' thrapezin' around ivrywhere a young liftnant in th' arrmy takes it into his head to stick a flag pole. It's too old. It's a home-stayin' constitution with a blue coat with brass buttons onto it, an' it walks with a goold-headed cane. It's old an' it's feeble an' it prefers to set on th' front stoop an' amuse th' childher. It wudden't last a minyit in thim thropical climes. 'T wud get a pain in th' fourteenth amindmint an' die befure th' doctors cud get ar-round to cut it out. No, sir, we'll keep it with us, an' threat it tenderly without too much hard wurruk, an' whin it plays out entirely we'll give it dacint buryal an' incorp'rate oursilves under th' laws iv Noo Jarsey.[14] That's what we'll do,' says he. 'But,' says th' other, 'if it wants to thravel, why not lave it?' 'But it don't want to.' 'I say it does.' 'How'll we find out?' 'We'll ask th' supreme coort. They'll know what's good f'r it.' . . ."

"Well, th' decision iv th' Coort (th' others dissentin') is as follows: First, that th' Disthrict iv Columbya is a state; second, that it is not; third, that New York is a state; fourth, that it is a crown colony; fifth, that all states ar-re states an' all territories ar-re territories in th' eyes iv other powers, but Gawd knows what they ar-re at home. In th' case iv Hogan varsus Mullins, th' decision is he must paper th' barn. (Hinnery VIII, sixteen, six, four, eleven.) In Wiggins varsus et al. th' cow belonged. (Louis XIV, 90 in rem.) In E. P. Vigore varsus Ad. Lib., the custody iv th' childher. I'll now fall back a furlong or two in me chair, while me larned but misguided collagues r-read th' Histhry iv Iceland to show ye how wrong I am. But mind ye, what I've said goes. I let thim talk because it exercises their throats, but ye've heard all th' decision on this limon case that'll get into th' fourth reader.' A voice fr'm th' audjeence, 'Do I get me money back?' Brown J.: 'Who ar-re ye?' Th' Voice: 'Th' man that ownded th' limons.' Brown J.: 'I don't know.' (Gray J., White J., dissentin' an' th' r-rest iv th' birds concurrin' but f'r entirely diff'rent reasons.)

"An' there ye have th' decision, Hinnissy, that's shaken th' intellicts iv th' nation to their very foundations, or will if they thry to read it. 'T is all r-right. Look it over some time. 'T is fine spoort if ye don't care f'r

14. A state much favored for incorporation purposes because of the looseness of its laws in the matter.

checkers. Some say it laves th' flag up in th' air an' some say that's where it laves th' constitution. Annyhow, something's in th' air. But there's wan thing I'm sure about."

"What's that?" asked Mr. Hennessy.

"That is," said Mr. Dooley, "no matther whether th' constitution follows th' flag or not, th' supreme coort follows th' iliction returns."

The Big Fine

[The subject of this piece was Judge Kenesaw Mountain Landis' ruling of 1907 that Rockefeller's "oil trust," the Standard Oil Company of New Jersey, had violated the Interstate Commerce Act in pressuring railroads into preferential tariff rebates. He subjected the corporation to the "big fine" that is Mr. Dooley's concern, an early step in government action leading to division of the corporation in 1911.]

• • •

"That was a splendid fine they soaked Jawn D. with," said Mr. Dooley.

"What did they give him?" asked Mr. Hennessy.

"Twinty-nine millyon dollars," said Mr. Dooley.

"Oh, great!" said Mr. Hennessy. "That's a grand fine. It's a gorjous fine. I can't hardly believe it."

"It's thrue, though," said Mr. Dooley. "Twinty-nine millyon dollars. Divvle th' cent less. I can't exactly make out what th' charge was that they arrested him on, but th' gin'ral idee is that Jawn D. was goin' around loaded up to th' guards with Standard Ile, exceedin' th' speed limit in acquirin' money, an' singin' 'A charge to keep I have' [15] till th' neighbors cud stand it no longer. The judge says: 'Ye're an old offender an' I'll have to make an example iv ye. Twinty-nine millyon dollars or fifty-eight millyon days. Call th' next case, Misther Clerk.'

"Did he pay th' fine? He did not. Iv coorse he cud if he wanted to. He wuddent have to pawn annything to get th' money, ye can bet on that. All he'd have to do would be to put his hand down in his pocket, skin twinty-nine millyon dollar bills off iv his roll an' hurl thim at th' clerk. But he refused to pay as a matter iv principle. 'Twas not that he needed th' money. He don't care f'r money in th' passionate way that you an' me do, Hinnissy. Th' likes iv us are as crazy about a dollar as a man is about his child whin he has on'y wan. Th' chances are we'll spoil it. But Jawn D., havin' a large an' growin' fam'ly iv dollars, takes

---

15. A familiar hymn of the day. Rockefeller was a notable Baptist layman.

on'y a kind iv gin'ral inthrest in thim. He's issued a statement sayin' that he's a custojeen iv money appinted be himsilf. He looks afther his own money an' th' money iv other people. He takes it an' puts it where it won't hurt thim an' they won't spoil it. He's a kind iv a society f'r th' previntion of croolty to money. If he finds a man misusing his money he takes it away fr'm him an' adopts it. Ivry Saturdah night he lets th' man see it f'r a few hours. An' he says h'es surprised to find that whin, with th' purest intintions in th' wurruld, he is found thryin' to coax our little money to his home where it'll find conjanial surroundings an' have other money to play with, th' people thry to lynch him an' th' polis arrest him f'r abduction.

"So as a matther iv principle he appealed th' case. An appeal, Hinnissy, is where ye ask wan coort to show its contempt f'r another coort. 'Tis sthrange that all th' pathrites that have wanted to hang Willum Jennings Bryan an' mesilf f'r not showin' proper respect f'r th' joodicyary, are now showin' their respect f'r th' joodicyary be appealin' fr'm their decisions. Ye'd think Jawn D. wud bow his head reverentially in th' awful presence iv Kenesaw Mt. Landis an' sob out: 'Thank ye'er honor. This here noble fine fills me with joy. But d'ye think ye give me enough? If agreeable I'd like to make it an even thirty millyons.' But he doesn't. He's like mesilf. Him an' me bows to th' decisions iv th' coorts on'y if they bow first.

"I have gr-reat respect f'r th' joodicyary, as fine a lot iv cross an' indignant men as ye'll find annywhere. I have th' same respect f'r thim as they have f'r each other. But I niver bow to a decision iv a judge onless, first, it's pleasant to me, an', second, other judges bow to it. Ye can't be too careful about what decisions ye bow to. A decision that seems agreeable may turn out like an acquaintance ye scrape up at a picnic. Ye may be ashamed iv it to-morrah. Manny's th' time I've bowed to a decree iv a coort on'y to see it go up gayly to th' supreem coort, knock at th' dure an' be kicked down stairs be an angry old gintleman in a black silk petticoat. A decree iv th' coort has got to be pretty vinrable befure I do more thin greet it with a pleasant smile.

"Me idee was whin I read about Jawn D.'s fine that he'd settle at wanst, payin' twenty-eight millyon dollars in millyon dollar bills an' th' other millyon in chicken-feed like ten thousand dollar bills just to annoy th' clerk. But I ought to've known betther. Manny's th' time I've bent me proud neck to a decision iv a coort that lasted no longer thin it took th' lawyer f'r th' definse to call up another judge on th' tillyphone. A judge listens to a case f'r days an' hears, while he's fig-urin' a possible goluf score on his blotting pad, th' argymints iv two or three lawyers that no wan wud dare to offer a judgeship to. Gin'rally speakin', judges are lawyers. They get to be judges because they have what Hogan calls th' joodicyal timp'ramint, which is why annybody gets a job. Th' other kind people won't take a job. They'd rather take a chance. Th' judge listens to a case f'r days an' decides it th' way he intinded to. D'ye find th' larned counsel that's just been beat climbin' up on th' bench an' throwin' his arms around th' judge? Ye bet ye don't. He gathers his law books into his arms, gives th' magistrate a look that means, 'There's an eliction next year,' an' runs down th' hall to another judge. Th' other judge hears his kick an' says he: 'I don't know annything about this here case except what ye've whispered to me, but I know me larned collague an' I wuddent thrust him to referee a roller-skatin' contest. Don't pay th' fine till ye hear fr'm me.' Th' on'y wan that bows to th' decision is th' fellow that won, an' pretty soon he sees he's made a mistake, f'r wan day th' other coort comes out an' declares that th' decision of th' lower coort is another argymint in favor iv abolishing night law schools.

"That's th' way Jawn D. felt about it an' he didn't settle. I wondher will they put him away if he don't pay ivinchooly? 'Twill be a long sen-tence. A frind iv mine wanst got full iv kerosene an' attempted to juggle a polisman. They thried him whin he come out iv th' emergency hos-pital an' fined him a hundhred dollars. He didn't happen to have that amount with him at th' moment or at anny moment since th' day he was born. But the judge was very lenient with him. He said he needn't pay it if he cudden't. Th' coort wud give him a letther of inthroduction to th' bridewell an' he cud stay there f'r two hundhred days. At that rate it'll be a long time befure Jawn D. an' me meet again on the goluf-links. Hogan has it figured out that if Jawn D. refuses to go back on his Puritan principles an' separate himsilf fr'm his money he'll be wan hundhred an' fifty-eight thousand years in cold storage. A man ought to be pretty good at th' lock step in a hundhred an' fifty-eight thou-sand years.

"Well, sir, glory be but times has changed whin they land me gr-reat an' good frind with a fine that's about akel to three millyon dhrunk an' disorderly cases. 'Twud've been cheaper if he'd took to dhrink arly in life. I've made a vow, Hinnissy, niver to be very rich. I'd like to be a little rich, but not rich enough f'r anny wan to notice that me pockets bulged. Time was whin I dhreamed iv havin' money an' lots iv it. 'Tis thrue I begun me dhreams at th' wrong end, spent th' money befure I got it. I was always clear about th' way to spend it but oncertain about th' way to get it. If th' Lord had intinded me to be a rich man He'd've turned me dhreams around an' made me clear about makin' th' money but very awkward an' shy about gettin' rid iv it. There are two halves to ivry dollar. Wan is knowin' how to make it an' th' other is not knowin' how to spend it comfortably. Whin I hear iv a man with gr-reat business capacity I know he's got an akel amount iv spending inca-pacity. No matter how much he knew about business he wuddent be rich if he wasn't totally ignorant iv a science that we have developed as far as our means will allow. But now, I tell ye, I don't dhream iv bein' rich. I'm afraid iv it. In th' good old days th' polis coorts were crowded with th' poor. They weren't charged with poverty, iv coorse, but with the results iv poverty, d'ye mind. Now, be Hivens, th' rich have invaded even th' coorts an' the bridewell. Manny a face wearin' side whiskers an' gold rimmed specs peers fr'm th' windows iv th' black Maria. 'What's this man charged with?' says th' coort. 'He was found in pos-session iv tin millyon dollars,' says th' polisman. An' th' judge puts on th' black cap."

"Well," said Mr. Hennessy, "'tis time they got what was comin' to thim."

"I'll not say ye're wrong," said Mr. Dooley. "I see th' way me frind Jawn D. feels about it. He thinks he's doin' a great sarvice to th' wor-ruld collectin' all th' money in sight. It might remain in incompetint hands if he didn't get it. 'Twud be a shame to lave it where it'd be mis-threated. But th' on'y throuble with Jawn is that he don't see how th' other fellow feels about it. As a father iv about thirty dollars I want to bring thim up mesilf in me own foolish way. I may not do what's right be thim. I may be too indulgent with thim. Their home life may not be happy. Perhaps 'tis clear that if they wint to th' Rockyfellar institution f'r th' care iv money they'd be in betther surroundings, but whin Jawn thries to carry thim off I raise a cry iv 'Polis,' a mob iv people that niver had a dollar iv their own an' niver will have wan, pounce on th' misguided man, th' polis pinch him, an' th' governmint condemns th' institution an' lets out th' inmates an' a good manny iv thim go to th' bad."

"D'ye think he'll iver sarve out his fine?" asked Mr. Hennessy.

"I don't know," said Mr. Dooley. "But if he does, whin he comes out at the end iv a hundhred an fifty-eight thousand years he'll find a great manny changes in men's hats an' th' means iv transportation but not much in annything else. He may find flyin' machines, though it'll be arly f'r thim, but he'll see a good manny people still walkin' to their wurruk."

Things Spiritual

"Th' latest thing in science," said Mr. Dooley, "is weighin' th' human soul. A fellow up in Matsachoosetts has done it. He weighs ye befure ye die an' he weighs ye afther ye die, an' th' diff'rence is what ye'er soul weighs. He's discovered that th' av'rage weight iv a soul in New England is six ounces or a little less. Fr'm this he argies that th' conscience isn't part iv th' soul. If it was th' soul wud be in th' heavyweight class, f'r th' New England conscience is no feather. He thinks it don't escape with th' soul, but lies burrid in th' roons iv its old fam'ly home—th' liver.

"It's so simple it must be true, an' if it ain't true, annyhow it's simple. But it's a tur-rble thing to think iv. I can't see anny money in it as an invintion. Who'll want to have his soul weighed? Suppose ye'er time has come. Th' fam'ly ar-re busy with their own thoughts, grievin' because they hadn't been as good to ye as they might, because they won't have ye with thim anny more, because it's too late f'r thim to square thimsilves, pityin' ye because ye'er not remainin' to share their sorrows with thim, wondhrin' whether th' black dhresses that were bought in honor iv what people might have said if they hadn't worn thim in mimry iv Aunt Eliza, wud be noticed if they were worn again f'r ye. Th' very young mimbers iv th' fam'ly ar-re standin' around, thryin' to look as sad as they think they ought to look. But they can't keep it up. They nudge each other, their eyes wandher around th' room, an' fr'm time to time they glance over at Cousin Felix an' expect him to make a laugh'ble face. He's a gr-reat frind iv theirs an' they're surprised he isn't gayer. Something must've happened to him. Maybe he's lost his job. There ar-re a gr-reat manny noises in th' sthreet. Th' undertaker whistles as he goes by, an' two iv th' neighbors ar-re at th' gate sayin' what a fine man ye were if ye didn't dhrink, an' askin' did ye leave much.

"An' little ye care. Everything is a millyon miles away fr'm ye. F'r th' first time in ye'er life ye're alone. F'r the first time in ye'er life ye ar-re ye'ersilf. F'r Hiven knows how manny years ye've been somebody else. Ye've been ye'er wife, ye'er fam'ly, ye'er relations, th' polisman on th' beat, th' doctor, th' newspaper reporther, th' foreman at th' mills, th' laws iv th' land, th' bartinder that gives ye dhrinks, th' tailor, th' barber, an' public opinion. Th' wurruld has held a lookin'-glass in front iv ye fr'm th' day ye were born an' compelled ye to make faces in it. But in this here particular business ye have no wan to please but ye'ersilf. Good opinyon an' bad opinyon ar-re alike. Ye're akelly unthroubled be gratichood an' revenge. No wan can help ye or stay ye. Ye're beyond th' sound iv th' alarm clock an' th' facthry whistle an' beginnin' th' Big Day Off whin th' man iv Science shakes ye be th' elbow an' says: 'Ye've got to weigh out.' An' he weighs figures: 'Wan hundhred an' forty-siven fr'm wan hundhred an' fifty. Siven fr'm naught can't be done; borry wan; siven fr'm ten leaves three. I find that th' soul iv our late laminted frind weighed a light three pounds avirdoopoise.'

"No, sir, it won't do. 'Twill niver be popylar. People won't have their souls weighed. I wudden't f'r all th' wurruld have th' wurrud go through th' ward: 'Did ye hear about Dooley's soul?' 'No, what?' 'They had to get an expert accountant to figure its weight, it was that puny.'

"D'ye suppose Dorgan, th' millyonaire, wud consint to it? Whin he entered th' race iv life he was properly handicapped with a soul to off-set his avarice an' his ability, so that some iv th' rest iv us wud have a kind iv a show again him. But as soon as he thinks no wan can see him he begins to get rid iv his weight an' comes rompin' home miles ahead. But th' judges say: 'Hold on, there; ye'll have to weigh out,' an' a little later a notice is posted up that Dorgan is disqualified f'r ridin' undher-weight in th' matther iv soul. On th' other hand, there's little Miss Mad-digan, th' seamstress. She's all but left at th' post; she's jostled all th' way around, an' comes in lame, a bad last. But she's th' only wan iv th' lot that's kept th' weight. She weighs ninety-six pounds—six iv it bein' tea an' toast an ninety iv it soul.

"No, sir, whin it comes to goin' up to th' scales to have their souls weighed people'll be as shy as they are in a Customs House. Th' people that wud make th' invintion pay wud be th' last to want to be tested by it. Th' pa-apers might keep records iv th' results: 'Misther So-an'-so, th' gr-reat captain iv finance, died yesterday, universally regretted. His estate amounts to nineteen millyon dollars. There ar-re two large bequests to charity. Wan is a thrust fund set aside f'r his maiden sister Annybelle, who will receive f'r life th' income on eight hundhred dollars in stock iv th' Hackensack Meadows Comp'ny. Th' other is forty-two dollars to buy a wooden leg f'r his brother Isaac, it bein' undherstood that no charge is to be made be th' estate against th' brother f'r a set iv false teeth bought f'r him in th' year nineteen four. Th' balance iv th' property is left in trust f'r th' minor childher until they ar-re 90 years old. Th' deceased requested that his soul be measured be troy weight. It tipped th' beam at wan pennyweight.'"

"D'ye think th' soul can be weighed?" asked Mr. Hennessy. "I know it's there, but I think—I kind iv feel—I wondher—I don't hardly know—"

"I see what ye mean," said Mr. Dooley. "Scales an' clocks ar-re not to be thrusted to decide annything that's worth deciding. Who tells time be a clock? Ivry hour is th' same to a clock an' ivry hour is diff'rent to me. Wan long, wan short. There ar-re hours in th' avenin' that pass between two ticks iv th' clock; there ar-re hours in th' arly mornin' whin a man can't sleep that Methusalah's age cud stretch in. Clocks ar-re habichool liars, an' so ar-re scales. As soon as annything gets good enough to weigh ye can't weigh it. Scales ar-re f'r th' other fellow. I'm perfectly willin' to take ye'er weight or ye'er soul's weight fr'm what th' scales say. Little I care. A pound or two more or less makes no dif-f'rence. But when it comes to measurin' something that's precious to me, I'll not thrust it to a slight improvement on a see-saw.

"But what do I know about it, annyhow? What do I know about annything? I've been pitchin' information into ye f'r more years thin anny wan iver wint to colledge, an' I tell ye now I don't know annything about annything. I don't like to thrust mesilf forward. I'm a modest man. Won't somebody else get up? Won't ye get up, Tiddy Rosenfelt; won't ye, Willum Jennings Bryan; won't ye, Prisidint Eliot; won't ye, pro-fissors, preachers, doctors, lawyers, iditors? Won't annybody get up? Won't annybody say that they don't know annything about annything worth knowin' about? Thin, be Hivens, I will. All alone I'll stand up befure me class an' say: 'Hinnissy, about annything that can't be weighed on a scales or measured with a tape line I'm as ign'rant as—ye'ersilf. I'll have to pay ye back th' money I took fr'm ye f'r ye'er schoolin'. It was obtained be false pretences.'

"How can I know annything, whin I haven't puzzled out what I am mesilf. I am Dooley, ye say, but ye're on'y a casual obsarver. Ye don't care annything about me details. Ye look at me with a gin'ral eye. Nawthin' that happens to me really hurts ye. Ye say, 'I'll go over to see Dooley,' sometimes, but more often ye say, 'I'll go over to Dooley's.' I'm a house to ye, wan iv a thousand that look like a row iv model wurrukin'men's cottages. I'm a post to hitch ye'er silences to. I'm always about th' same to ye. But to me I'm a millyon Dooleys an' all iv thim sthrangers to ME. I niver know which wan iv thim is comin' in. I'm like a hotel keeper with on'y wan bed an' a millyon guests, who come wan at a time an' tumble each other out. I set up late at night an' pass th' bottle with a gay an' careless Dooley that hasn't a sorrow in th' wurruld, an' suddenly I look up an' see settin' acrost fr'm me a gloomy wretch that fires th' dhrink out iv th' window an' chases me to bed. I'm just gettin' used to him whin another Dooley comes in, a cross, cantankerous, crazy fellow that insists on eatin' breakfast with me. An' so it goes. I know more about mesilf than annybody knows an' I know nawthin'. Though I'd make a map fr'm mem'ry an' gossip iv anny other man, f'r mesilf I'm still uncharted.

"So what's th' use iv thryin' to know annything less important. Don't thry. All ye've got to do is to believe what ye hear, an' if ye do that enough, afther a while ye'll hear what ye believe. Ye've got to start in believin' befure ye can find a reason f'r ye'er belief. Our old frind Christopher Columbus hadn't anny good reason f'r believin' that there was anny such a place as America. But he believed it without a reason an' thin wint out an' found it. Th' fellows that discovered th' canals on Mars which other fellows think cud be cured be a good oculist, hadn't anny right to think there were canals on Mars. But wan iv thim said: 'I wondher if there ar-re canals on Mars; I believe there ar-re. I'll look an' see. Be Hivens, there ar-re.' If he'd wondhered an' thin believed about clothes poles he'd've found thim too. Anny kind iv a fact is proof iv a belief. A firm belief atthracts facts. They come out iv holes in th' ground an' cracks in th' wall to support belief, but they run away fr'm doubt.

"I'll niver get anny medal f'r makin' anny man give up his belief. If I see a fellow with a chube on his eye and hear him hollerin', 'Hooray, I've discovered a new planet,' I'll be th' last man in th' wurruld to brush th' fly off th' end iv th' telescope. I've known people that see ghosts. I didn't see thim, but they did. They cud see ghosts an' I cudden't. There wasn't annything else to it. I knew a fellow that was a Spiritualist wanst. He was in th' chattel morgedge business on week days an' he was a Spiritualist on Sunday. He cud understand why th' spirits wud always pick out a stout lady with false hair or a gintleman that had his thumb mark registhered at Polis Headquarthers to talk through, an' he knew why spirits liked to play on banjoes an' mandolins an' why they convarsed be rappin' on a table in th' dark. An' there was a man that wud bite a silver dollar in two befure he'd take it f'r good."

"My aunt seen a ghost wanst," said Mr. Hennessy.

"Ivrybody's aunt has seen a ghost," said Mr. Dooley.

Part Three
The World Changes

From an illustration by Herman Rosse for Ben Hecht's *1001 Afternoons in Chicago*.

Introduction

Across its breadth, the heyday of Chicago's public wit represented a remarkable flowing together of the comic spirit and the spirit of the city that nourished it. Field had moved from the buoyant if often still crude efforts of his Denver days to a sophisticated humor and sentiment then rare in American comic writing. Chicago and its newly fledged city life became for him the milieu of a pointed but still genial imagination. Ade, the young newcomer to town, had sharpened eye and ear to observe the city's doings and from them evolved the comic focus of his work. As he gave himself to the city, it in turn conferred a public identity on him. Dunne, the native born and bred, had found dramatic reality in an obscure corner of town, one as little favored in its day for literary or even literate resource as any the city offered, yet one that allowed him to become a voice heard across the nation. In the years between Field's arrival in 1883 and the vacating of Chicago by its heyday wits about 1900, a segment of American humorous writing unparalleled for the warmth of its relation to its time and location had been put into place.

The attainment was not to be continued or repeated. The reasons for change are far from clear, but the newspaper humorists who made their debut in the early years of the century did indeed proceed along a contrasting line of speaking for particularized and selective attitudes. Perhaps the city as a whole seemed less manageable and phrasable. Certainly the number of newspapers declined, and those that survived faced pressures apparently beyond the resources of wit to confront. Not surprisingly, perhaps, wit would seek out specialized areas of understanding and response and, in the process, increasingly loosen its Chicago congenialities.

The history of Chicago papers in later decades suggests a search for liveliness quite different from earlier times. The ascendance of yellow journalism in Chicago marked by the appearance of "comics" pages, pictorial reportage, sensation mongering, and strong-arm efforts to promote circulation was furthered by the appearance in 1900 of Hearst's *American*, which was published in shifting morning and evening editions under a variety of names and made an impact on the tone of the *Tribune* and the *Daily News*. Its chief morning competitor, the *Tribune*, with forty years to come of eccentric but highly successful editing and management, brandished an ever more blazing sword of local and national chauvinism and partisan writing to emerge as the commanding morning paper of the city. A number of the older papers faded altogether—discontinued or merged with competitors. The *Daily News* made its tone more strident and dominated the afternoon field for some time still. But despite its efforts, changes of ownership and the additional competition of television took a toll that forced it to an end in 1978.

Again the curve of history, this time from the era of the First World War, turned in directions that paralleled the growing segmentation of public wit. Chicago, in brief, was becoming more difficult to treat as a community of the whole. The physical signs could be dramatic. Corrupt municipal government had plagued the town from its earliest days, and the crooked "boodler," the alderman who sought election only to sell his votes to the highest bidder, had become a public scandal by the nineties. By 1916, however, and the first of the several elections of William Hale Thompson to the mayoralty, corrupter and corrupted were to become more extended menaces.

The story is long and complex. It may be simplified by relating that when the traction magnate, Charles T. Yerkes, was seen as a major force for harm in the nineties, buying city council votes and making a strong effort, even, to purchase those of the state legislature to defend his interests, the Civic Federation of that day could bring legal action forcing Yerkes to flee Chicago despite his placating gift of an observatory to the University of Chicago and his purchase of the *Inter-Ocean* as a public relations organ. Under Thompson and his long if occasionally interrupted sway, however, it became more difficult to separate the sheep from the goats.

Thompson had gained his first election partly by violent anti-Irish

smears and, to compensate, went on to become a professional if point-
less enemy of the King of England. In 1919 Chicago was rocked by the
first of its vicious race riots, the earliest mass violence in a war that
smoldered for long years to come. Slason Thompson's *America* had
accented an anti-Catholic and generally antiforeign campaign in the
nineties. By the early 1920s and the rise of Colisimo, Torrio, Capone,
and other Italian gangsters, Italians as such were singled out as "un-
desirable aliens." Capone, however, appeared to enjoy the protection
of the mayor, who seemed thus to have the support of both the crimi-
nals and their accusers. Thompson was the builder of the complex
bridge that was to make the extended splendor of Michigan Avenue
possible. At the same time, he was thought to be in the pay of the railroads that controlled the lakefront and opposed its further improvement. And to cap the matter, he and his henchmen were rumored to
have profited from the bridge construction to the amount of some
$800,000.

The whole spectacle of the affluent, unruly 1920s and earlier may
have called for humor, but focus was difficult. One sometimes hardly
knew whether leading citizens were industrial geniuses or confidence
men. In the early years of the century, Samuel Insull secured control of
the Chicago Edison Company and other utilities and extended elec-
trification of the city by innovative engineering and construction. He
supported the civic opera and built its overpowering building. Soon,
however, he was to be revealed as a swindling manipulator of stock in
pyramided holding companies and was declared bankrupt. Chicago's
workers felt themselves to be victims of the city's whole power. Massive
construction strikes in the early twenties hampered building, and during the thirties' depression the workers at Chicago's immense steel
furnaces were in the throes of unionization and open riot. On the
other side, business owners complained that they could not appeal to
the city for support for fear of having taxes or other regulations im-
posed to a confiscatory point and their affairs handed on to city hall
favorites. In increasing numbers, and with heavy purses, Chicago's
wealthy withdrew from residence in the city to remote suburbs.
Middle- and lower-class citizens were compacted into drab ethnic
communities. The town's poor were huddled into unrelieved blocks of
squalor and ugliness.

The phenomenon of public wit seemed largely in retreat from Chicago's daily papers by 1930. That year was to mark the onset of a decade of crippling economic depression affecting Chicago and the nation. Mayor Anton Cermak's death in 1933 at the hands of an assassin attacking President Roosevelt delivered the city into the control of an Irish-dominated political machine (with roots extending deeply and widely into the city's other ethnic communities) led first by Edward J. Kelly and later, for many years, by Richard J. Daley. The two appeared to spare Chicago some of the worst capering of what had been an almost farcical history of venality and mismanagement under Thompson. Kelly was cofounder of the Kelly-Nash Democratic machine which Daley in his time converted into a monolithic power that was to change the physical face of much of the city and also do much to alter its spirit and its material fortunes for the better. Both, however, held a grip on political power that allowed them to dominate and profit from countless details of the city's life. In the eyes of many commentators, Daley's organization was simply a more efficient reconstitution of the older municipal graft and corruption (his personal ethic, according to Mike Royko, was "Don't steal, and don't blow the whistle on those that do"), though many, too, could bring themselves to see the qualities of such defects and pronounce Chicago to be a "city that works"—at what cost was perhaps not so plain.

The town had briefly rallied from depression in 1933 and 1934 to stage a second world's fair, "A Century of Progress," which was highly successful even in those sad years. Still, Chicago's population and business importance continued to grow only haltingly at best. For the most part the thirties and early forties marked a period of decay or of line holding. Much of the South Side stretched out in blight that surrounded the island neighborhood of the University of Chicago and its adjacent parks. Slum and near slum spread over substantial parts of the inner West Side. The wealth that had thrown up the monumental residences on the Near North Side to create another "Gold Coast" largely melted away during the thirties and forties to seek refuge in out-of-town locations. The city itself looked increasingly drab, and there was much talk of Chicago as a case of "urban rot."

It would not be until after the Second World War that the "I Will" spirit would again make itself felt, then to erect the astonishing sight that is modern downtown Chicago and its lakefront environs and to rebuild substantially in other sections. Under the renewed interest of the Chicago business community, the intense concern of Mayor Daley for heightening the city's affluence, and the funding available to and stimulated by federal urban renewal programs, Chicago has risen from its period of decay to present a brave face to the world once more. O'Hare Airport was completed to reaffirm the city's traditional role as transportation junction for the nation. Lakefront development brought into existence large areas of filled land, new and dramatic buildings, and a network of superhighways focusing on the area. The Near North Side was revived as a glamorous residential, shopping, and recreation area studded with high-rise buildings. The Loop itself was marked by new and striking construction. Large areas of urban blight both north and south were replaced with elaborate housing developments. Across the whole, however, lay an uneasy suggestion that such resurrection was more dramatic in its impact than real, but it was true that, early and late, Chicago had been a city in which attainment of a high urban tone had been a bellwether of general prosperity.

Out of this complex of changing fortunes for the city a diverse pattern of writing emerged, characterized by a shifting sense of relationship between town and writer. In one of its several aspects, here labeled "The Superior Eye," wits stood aloof from the city's everyman. Thus, in the newspaper "colyums" of Bert Leston Taylor and Keith Preston the writer offered himself as a still genial but clearly superior spirit appealing to others of such higher caste. In Ring Lardner superiority took the form of lampooning the average "boob" and his ways, implicitly asserting the position of writer and reader above such buffoonery. A second aspect of special appeal was marked by the approximately fifteen-year span of informed and irreverent writing impelled by the new literature of the day (along with many gibes at prevailing social mores and values), illustrated especially by the literary wits of the *Evening Post*, the *Daily News*, the *Tribune*, and, briefly, by Ben Hecht's *Chicago Literary Times*. In a third and still contemporary mode, wit has in a sense converted itself into a hard-eyed irony of perception directed against the often harsh grain of contemporary urban reality. In varying ways, Langston Hughes, Nelson Algren, and Mike Royko have held to the combined victimage, waywardness, and, still, resilience, of the man in the street amid the merciless pressure of the town around him.

The Superior Eye _____

The first two decades of the century saw a continuation of newspaper column writing but in a new vein—most notably in Bert Leston Taylor of the *Tribune* and Keith Preston of the *Daily News*—now seeking upper-class and sophisticated interest and approval. Excepting an interim period, Taylor produced his popular "A Line O' Type or Two" for some twenty years, and the column would be continued for years afterward by others. Keith Preston, beginning as a contributor to Taylor and possessor of a doctorate in Latin literature, became a professional writer for the *News*'s weekly book page and added to that concern the assumption of an existing daily humor column, "Hit or Miss." Both men wrote a part of their own material, but they also solicited work from like-minded contributors. Their columns were complemented in an inverse fashion by Ring Lardner's assignment to a column in the *Tribune* begun by Hugh E. Keough, "In the Wake of the News," out of which he generated the attitudes coloring his early books and their sardonic feel for ordinary Chicago life.

Despite their contrasts, we have classified these figures together to suggest that the work of the first two found a superior vantage on the day's common man in a playful but elaborately sustained sophistication, and the work of the last farcically lampooned the citizen who personified that common man. Whether as spokesman for a lettered and informed elite or as a disillusioned observer of *hoi polloi*, all three valued a superiority to what Taylor often referred to as "the so-called human race," and they sought and found readers who shared that sense of elevation above the mass.

The "Colyum": Bert Leston Taylor and Keith Preston

Bert Leston Taylor (1866–1921) was born in Goshen, Massachusetts. He learned the fundamentals of his trade in a number of eastern jobs and then moved west to become the editorial writer on the Duluth *News-Tribune*. From that post he contributed miscellanea to a column of the Chicago *Journal*, "A Little Bit of Everything"—material of such quality that he was hired by Finley Peter Dunne, then an editor of the *Journal*, primarily to conduct the department. In 1901 the *Tribune* lured him away to found his own "A Line O' Type or Two." Until his death in 1921, and with a few years' interruption for service on *Judge* magazine, Taylor rode the crest of a wave he thus originated in his conversion of a standard newspaper feature, the column of jokes, into a bookish and idiosyncratic contributors' "colyum," as he called it, one that found quick imitation in the work of Franklin P. Adams (who succeeded Taylor at the *Journal* but soon carried Taylor's style to New York), the Chicago *Daily News*'s Keith Preston, the Cleveland *Plain Dealer*'s Ted Robinson, the New York *Evening Post*'s Christopher Morley, and others. In this mode, the column conductor wrote a variety of light verse, essays, and short squibs, reprinted amusing slips and gaffes from provincial newspapers, advertisements, or whatever else came his way, and in general established a tone of genial but rather superior taste, sophistication, and literacy. He accepted and printed items in a variety of forms from his "contribs," readers of temperament and talents similar to his, identified only obliquely by initials or pen names but presumably valuing even that much recognition.

Keith Preston (1884–1927) was born in Chicago and moved through local schools to the University of Chicago, where he completed a doctorate in classical studies. As a popular author he was to shade much of his verse with the tone of Latin epigrammatic styles. He taught briefly at Princeton, which, he said, taught him chiefly "the intellectual importance of luxurious surroundings," and later at Northwestern University. He began as a contributor to Taylor's column, and then contributed to the *Daily News* book page, but in 1918 he was assigned a weekly column of his own in the *News* book section called "The Periscope" and was made the page's editor in 1926. In 1922 he had also been assigned to the daily humor column in the *News* begun by Tubman K. Hedrick and called "Hit or Miss" and continued there until his death.

Our selection from Taylor reflects an early twentieth-century flow of events and experiences, with allusions to the "European War" of 1914, as it then seemed to be; the still modest shortening of women's skirt lines and a growing ease and informality in their dress; a reliance on electric interurban lines for a weekend jaunt out of Chicago; and the founding in 1912 of the Chicago Little Theatre by Maurice Browne. Following Taylor's lead, Keith Preston's verses and squibs extend the columnist's interest to popular subjects of the 1920s, including the death of the film star Rudolph Valentino, the frequent and often scandalous appearance of chorus girls from Ziegfeld's famous "Follies" in newspaper stories, the razing of the old Palmer House Hotel to make room for the existing structure, the sudden popularity of F. Scott Fitzgerald, the appearance of new literary fashions and modes, and the secularizing of American idealism in the affluent and materialistic decade at hand.

Taylor published a variety of volumes of prose humor and light verse during his lifetime. After his death, selections from his column were edited by Franklin P. Adams, *A Penny Whistle, Together with the Babbette Ballads* (1921), Henry B. Fuller, *The So-Called Human Race* (1922), Chick Evans, *A Line of Gowf or Two* (1923), and James Rowland Angell, *The East Window and the Car Window* (1924). Keith Preston composed and edited a number of volumes of column material during his lifetime. After his death a selection was edited by Christopher Morley, *Pot Shots from Pegasus* (1929).

Bert Leston Taylor: From "A Line O' Type or Two"

Arms and the Colyum

I sing of arms and heroes, not because
I'm thrilled by what these heroes do or die for:
The Colyum's readers think they make its laws,
And I make out to give them what they cry for.

And since they cry for stuff about the war,
Since war at this safe distance not to *them*'s hell,
I have to write of things that I abhor,
And far, strange battlegrounds like Ypres and Przemysl.

War is an almost perfect rime for bore;
And, 'spite my readers (who have cursed and blessed me),
Some day I'll throw the war junk on the floor,
And write of things that really interest me:

Of books in running brooks, and wilding wings,
Of music, stardust, children, casements giving
On seas unvext by wars, and other things
That help to make our brief life worth the living.

I sing of arms and heroes, just because
All else is shadowed by that topic fearful;

> But I've a mind to chuck it [Loud applause],
> And tune my dollar harp to themes more cheerful.

•••

Though there has been little enough to encourage it, the world is growing kinder; at least friendliness is increasing. Every other day we read of some woman living pleasantly in a well appointed apartment, supplied with fine raiment and an automobile, the fruit of Platonism. "No," she testifies, "there was nothing between us. He was merely a friend."

•••

What heaven hath cleansed let no man put asunder. Emma Durdy and Raymond Bathe, of Nokomis, have been j. in the h. b. of w.[1]

The Tracers Are at Work

Sir: Please consult the genealogical files of the Academy and advise me if Mr. Harm Poppen of Gurley, Nebraska, is a lineal descendant of the w. k. Helsa Poppen, famous in profane history.

E. E. M.

•••

Our opinion, already recorded, is that if Keats had spent fifteen or twenty minutes more on his Grecian Urn, all of the stanzas would be as good as three of them. And so we think that if A. B. had put in, say, a half hour more on her sonnet she would not have rhymed "world-liness" and "moodiness." Of the harmony, counterpoint, thoroughbass, etc., of verse we know next to nothing—we play on *our* tin whistle entirely by ear—but there are things which we avoid, perhaps needlessly. One of these is the rhyming of words like utterly, monody, lethargy, etc.; these endings seem weak when they are bunched. Our assistants will apprehend that we are merely offering a suggestion or two, which we hope they will follow up by exploring the authorities.

•••

Music like Brahms' Second Symphony is peculiarly satisfying to the listener. The first few measures disclose that the composer is in complete control of his ideas and his expression of them. He has something to say, and he says it without uncertainty or redundancy. Only a man who *has* something to say may dare to say it only once.

•••

Those happy beings who "don't know a thing about art, but know what they like," are restricted to the obvious because of ignorance of

---

1. Taylor affected the use of lowercase initials for much used phrases: here "joined in the holy bond of wedlock," or, below, "w. k." for "well known."

form; their enjoyment ends where that of the cultivated person begins. Take music. The person who knows what he likes takes his pleasure in the tune, but gets little or nothing from the tune's development; hence his favorite music is music which is all tune.

We recall a naïve query by the publisher of a magazine, at a musicale in Gotham. Our hostess, an accomplished pianist, had played a Chopin Fantasia, and the magazine man was expressing his qualified enjoyment. "What I can't understand," said he, "is why the tune quits just when it's running along nicely." This phenomenon, no doubt, has mystified thousands of other "music lovers."

· · ·

A Boston woman complains that school seats have worn out three pairs of pants (her son's) in three months. "Is a wheeze about the seat of learning too obvious?" queries Genevieve. Oh, quite too, my dear!

"Nothing to Wear"[2]

    Miss Flora McFlimsy of Michigan Boul.
        In spite of hot weather is perfectly cool.
    She has it all over her namesake, the fair
    Miss Flora McFlimsy of Madison Square,
        Who, ages ago,
        As most of you know,
    Lamented the fact she had "nothing to wear."
    Miss Flora of old bought her drygoods in Paris;
    She shopped (you recall) with her friend Mrs Harris.
    Her garments were many, and costly and rare,
    And yet she complained she had nothing to wear.

    But Flora McFlimsy of Boulevard Mich.
    Dispenses with ev'ry superfluous stitch,
    And clad in a single diaphanous gown
    Parades in the sunlight, the joy of the town.
        "And if I show through,
        What harm does it do?"
    Says Flora McFlimsy; "I leave it to you."

---

2. Taylor here adapts his verse from a famous 1857 poem by William Allen Butler resetting the scene in Chicago and turning Butler's randomly deft lines and construction to his own purposes.

Why, none whatsoever, we beg to reply.
You are all to the good to our critical eye.
Proceed, Miss McFlimsy, as far as you wish;
Parade in the sunlight on Boulevard Mich.,
And let, if it please you, your vanishing dress
Grow fine by degrees and delightfully less,
  Until, like the dame
  Of evergreen fame.
You *really* have nothing whatever to wear,
Excepting a hank of remarkable hair.
And should you appear as the Lady Godiva,
We'll stand on the corner and hand you a "Viva!"

    ...

Arethusa was studying the trolley map again. "We might go to Aurora," she said presently.

"Anything," I agreed, "to get away from here. The breeze has been flapping the window curtains all morning, and it's becoming a trifle annoying."

"I simply must get into the country," said Arethusa, "I can't be cooped up in town another day."

"How does one get to Aurora—by the Twenty-second Street line?" I inquired.

"No; we take a fast electric train at Fifth Avenue and something," said Arethusa, "and go all the way to Aurora without change. Then comes a beautiful ride along the Fox River to Elgin, and thence back to Chicago."

"Let us fare forth into the merry sunshine," said I. The thermometer can't be a notch above 80 degrees.

"I feel so sorry for the poor people who can't get out in the air," said Arethusa, as we set forth. "You would best put up the umbrella—the sun is a little strong."

We reached the station at Fifth Avenue and something a little after twelve o'clock. The next train for Aurora left at one. We sought luncheon and found a bad one.

By one o'clock half of Chicago seemed bent on going to Aurora. A perspiring throng filled the waiting room. It was Saturday—we had forgotten that. "Perhaps," said Arethusa, "we would better go to Evanston instead, and trolley along the North Shore."

I assented, and we climbed to an "L" platform. Here we found most of the people in Chicago who were not going to Aurora. The shops were letting out, and bright faced lads and lasses were swarming up the "L" stairs. Train after train went by, loaded to the limit.

"Perhaps we would better go home," said I. So again we footed it across the city. The heat was terrific, but the people were rushing madly through the streets—some headed for Aurora, others for Evanston.

Shall we ever get into the country? sighed Arethusa.

Eventually we did.[3]

• • •

There is a stage in almost everybody's musical education when Chopin's Funeral March seems the most significant composition in the world.

• • •

The two stenogs in the L coach were discussing the opera. "I see," said one, "that they're going to sing 'Flagstaff.'" "That's Verdi's latest opera," said the other. "Yes," contributed the gentleman in the adjacent seat, leaning forward; "and the scene is laid in Arizona."

• • •

Mr. Shanks voxpops that traffic should be relieved, not prevented, as "the automobile is absolutely important in modern business life." Now, the fact is that the automobile has become a nuisance; one can get about much faster and cheaper in the city on Mr. Shanks' w. k. mare. Life to-day is scaled to the automobile, whereas, as our gossip Andy Rebori contends, it ought to be scaled to the baby carriage. Many lines of industry are short of labor because this labor has been withdrawn for the care of automobiles.

• • •

"Do you remember," asks a fair correspondent (who protests that she is only academically fair), "when we used to read 'A Shropshire Lad,' and A. E., and Arthur Symons, and Yeats? And you used to print so many of the beautiful things they wrote?" Ah, yes, we do remember; but that, my dear, was a long, long time ago, in the period which has just closed, as Bennett puts it. How worth while those things used to seem, and what pleasant days those were. Men say that they will come again. But men said that Arthur would come again.

• • •

3. This is the first installment of a longer account of the city dweller's efforts "to get into the country." It was continued in later columns in the original.

Our method: We select only things that interest us, assuming that other people will be interested; if they are not—why, chacun à son goût, as the cannibal king remarked, adding a little salt. We printed "The Spires of Oxford" a long time ago because it interested us exceedingly.

• • •

A valued colleague quotes the emotional line—

"This is my own, my native land!"—

as palliation, if not justification, for the "simple, homely, and comprehensive adjuration, 'Own Your Own Home.'" We acknowledge the homeliness and comprehensiveness, but we deny the value of poetic testimony. Said Dr. Johnson:

"Let observation with extensive view
Survey mankind from China to Peru,"

which, De Quincey or Tennyson declared, should have run: "Let observation with extended observation observe mankind extensively." Poets and tautology go walking like the Walrus and the Carpenter.

• • •

Announcement is made of a Little Theatre[4] that is "to create and produce a poetic drama and to promote a full discussion of life and the arts." The plans are attractive and full of promise, and the best luck one can wish the enterprise is that it may not start off handicapped by the blighting appellation "highbrow." The label will be applied, by those that wish the venture well and by those that wish it ill; but if the management disclaim the label and be industrious in getting rid of it, the Little Theatre may become more than a social incident and a season's novelty.

It is a mistake to assume that the approval of the pundits of culture is of value in commending an artistic experiment to the consideration of the multitude; the moment such impression is conveyed, that moment the enterprise is on the defensive. It invites and receives the antagonism of the general public and the polite derision of the really cultured minority, whose culture has passed the stage of tea table discussion of matters that, in an enlightened society, are taken for granted.

It is human nature to resent the conscious "uplift" and the air of

4. Taylor here refers to Maurice Browne's founding of the Chicago Little Theatre in 1912.

superiority that surrounds such ventures. If a thing be good it is sufficient to offer it as such or to cry it up as better than something else. Appreciation may be slow in coming, or may not come at all, but at least the enterprise will have a chance to succeed, unimpeded by oracular pronouncements and infusions of Orange-Pekoe culture.

Keith Preston: From "Hit or Miss"

Lines Written While Opening Our Column Mail

> The oyster man opens full many
> > An oyster to find a few pearls,
> And some days he doesn't find any;
> > It's then that he angrily hurls
> His oyster knife at his assistant
> > And utters a horrible yell,
> As he curses the shortage persistent
> > That's shooting his trade all to shell.

> The columnist sits in his cloister
> > And, cleverly doing his stint,
> Slits open each pearl like an oyster
> > And peers for a pearl fit to print.
> He beams when a bivalve yields verses,
> > He giggles with glee at a wheeze,
> But some days he bursts into curses
> > And scribbles some verses like these.

• • •

The idea that radio and other devices to tie humanity closer together promote international peace is one to which we cannot altogether subscribe. Consider the Kilkenny cats. The shorter their rope the harder they scratched. Improved communication makes it easier for us to misunderstand one another. That putting the human family in a single bed will guarantee close harmony is not borne out by small scale experiments.

• • •

Rudolph Valentino perfectly represented American woman's ideal of a romantic lover, and it seems to us that his vast popularity is just indictment of the American business man as a love-maker. Babbitt is a good bread winner but a poor worshiper. His lady has to fly to the screen for

what she can't get in the home. Love in the home is bread and pud-
ding and applesauce. Love at the movies is double bitter-sweet and
Peach Melba. The cinema is the soda parlor of sentiment.

· · ·

    Among our literary scenes
      Saddest this sight to me:
    The graves of little magazines
      That died to make verse free.

· · ·

A point that future historians will ponder is the unique importance of
Mr. Ziegfeld's choruses in the life of present-day America. Each member of a Follies chorus has an ex-officio news value ten times that of
an ordinary senator. Whether wooed or wedded, match-making or
match-breaking, she is good for first or second page publicity. In all
history no body of young women has claimed such importance in the
life of a state—unless it be the College of Vestal Virgins in Rome, and
even this analogy seems not entirely satisfactory.

Some will remember the old Palmer house for the barber shop, paved
with silver simoleons, the delight of rubes and one of the seven wonders of the west, the others being Heinegebubeler's, the Masonic
Temple, the cataract at Niagara, the vats of Milwaukee, Bubbly Creek
and the Mammoth Cave of Kentucky. Others will recall the Palmer
house bar with its colossal battery of taps from which, like Pharphar
and Abana, flowed, two by two, Bud and Blatz, Schlitz and Pabst, High
Life and Alma Mater, each and all the boasted drafts of the brewmakers
of the western world. Then there was the Palmer house restaurant
with its choice hot breads. We used to breakfast there with an Indiana
Humorist, who always concluded the meal in the same way. As he
tipped the waiter he would hand out his card saying, "Please give this
to Mrs. Palmer[5] and tell her she makes the best biscuits." The waiter
always dropped the dime and sometimes a tray of dishes.

Effervescence and Evanescence
    We've found this Scott Fitzgerald chap
      A chipper, charming child;

---

5. Mrs. Potter Palmer, notable for her leadership of Chicago's fashionable society.
She was often referred to by her social rivals as "the innkeeper's wife."

He taught us how the flappers flap,
And why the whipper-snappers snap,
　　What makes the women wild.
But now he should make haste to trap
　　The ducats in his dipper.
The birds that put him on the map
Will shortly all begin to rap
　　And flop to something flipper.

Deep Stuff

Sampling the books the moderns bring,
　　In honesty I must confess
I like the old Pierian spring
　　More than the "stream of consciousness."

• • •

"I think," says Bobby Jones'[6] literary collaborator, "that he is going to do a very fine bunch of articles. He is a much better writer than he thinks he is."

Bobby's modesty is engaging, but we fear it bodes ill for his success as a writer. When Sinclair Lewis was in the first flush of his *Main Street* success an anonymous article appeared in the Bookman charging him with extreme and offensive egocentricity, which is the lit'ry lingo for what in vulgar parlance is known as a swelled head. Mr. Lewis was touched to the quick by the article. He showed it to us, asking plaintively, "Am I egotistical and, if I am egotistical, don't I need it in my business?"

We honestly agreed that he needed it in his business. There is no business that requires more egotism than the writing game. If a writer doesn't know that he is good how will he get by the office boys and secretaries, not to mention the editors and publishers?

Another distinguished writing man, Joseph Hergesheimer, once spoke to us with delightful candor on this topic. "A first-rate writer," he said, "never wants to meet other first-rate writers. When he sees a first-class piece of work all he says is 'Why the h—l didn't I think of that first?' All a first-class man wants is a megaphone, a spotlight and a reflector."

6. A notable golfer of the day.

Lines Written on the Eve of a National Election
>Whither the trend has been trending
>>Which way the tide was to turn
>Whom was the undertow towing,
>>Friends, we shall presently learn.

>All things at last have an ending
>>Soon the landslide will have slid
>Whither the silent vote's going
>>Cannot much longer be hid.

>Soon they will shut off the spouters,
>>Can all the old stuff again;
>The ins will be in till the outers
>>Can-open another campaign.

• • •

Millennial ideas change with the times. Up to a decade or two back the millennium was a religious conception. When clergymen and sages came together in synods and conferences, they saw rosy visions of an earthly paradise in which peace, piety, and prosperity should prevail on earth almost as they do in heaven.

Lately the clergy have seemed to lose faith in an earthly millennium. Post-war disillusion may have affected some. The dubious results of prohibition perhaps dishearten others. Whatever the cause, one finds pessimism rife among preachers and social philosophers. Jeremiads against jazz, diatribes against dancing, have replaced utopian predictions.

Does this mean that the millennial dream is lost to humanity? Far from it. When Religion lost faith in the earthly paradise Science took it over. From every congress of chemists come jubilees, hosannas, and visions more marvelous than the prophets of old ever dreamed of.

In the chemical millennium the irresistible force will lie down with the immovable object and a little electron will lead them. We shall see a diseaseless, sleepless world in which men will live on the fat of the laboratory beyond the years of Methuselah. Best of all, men will live without working. The objection to all religious and philosophical schemes for the millennium was that they wouldn't work. The beauty of the chemical millennium is that they won't have to.

From an illustration by Herman Rosse for Ben Hecht's *1001 Afternoons in Chicago*.

Ring Lardner

Ringgold Lardner (1885–1933) grew up in a well-to-do family of Niles, Michigan (where he had been born on March 6), and his family provided a center for him during the years in which he scraped through high school, failed as a student at Armour Technical Institute in Chicago, and worked through a variety of odd jobs. By accident, in 1905 he landed a place as reporter on the South Bend, Indiana, *Times* and so launched his career. He moved on to become a sports writer on the Chicago *Inter-Ocean* in 1907 and by 1913 had attained sufficient reputation there and elsewhere to be asked to continue the widely admired sports page column, "In the Wake of the News," begun by Hugh E. Keough and continued by Hugh Fullerton for the Chicago *Tribune*. He held this post until 1919 when he moved to the New York publishing world. The "Wake," as the column was commonly called, appeared daily. Sports were its large concern, but Lardner's writing expanded to include general satire, nonsense, and verse as well. As a result of this variety, and at the special behest of friends who admired his ear for colloquial speech, he developed during his first year with the column a series of anecdotes, declined by the *Tribune* but accepted by the *Saturday Evening Post*, couched as letters from a rookie baseball pitcher who moves to the Chicago White Sox and a checkered career as ballplayer, lover, husband, and father. Jack Keefe, as he was called, faithfully writes of his adventures to his old friend, "Al," who lives at home in the small town of "Bedford." Just as faithfully, if with never-failing blindness to the truth of himself and nearly everything he encounters, he opens himself to the reader.

These "letters" appeared in book form in 1916 as *You Know Me, Al* and were so warmly received that Lardner revived Jack Keefe for later if generally less interesting adventures in *Treat 'Em Rough* and *The Real Dope*. He published two further books, *Own Your Own Home* and *Gullible's Travels, Etc.*, before moving from Chicago and the *Tribune* to become a syndicated variety writer and the author of a total of 120 short stories.

During the Chicago years Lardner decisively established his literary character with his creation of lowbrow characters, either obtuse with a blend of the farcical and the repellent, like Keefe, or like the narrator of the third book, Gullible, more likable but at the mercy of others' low-visioned and futile ambitions. The results are, technically, humorous. Sometimes they are sardonic, sometimes comic, sometimes even pathetic. Sometimes they verge on a nihilistic sense of modern life and its average man in which hope for the subject seems largely abandoned.

There are differences among Lardner's critics and biographers as they try to find the source for the fascinating if frequently appalling view of reality he provides. Some locate its source in temperament whereas others point out that Lardner himself was a warm-hearted and gregarious man. Still others suggest that the protectiveness of family he had known in his early years was stripped from him too violently by his later life as he moved into a hard-bitten newspaper world bound by its professional calling to the incessant stupidities and meannesses of existence. The result, in any case, was the attainment of a marked originality of vision. H. L. Mencken's gibes at boobocracy were contemporary with Lardner's but afford little parallel to the latter's lifelong immersion in writing of the dismally average. Sinclair Lewis may have learned from Lardner. Ernest Hemingway certainly did. Such association puts him near the root of a recognizably "modern" awareness of life in popular twentieth-century writing. With all this, Lardner's reception in his own day was immense. He found large sales, high income, and sophisticated approval early and did not lose them despite the prevailing hardness of his tone. Like numbers of American humorists of the nineteenth century, he found an appeal to the public that had its ultimate power in a merciless debunking of the very possibility of virtue and resource in the average man. He published some twenty volumes of short stories, light verse, essays, plays, and miscellanea during his lifetime. A sampling is available in *The Ring Lardner Reader* (1947). A full account of his life and work is to be found in Jonathan Yardley, *Ring* (1977).

From You Know Me, Al

[The following excerpts are taken from the first group of Jack Keefe letters Lardner originally published in the *Saturday Evening Post* in 1914. They record Jack's transfer to Chicago from his minor league team and his subsequent misfortunes. Charles Comiskey, who is mentioned in them, was the actual owner of the White Sox. The team's present-day stadium in Chicago is named in his honor.]

•••

Chicago, Illinois, December 16

DEAR FRIEND AL: Well I will be home in a couple of days now but I wanted to write you and let you know how I come out with Comiskey. I signed my contract yesterday afternoon. He is a great old fellow Al and no wonder everybody likes him. He says Young man will you have a drink? But I was to smart and wouldn't take nothing. He says You was with Terre Haute? I says Yes I was. He says Doyle tells me you were pretty wild. I says Oh no I got good control. He says Well do you want to sign? I says Yes if I get my figure. He asks What is my figure and I says three thousand dollars per annum. He says Don't you want the office furniture too? Then he says I thought you was a young ball-player and I didn't know you wanted to buy my park.

We kidded each other back and forth like that a while and then he says You better go out and get the air and come back when you feel better. I says I feel O. K. now and I want to sign a contract because I have got to get back to Bedford. Then he calls the secretary and tells him to make out my contract. He give it to me and it calls for two hundred and fifty a month. He says You know we always have a city serious[7] here in the fall where a fellow picks up a good bunch of money. I hadn't thought of that so I signed up. My yearly salary will be fifteen hundred dollars besides what the city serious brings me. And that is only for the first year. I will demand three thousand or four thousand dollars next year.

I would of started home on the evening train but I ordered a suit of cloths from a tailor over on Cottage Grove and it won't be done till to-morrow. It's going to cost me twenty bucks but it ought to last a long time. Regards to Frank and the bunch. Your pal, JACK.

•••

Oklahoma City, April 4

FRIEND AL: Coming out of Amarillo last night I and Lord and Weaver was sitting at a table in the dining car with a old lady. None of us were talking to her but she looked me over pretty careful and seemed to kind of like my looks. Finally she says Are you boys with some football

---

7. "City series," between the White Sox and the Cubs.

club? Lord nor Weaver didn't say nothing so I thought it was up to me and I says No mam this is the Chicago White Sox Ball Club. She says I knew you were athaletes. I says Yes I guess you could spot us for athaletes. She says Yes indeed and specially you. You certainly look healthy. I says You ought to see me stripped. I didn't see nothing funny about that but I thought Lord and Weaver would die laughing. Lord had to get up and leave the table and he told everybody what I said.

All the boys wanted me to play poker on the way here but I told them I didn't feel good. I know enough to quit when I am ahead Al. Callahan and I sat down to breakfast all alone this morning. He says Boy why don't you get to work? I says What do you mean? Ain't I working? He says You ain't improving none. You have got the stuff to make a good pitcher but you don't go after bunts and you don't cover first base and you don't watch the baserunners. He made me kind of sore talking that way and I says Oh I guess I can get along all right.

He says Well I am going to put it up to you. I am going to start you over in St. Joe day after to-morrow and I want you to show me something. I want you to cut loose with all you've got and I want you to get round the infield a little and show them you aren't tied in that box. I says Oh I can field my position if I want to. He says Well you better want to or I will have to ship you back to the sticks. Then he got up and left. He didn't scare me none Al. They won't ship me to no sticks after the way I showed on this trip and even if they did they couldn't get no wavers on me.

Some of the boys have begun to call me Four Sevens but it don't bother me none. Yours truly, JACK.

...

Chicago, Illinois, April 19

DEAR OLD PAL: Well Al it's just as well you couldn't come. They beat me and I am writing you this so as you will know the truth about the game and not get a bum steer from what you read in the papers.

I had a sore arm when I was warming up and Callahan should never ought to of sent me in there. And Schalk kept signing for my fast ball and I kept giving it to him because I thought he ought to know something about the batters. Weaver and Lord and all of them kept kicking them round the infield and Collins and Bodie couldn't catch nothing.

Callahan ought never to of left me in there when he seen how sore my arm was. Why, I couldn't of threw hard enough to break a pain of glass my arm was so sore.

They sure did run wild on the bases. Cobb stole four and Bush and Crawford and Veach about two apiece. Schalk didn't even make a peg half the time. I guess he was trying to throw me down.

The score was sixteen to two when Callahan finally took me out in the eighth and I don't know how many more they got. I kept telling him to take me out when I seen how bad I was but he wouldn't do it. They started bunting in the fifth and Lord and Chase just stood there and didn't give me no help at all.

I was all O. K. till I had the first two men out in the first inning. Then Crawford come up. I wanted to give him a spitter but Schalk signs me for the fast one and I give it to him. The ball didn't hop much and Crawford happened to catch it just right. At that Collins ought to of catched the ball. Crawford made three bases and up come Cobb. It was the first time I ever seen him. He hollered at me right off the reel. He says You better walk me you busher. I says I will walk you back to the bench. Schalk signs for a spitter and I gives it to him and Cobb misses it.

Then instead of signing for another one Schalk asks for a fast one and I shook my head no but he signed for it again and yells Put something on it. So I throwed a fast one and Cobb hits it right over second base. I don't know what Weaver was doing but he never made a move for the ball. Crawford scored and Cobb was on first base. First thing I knowed he had stole second while I held the ball. Callahan yells Wake up out there and I says Why don't your catcher tell me when they are going to steal. Schalk says Get in there and pitch and shut your mouth. Then I got mad and walked Veach and Moriarty but before I walked Moriarty Cobb and Veach pulled a double steal on Schalk. Gainor lifts a fly and Lord drops it and two more come in. Then Stanage walks and I whiffs their pitcher.

I come in to the bench and Callahan says Are your friends from Bedford up here? I was pretty sore and I says Why don't you get a catcher? He says We don't need no catcher when you're pitching because you can't get nothing past their bats. Then he says You better leave your uniform in here when you go out next inning or Cobb will steal it off your back. I says My arm is sore. He says Use your other one and you'll do just as good.

Gleason says Who do you want to warm up? Callahan says Nobody. He says Cobb is going to lead the league in batting and basestealing anyway so we might as well give him a good start. I was mad enough to punch his jaw but the boys winked at me not to do nothing.

Well I got some support in the next inning and nobody got on. Between innings I says Well I guess I look better now don't I? Callahan says Yes but you wouldn't look so good if Collins hadn't jumped up on the fence and catched that one off Crawford. That's all the encouragement I got Al.

Cobb come up again to start the third and when Schalk signs me for a fast one I shakes my head. Then Schalk says All right pitch anything you want to. I pitched a spitter and Cobb bunts it right at me. I would of threw him out a block but I stubbed my toe in a rough place and fell down. This is the roughest ground I ever seen Al. Veach bunts and for a wonder Lord throws him out. Cobb goes to second and honest Al I forgot all about him being there and first thing I knowed he had stole third. Then Moriarty hits a fly ball to Bodie and Cobb scores though Bodie ought to of threw him out twenty feet.

They batted all round in the forth inning and scored four or five more. Crawford got the luckiest three-base hit I ever see. He popped one way up in the air and the wind blowed it against the fence. The wind is something fierce here Al. At that Collins ought to of got under it.

I was looking at the bench all the time expecting Callahan to call me in but he kept hollering Go on and pitch. Your friends wants to see you pitch.

Well Al I don't know how they got the rest of their runs but they had more luck than any team I ever seen. And all the time Jennings was on the coaching line yelling like a Indian. Some day Al I'm going to punch his jaw.

After Veach had hit one in the eight Callahan calls me to the bench and says You're through for the day. I says It's about time you found out my arm was sore. He says I ain't worrying about your arm but I'm afraid some of our outfielders will run their legs off and some of them poor infielders will get killed. He says The reporters just sent me a message saying they had run out of paper. Then he says I wish some of the other clubs had pitchers like you so we could hit once in a while.

He says Go in the clubhouse and get your arm rubbed off. That's the only way I can get Jennings sore he says.

Well Al that's about all there was to it. It will take two or three stamps to send this but I want you to know the truth about it. The way my arm was I ought never to of went in there. Yours truly, JACK.

•••

Chicago, Illinois, April 25

FRIEND AL: Just a line to let you know I am still on earth. My arm feels pretty good again and I guess maybe I will work at Detroit. Violet writes that she can't hardly wait to see me. Looks like I got a regular girl now Al. We go up there the twenty-ninth and maybe I won't be glad to see her. I hope she will be out to the game the day I pitch. I will pitch the way I want to next time and them Tigers won't have such a picnic.

I suppose you seen what the Chicago reporters said about that game. I will punch a couple of their jaws when I see them. Your pal, JACK.

•••

Chicago, Illinois, April 29

DEAR OLD AL: Well Al it's all over. The club went to Detroit last night and I didn't go along. Callahan told me to report to Comiskey this morning and I went up to the office at ten o'clock. He give me my pay to date and broke the news. I am sold to Frisco.

I asked him how they got wavers on me and he says Oh there was no trouble about that because they all heard how you tamed the Tigers. Then he patted me on the back and says Go out there and work hard boy and maybe you'll get another chance some day. I was kind of choked up so I walked out of the office.

I ain't had no fair deal Al and I ain't going to no Frisco. I will quit the game first and take that job Charley offered me at the billiard hall.

I expect to be in Bedford in a couple of days. I have got to pack up first and settle with my landlady about my room here which I engaged for all season thinking I would be treated square. I am going to rest and lay round home a while and try to forget this rotten game. Tell the boys about it Al and tell them I never would of got let out if I hadn't worked with a sore arm.

I feel sorry for that little girl up in Detroit Al. She expected me there today. Your old pal, JACK.

P. S. I suppose you seen where that lucky lefthander Allen shut out Cleveland with two hits yesterday. The lucky stiff.

From Gullible's Travels, Etc.

[Early sections of the tale have Gullible recounting how "I and wife was both hit by the society bacillus" and how a travel agent persuaded them that the best way to make an entree would be to pay a winter visit to a fashionable Palm Beach hotel. Gullible loses his taste for high life as soon as the bills begin to arrive, but his wife is harder to convince.]

v

In our mail box the next mornin' they was a notice that our first week was up and all we owed was one hundred and forty-six dollars and fifty cents. The bill for room and meals was one hundred and nineteen dollars, the rest was for gettin' clo'es pressed and keepin' the locker damp.

I didn't have no appetite for breakfast. I told the Wife I'd wait up in the room and for her to come when she got through. When she blew in I had my speech prepared.

"Look here," I says; "this is our eighth day in Palm Beach society. You're on speakin' terms with a maid and I've got acquainted with half a dozen o' the male hired help. It's cost us about a hundred and sixty-five dollars, includin' them private rooms down to the Casino and our Afromobile trips, and this and that. You know a whole lot o' swell people by sight, but you can't talk to 'em. It'd be just as much satisfaction and hundreds o' dollars cheaper to look up their names in the telephone directory at home; then phone to 'em and, when you got 'em, tell 'em it was the wrong number. That way, you'd get 'em to speak to you at least.

"As for sport," I says, "we don't play golf and we don't play tennis and we don't swim. We go through the same program o' doin' nothin' every day. We dance, but we don't never change partners. For twelve dollars I could buy a phonograph up home and I and you could trot round the livin'-room all evenin' without no danger o' havin' some o' them fancy birds cave our shins in. And we could have twice as much liquid refreshments up there at about a twentieth the cost.

"That Gould I met on the train comin' down," I says, "was a even bigger liar than I give him credit for. He says that when he was here people pestered him to death by comin' up and speakin' to him. We ain't had to dodge nobody or hike behind a cocoanut tree to remain exclusive. He says Palm Beach was too common for him. What he should of said was that it was too lonesome. If they was just one white man here that'd listen to my stuff I wouldn't have no kick. But it ain't no pleasure tellin' stories to the Ephs. They laugh whether it's good or not, and then want a dime for laughin'.

"As for our clo'es," I says, "they would be all right for a couple o' days' stay. But the dames round here, and the men, too, has somethin' different to put on for every mornin', afternoon, and night. You've wore your two evenin' gowns so much that I just have to snap my finger at the hooks and they go and grab the right eyes.

"The meals would be grand," I says, "if the cook didn't keep gettin' mixed up and puttin' puddin' sauce on the meat and gravy on the pie.

"I'm glad we've been to Palm Beach," I says. "I wouldn't of missed it for nothin'. But the ocean won't be no different to-morrow than it was yesterday, and the same for the daily program. It don't even rain here, to give us a little variety.

"Now what do you say," I says, "to us just settlin' this bill, and whatever we owe since then, and beatin' it out o' here just as fast as we can go?"

The Missus didn't say nothin' for a w'ile. She was too busy cryin'. She knowed that what I'd said was the truth, but she wouldn't give up without a struggle.

"Just three more days," she says finally. "If we don't meet somebody worth meetin' in the next three days I'll go wherever you want to take me."

"All right," I says; "three more days it is. What's a little matter o' sixty dollars?"

Well, in them next two days and a half she done some desperate flirtin', but as it was all with women I didn't get jealous. She picked out some o' the E-light o' Chicago and tried every trick she could think up. She told 'em their noses was shiny and offered 'em her powder. She stepped on their white shoes just so's to get a chance to beg their pardon. She told 'em their clo'es was unhooked, and then unhooked 'em so's she could hook 'em up again. She tried to loan 'em her finger-nail tools. When she seen one fannin' herself she'd say: "Excuse me, Mrs. So-and-So; but we got the coolest room in the hotel, and I'd be glad to have you go up there and quit perspirin'." But not a rise did she get.

Not till the afternoon o' the third day o' grace. And I don't know if I ought to tell you this or not—only I'm sure you won't spill it nowheres.

We'd went up in our room after lunch. I was tired out and she was discouraged. We'd set round for over an hour, not sayin' or doin' nothin'.

I wanted to talk about the chance of us gettin' away the next mornin', but I didn't dast bring up the subject.

The Missus complained of it bein' hot and opened the door to leave the breeze go through. She was settin' in a chair near the doorway, pretendin' to read the *Palm Beach News*. All of a sudden she jumped up and kind o' hissed at me.

"What's the matter?" I says, springin' from the lounge.

"Come here!" she says, and went out the door into the hall.

I got there as fast as I could, thinkin' it was a rat or a fire. But the Missus just pointed to a lady walkin' away from us, six or seven doors down.

"It's Mrs. Potter," she says; "*the* Mrs. Potter from Chicago!"

"Oh!" I says, puttin' all the excitement I could into my voice.

And I was just startin' back into the room when I seen Mrs. Potter stop and turn round and come to'rd us. She stopped again maybe twenty feet from where the Missus was standin'.

"Are you on this floor?" she says.

The Missus shook like a leaf.

"Yes," says she, so low you couldn't hardly hear her.

"Please see that they's some towels put in 559," says *the* Mrs. Potter from Chicago.

vi

About five o'clock the Wife quieted down and I thought it was safe to talk to her. "I've been readin' in the guide about a pretty river trip," I says. "We can start from here on the boat to-morrow mornin'. They run to Fort Pierce to-morrow and stay there to-morrow night. The next day they go from Fort Pierce to Rockledge, and the day after that from

Rockledge to Daytona. The fare's only five dollars apiece. And we can catch a north-bound train at Daytona."

"All right, I don't care," says the Missus.

So I left her and went down-stairs and acrost the street to ask Mr. Foster. Ask Mr. Foster happened to be a girl. She sold me the boat tickets and promised she would reserve a room with bath for us at Fort Pierce, where we was to spend the followin' night. I bet she knowed all the w'ile that rooms with a bath in Fort Pierce is scarcer than toes on a sturgeon.

I went back to the room and helped with the packin' in an advisory capacity. Neither one of us had the heart to dress for dinner. We ordered somethin' sent up and got soaked an extra dollar for service. But we was past carin' for a little thing like that.

At nine o'clock next mornin' the good ship *Constitution* stopped at the Poinciana dock w'ile we piled aboard. One bellhop was down to see us off and it cost me a quarter to get that much attention. Mrs. Potter must of overslept herself.

The boat was loaded to the guards and I ain't braggin' when I say that we was the best-lookin' people aboard. And as for manners, why, say, old Bill Sykes could of passed off for Henry Chesterfield in that gang! Each one o' them occupied three o' the deck chairs and sprayed orange juice all over their neighbors. We could of talked to plenty o' people here, all right; they were as clubby a gang as I ever seen. But I was afraid if I said somethin' they'd have to answer; and, with their mouths as full o' citrus fruit as they was, the results might of been fatal to my light suit.

We went up the lake to a canal and then through it to Indian River. The boat run aground every few minutes and had to be pried loose. About twelve o'clock a cullud gemman come up on deck and told us lunch was ready. At half past one he served it at a long family table in the cabin. As far as I was concerned, he might as well of left it on the stove. Even if you could of bit into the food, a glimpse of your fellow diners would of strangled your appetite.

After the repast I called the Missus aside.

"Somethin' tells me we're not goin' to live through three days o' this," I says. "What about takin' the train from Fort Pierce and beatin' it for Jacksonville, and then home?"

"But that'd get us to Chicago too quick," says she. "We told people how long we was goin' to be gone and if we got back ahead o' time they'd think they was somethin' queer."

"They's too much queer on this boat," I says. "But you're goin' to have your own way from now on."

We landed in Fort Pierce about six. It was only two or three blocks to the hotel, but when they laid out that part o' town they overlooked some o' the modern conveniences, includin' sidewalks. We staggered through the sand with our grips and sure had worked up a hunger by the time we reached Ye Inn.

"Got reservations for us here?" I ast the clerk.

"Yes," he says, and led us to 'em in person.

The room he showed us didn't have no bath, or even a chair that you could set on w'ile you pulled off your socks.

"Where's the bath?" I ast him.

"This way," he says, and I followed him down the hall, outdoors and up an alley.

Finally we come to a bathroom complete in all details, except that it didn't have no door. I went back to the room, got the Missus and went down to supper. Well, sir, I wish you could of been present at that supper. The choice o' meats was calves' liver and onions or calves' liver and onions. And I bet if them calves had of been still livin' yet they could of gave us some personal reminiscences about Garfield.

The Missus give the banquet one look and then laughed for the first time in several days.

"The guy that named this burg got the capitals mixed," I says. "It should of been Port Fierce."

And she laughed still heartier. Takin' advantage, I says:

"How about the train from here to Jacksonville?"

"You win!" says she. "We can't get home too soon to suit me."

vii

The mornin' we landed in Chicago it was about eight above and a wind was comin' offen the Lake a mile a minute. But it didn't feaze us.

"Lord!" says the Missus. "Ain't it grand to be home!"

"You said somethin'," says I. "But wouldn't it of been grander if we hadn't never left?"

"I don't know about that," she says. "I think we both of us learned a lesson."

"Yes," I says; "and the tuition wasn't only a matter o' close to seven hundred bucks!"

"Oh," says she, "we'll get that back easy!"

"How?" I ast her. "Do you expect some tips on the market from Mrs. Potter and the rest o' your new friends?"

"No," she says. "We'll win it. We'll win it in the rummy game with the Hatches."

The Literary Wits

The appeal of Lardner and the column writers to a somewhat specialized audience was to find an even more particularized line in the development of elaborate "literary sections" in three of the city's newspapers during the second and third decades of the century. This sudden flowering was spurred by the advent of a twentieth-century spread of writing often diverging from established nineteenth-century admirations and from the "popular" literature of the day alike. Nevertheless, it was one that commanded journalistic interest for some years.

There is no single label adequate to embrace the breadth of the literary phenomena that came in for comment pro and con. It included interest in such figures as George Bernard Shaw, H. G. Wells, and John Galsworthy in addition to a number of innovative Continental writers like Henrik Ibsen, Guy de Maupassant, and Gabriele D'Annunzio. Attention was extended to Theodore Dreiser and Stephen Crane in America in addition to a second generation of native "realists" including Henry Fuller, Robert Herrick (both from Chicago), and James Branch Cabell. The phenomenon of a radical avant-garde suggested itself to Chicago by such figures as Ezra Pound and his enthusiasm for T. S. Eliot and James Joyce (reflected in Chicago's *Poetry* and *Little Review*), by such other contributors to *Poetry* as Carl Sandburg and Vachel Lindsay, by Sherwood Anderson, and by Edgar Lee Masters' *Spoon River Anthology*. Across its breadth the period was marked for Chicago interest by the spread of more than fifteen years separating the first appearance of the copiously titled "Chicago Evening Post Friday Literary Review" in 1909 to the flourishing of "book pages" in the

Tribune and *Daily News*, and, on into the 1920s, the brief, zany run of Ben Hecht's *Chicago Literary Times*.

Literary innovation had been a bone of newspaper contention since Eugene Field's day and a standard butt of the column conductors. Now, in its behalf, newspaper wit reflected an openness to twentieth-century innovation and change, both wooing and lampooning the conventional taste it opposed and using as much cleverness as was at hand to help fulfill its role. Both the newspaper men themselves and the writing they discussed were in their youth, proud of their newly acquired sophistication and pleased with the opportunity at hand for demonstrating it. Such an exchange as that on Joyce's *Ulysses*, for example, could be plotted in advance during a Saturday afternoon at Schlogl's restaurant or some other favorite gathering spot and then executed during the ensuing weeks to the mutual notoriety and benefit of all concerned.

The Friday Literary Review of the Chicago *Evening Post*

The review first appeared in 1909 as a weekly supplement to a conventional upper-class newspaper with a reputation for "literary" interests, the *Evening Post*. It was originated by Francis Hackett, who, Irish born, had departed London journalism for adventuring in America, which led him to Chicago's Hull House Theater, the *Post*, and later to the literary editorship of the *New Republic* in New York. Floyd Dell, the second editor, had educated himself in Socialist and literary circles in Davenport, Iowa. He appeared as "Associate" to Hackett in January of 1910. When Hackett resigned his post in 1911, Dell succeeded him as editor, appointing one of his erstwhile Davenport tutors, George Cram Cook, as associate. After a brief stint with the review, Cook was to leave for the East and become a founder of the Provincetown Players. Dell, departing Chicago for New York, the *Masses* magazine, and a career as a novelist, was followed by Lucien Cary in 1912, and Cary was succeeded by Llewellyn Jones in 1913, who swung the review into more ordinary "book page" channels.

The review under Hackett reflected an interest in London and Continental literary groupings and their espousal by the unpredictably Socialist journal, the London *New Age*, for which Hackett often expressed admiration. Dell brought a greater attention to American writing into play and his own inclination toward a native Socialist intellectuality was combined with psychological enthusiasms, feminism, William James's pragmatism, and a variety of new social and intellectual impulses which Cary would continue. All three assumed a tone of literary wit and sophistication in their editorial style. Such unpredictable and often rather inconsistent blending of interests gave the journal a ground toward which it sought to woo its readers from the conventional and so spur them on to new awareness.

Francis Hackett's later book publication was highly diversified; most notable was his highly popular volume, *The Private Life of Henry VIII* (1929). Dell was to have a noteworthy later career perhaps most distinguished by his novels, *Moon Calf* (1920) and *The Briary Bush* (1921), and by his autobiography, *Homecoming* (1933).

Predigested Opinions

An esteemed contemporary ends up one of its literary criticisms with the following: "You may quarrel with his philosophy of life, disapprove of many of his opinions, but one thing you cannot deny, and that is the vastly entertaining character of all he produces. For brilliancy of dialectic, for unexpectedness of humor, for trenchancy of wit, he has few compeers."

This is good, but should it not also hint that he is something of a mountebank, an *enfant terrible* and a *farceur*?

An ingenious volume might be arranged on the principle of this quotation for ladies who are tired after shopping. Instead of having to converse at a moment's notice about Messrs. Chesterton, Wells and Shaw, they could turn to their "Predigested Opinions" and read the general verdict, with appropriate remarks on all volumes printed within the last week.

The essayist who named his recent books, "On Everything," "On Anything," "On Nothing," gave an unmistakable clew to the modern essayist's[1] state of mind. They are discussing everything, anything and nothing. For this reason casual conversation on their philosophy or their art is apt to begin and end everywhere, anywhere and nowhere. All that is certain is that Mr. Wells is brilliant, Mr. Shaw is brilliant and Mr. Chesterton is brilliant. But, from the standpoint of the pathetic

---

1. The word is here used as a synonym for "book reviewer."

lady who does read these gentlemen, a little prearrangement of ideas might be desirable. And the man to do it is surely he who summed up Bernard Shaw so—well, So Brilliantly—in the quotation above.

Mrs. Grundy

Since publishers were, they have been of two classes; some have printed what they chose and the others have printed what Mrs. Grundy let them. Somewhat late in the day an exception has been discovered—a publisher who prints something of which Mrs. Grundy disapproves, accompanying it with an elaborate apology to that venerable dame.

Mr. W. Heinemann, an English publisher, is the one who has achieved this epicene distinction. He may be remembered as the man who at a recent publishers' convention, characterized the works of Henry George, Karl Marx and Friedrich Nietzsche as "noxious literature"—adding with some pride that all three were "foreigners." It is in the case of another foreigner that Mr. Heinemann performs his unique apologetics. On the paper cover of a translation of Maupassant's "Boule de Suif" he has caused to be printed these words.

> In offering this English translation of a story universally recognized as the finest and most artistic short story ever written, the publisher has to justify his action so far as concerns the existing prejudice in England against subjects such as those chosen and treated by De Maupassant. He wishes therefore to say that he appeals only to that small section of the public interested in a work of art for the sake of art, regardless of so-called morality or ethics. This book is not intended to be placed indiscriminately in the hands of those unlikely to judge of and appreciate the beauty of workmanship quite independently of its subject, or of those who distrust the realism of this author.

What one thinks of this artful little composition depends on whether one is on the side of Mrs. Grundy or of De Maupassant. In the latter case one is amused, in the former unconvinced: in either case, Mr. Heinemann's ingenuity seems wasted. Since when have honest men believed they had to justify a worthy action against the prejudice of the crowd. Or how can an honest man take the responsibility of distributing an article on which he is compelled to put a poison label?

If what Mr. Heinemann desired was to warn Philistines away—if he really believed "Boule de Suif" to be the "finest and most artistic short story ever written"—there was a phrase ready to his hand which he could have used with the happiest effect, leaving no doubt among intelligent people as to his attitudes and motives: "this is not meat for little people or for fools."

The Average Reader

A correspondent inquires: "What is your attitude toward the Average Reader?" He wonders if we vainly imagine that THE FRIDAY LITERARY REVIEW suits this hypothetical personage—or if, on the other hand, we flout, or even ignore him. . . .

This conception has had for many minds a singular fascination. It satisfies the mental craving for all-inclusiveness and finality. If one can understand the nature of the Average Man, it is unnnecessary to study people in particular. And so the restless curiosity is drugged into a peaceful slumber.

Our correspondent inquires concerning the estimation in which this journal and an imaginary being, with miraculous attributes of general representativeness, hold each other. Him and his imaginary opinions we certainly ignore. But in our real readers and their real opinions, in all their bewildering variety, we have a most lively and respectful interest. . . .

There is, first, the young man who gives us no little uneasiness by his enthusiastic approval of the Review. He is anywhere between 18 and 25 years old, and he usually writes verse. His interest in literature is secondary to his interest in ideas—and a rather narrow set of ideas he has. He conceives of books as the weapons in a battle—or, rather, as arguments in a huge and noisy debate. On one side is ranged the world of ignorance and reaction; on the other himself and a few other heroic champions of progress.

When this young man sees THE FRIDAY LITERARY REVIEW he hails it, in a manner most embarrassing, as an ally, and proceeds to deluge its editor with controversial articles and poems. Also with advice. He wants us to print more about Bernard Shaw, H. G. Wells, Mrs. Charlotte Perkins Gilman[2] and Nietzsche. He counts that issue lost which is devoted to such writers as Scott, Thackeray, and Dickens—people, he insists, of no vital significance. After a time when his favorite philosopher

---

2. An American writer on labor economics and women's rights.

is "roasted" in our columns, he concludes that he was mistaken. We are not on the side of the angels, after all. He alludes to us thenceforth, in his private conversation, as "that reactionary sheet."

Then there is the woman of middle age. She does not tell us what she thinks of the Review, but nevertheless we think we understand her feelings. She is a little scornful of us, and yet, perhaps, a little piqued. She is scornful because we do not show what she calls a real love of literature; piqued because out of those new books and plays by Wells and Shaw—which she often really reads—we apparently manage to get so much pleasure.

Her attitude toward literature is quite different from that of the young man. She has been young, and she is becoming old. She has seen life, and it is not a beautiful thing. So she turns to literature as to something in which life is mysteriously ennobled. Hawthorne and Howells seem to her truer than the actual domestic and social life in which she finds herself immersed. Nevertheless it is as a reflection of that life that literature essentially interests her.

The middle-aged woman has in the youth a kindly interest. But she thinks: "Wait ten years." And the young man, with his youthful trait of phrasemaking, says of her, somewhat harshly: "She wishes to intoxicate herself with dreams, so as to forget the actual world."

And, just as the young man reproaches us for our too little interest in ideas, the woman reproaches us silently for our too great interest. Ideas make her vaguely uncomfortable. If she could or would translate that discomfort into words, she would say: "Ideas have no such overweening importance as you imagine."

Between these two readers we cannot attempt to arbitrate. But we confess that, under the stress of the egotistic intellectuality of the youth, we have growing sympathy for the woman of middle age. In so far as her attitude is a reaction against pain and disappointments which the young man has not experienced, it has a real justification: and that beauty which life has failed to yield she has the highest right to look for in literature.

The *Daily News* Book Page

Under Francis Hackett, the *Post*'s "Friday Literary Review" had begun as a venture in exploratory social and literary attitudes. The *Daily News* book page was originated in 1916 by Henry Blackman Sell almost as a publicist's concept. He persuaded the paper's editor that if given charge of the department he could sell enough advertising to make it pay. This was not quite the first of Sell's promotions, but it was the first to achieve major success and led directly to his later career as editor of *Harper's Bazaar*, the *Delineator*, and *Town and Country*, to his ownership of an advertising agency, and to a life identified with the international smart set of New York, Paris, and the Riviera. Although he was a competent reviewer, Sell's particular skill was that of editor and organizer. The quality of his book page reflected the variety and freshness of the contributions he attracted and encouraged.

He began with the advantage of having Carl Sandburg and Ben Hecht directly at hand on the *News* staff, while Sherwood Anderson was a Chicago resident anxious to achieve public notice. They and other Chicagoans were pressed into service. Keith Preston began his years on the *News* by writing a weekly column for the page, "The Periscope." Eunice Tietjens, for a time assistant editor of *Poetry* magazine, was a regular contributor. During Sell's frequent trips to New York to interest eastern publishers in advertising on the page he persuaded Alfred Kreymborg, Conrad Aiken, and others to contribute. The result was a lively and various mixture of literary opinion, self-expression, and gossip ranging across Sell's time as editor, from 1916 to 1920, and continuing under Harry Hansen and then Keith Preston until 1927.

Sell was born in Chicago and first came to newspaper success as author of a self-originated series, again specially sold to the *News*, which he called "Nations in Council" and which featured articles on the lives and character of Chicago's numerous ethnic communities. Harry Hansen, his successor as editor, had been a hard-working reporter for the *News* abroad during the First World War and the Versailles Conference. In 1923 his book *Midwest Portraits* appeared, a warm and perceptive account of Chicago's literary renaissance of the day. After leaving the *News* in 1926 he proceeded to the staffs of the New York *World* and later the *World-Telegram* and thence became editor of *The World Almanac*. Keith Preston's career as a column "conductor" has been sketched earlier in this volume.

Alfred Kreymborg: The Stevens Fadeaway

[Kreymborg, born and raised in New York City and mainly active there, was a poet and a major figure in the early little magazine movement. He was founder of the *Glebe* (1913) and *Others* (1914). In 1927 he established the literary annual, *The American Caravan*. He had met Henry Sell in New York and came to Chicago in 1916 reporting the Republican convention of that year. As a result, he spent some time in the city in 1916 and 1917 associating with the *Poetry* magazine circle and other Chicago groups.]

...

M'sieu Aiken and Mynheer Hecht, critics extraordinaires, have both overlooked el Senor Stevens, whimsical perpetrator of the monologue play, "Carlos Among the Candles," in the December issue of *Poetry*. Brother Conrad [Aiken] once termed Stevens a composer of half poems, while Cousin Ben [Hecht]—well, in a recent symposium on Ezra Pound, he fell into that antiquated trap, the selection of an Anglo-American team of poets, in this instance made up of the infield only, Pound, Sandburg, Aldington and Bodenheim. Why he neglected the outer garden with such stern folk as Amy Lowell, Eunice Tietjens and Mina Loy ever ready to chase fungos, is a poser I will have to refer to Grantland Rice or Bozeman Bulger.[3] Recently, Miss Lowell elected Messrs. Masters, Frost, Sandburg, Robinson, Fletcher and Mrs. H. D. Aldington[4] to sing in the Jammermoor sextet. Ezra[5] himself used to air a love for teams. And so it goeth, when poets criticize.

I too am one of those hapless folk who is prone to base his judgments, or debase them, on emotions of friendship or recognition of kinship. Hence my rooting for the curves of Wallace Stevens—and since one must always indulge the superlative, there are none better, more serpentine, more elusive, none so like the Mathewson fadeaway.[6] Is Carlos a play—isn't it a play? Is it prose or poetry? It is writ in prose, but it sounds like poetry. Well—it gets me. I have read it four times,

3. Kreymborg here teases Hecht for neglecting women poets. Rice and Bulger were notable contemporary sports writers.
4. The poetess H. D. (Hilda Doolittle), now married to the English poet, Richard Aldington. Kreymborg here refers to Amy Lowell's grouping of these figures in her recently published book referred to later in the article.
5. Ezra Pound, who had lost the leadership of the Imagist grouping of poets to Amy Lowell.
6. The special pitch of Christy Mathewson, a notable contemporary baseball figure.

and I saw it performed in New York by the Wisconsin players at the Neighborhood Playhouse. A play concerning a whimsical pedant lighting and blowing out four candles—a creature created by a Hartford lawyer, embodied by an Italian actor, Signor Ioucelli, from Milwaukee, on the east side in Manhattan. Who would say art is national? The play was guffawed off the stage by erudite New York, and Chicago has guffawed through the person of a Herald editorial. Me, it intrigues, captivates, de-egotizes. Exquisite melodic contours, provocative splashes of line and color, and the smell of good ripe thought—so patronizingly scorned by Cousin Ben. Well—the fact that I didn't know what the play was about made me think when I first read it; the fact, now, that I don't care what it is about, makes me think still harder. And with growing cheerfulness.

For me, the December "Poetry" begins at the top of page 115 and ends at the bottom of page 123. There are some mediocre contributions, including a Chicago group by John Gould Fletcher and some conventional moods along various lines and in conventional molds, whether rhymed or free, by the Dudley sisters, Clement Wood, Grace Hazard Conkling, Florence Kiper Frank, Florence K. Mixter and Earl Marlatt. Nay, Louis Grudin was worth "discovering."[7] Several of his "miniatures" are unique. In the Review section, Miss Lowell is deservedly taken to task by Miss Monroe for her "Tendencies in Modern American Poetry." Had I perpetrated the book, and been confined to a six poet team, I would have chosen for my side Friend Wallace Stevens, Friend William Carlos Williams, Friend Carl Sandburg, Friend Orrick Johns, Friend Maxwell Bodenheim and a man on behalf of whose modesty I wouldn't have perpetrated the book. Well—toss the hat. Fist over fist, no cheating, no inching. You win? Whom do you choose—Ty Cobb?[8] I don't blame you.

Carl Sandburg: A Middle-West Man

There is only one weekly paper I have read every week for thirteen years without missing a week. Its name is Reedy's Mirror of St. Louis, Missouri. There are papers with higher priced contribs, star special

---

7. In general, Kreymborg is asserting a taste for the more notably avant-garde poets among his friends.

8. Another notable baseball contemporary.

From a cartoon by Morey Schwartz in the Chicago *Daily News*, June 13, 1917.

scribblers, whose names are on the billboards—but none has more honest thought, more frank and fresh liars, more original and careless players with the foolery of life, more somber and earnest pilgrims, hunting the finalities that do not turn ashen at our hands under the fire of the years.

William Marion Reedy, the editor of this paper, better known to a wide flung clan as "Bill" Reedy, is not only a personality but an institution. Situated in the heart of the world's greatest mule breeding region, he has never balked at facing any problem of life shoved up front stage by the props and flymen of time. A philosopher with a series of revolving mirrors down the corridor of his brain, those who write of him are led into the fallacies and contortions of Irish bulls. Elbert Hubbard[9] called Reedy the best all round writing man in America, and during fifteen years of writing Hubbard at regular intervals repeated his declaration that nobody else was getting anything on Reedy in the art of scribendi furoribus.

Among ink writing men Reedy stands about as John L. Sullivan does among fist fighting men. Each is a tradition with a wealth of personalia and a proven reputation for fair play. Amid the highbrow elements of our population there will be no understanding of this comparison of Reedy with John L. Sullivan, but in the sporting world, weary of fixed fights and fake bouts, there will be a gleam of response. It is into Irish analogies that one runs in hitting off Reedy. And I hope some day we will get more complete and authoritative pictures of "The Patch" in St. Louis, the shantytown where Reedy grew up with a gang of Huck Finns of whom another was Frank P. Walsh, who is to industrial economics what Reedy is to journalism.

It was Reedy who first in any American magazine printed stories and sketches by John Galsworthy. He first picked up R. B. Cunningham-Grahame.[10] He is to the middle west what James Huneker[11] and Henry L. Mencken are to the Atlantic coast. While he is lacking some of the broad suavity, didactic art discriminations and musical prescience of the seaboard promulgators, he has them backed off the boards in the special fields of politics, literature, people and the whirl-

9. A friend of Sandburg's, editor of a literary paper called the *Philistine*, and a notable literary promoter of the day.
10. A British writer of fiction, travel, and adventure set chiefly in South America.
11. American critic, essayist, and wit of the early twentieth century.

amarig of life in the present and actual. He discovered Edgar Lee Masters for Chicago.[12] He printed Harry Marion Lyon's book of short stories. He has published the first pragmatic consideration relevant to Clifford Raymond of Chicago as man, stylist, and friend of the Ravinia oven bird.[13]

The Henley poem, "Out of the Night that Covers Me," had its first publication in America in Reedy's Mirror, Dunsany[14] plays and sketches were in the Mirror before other magazines. It is here only that short stories have been printed from Tubman K. Hedrick, owner of the initials "T. K. H.," at the foot of the "Hit or Miss" column of The Daily News.

There is a clairvoyance about Reedy's envisioning of current events. He has a gift for handling the news facts of the day in a manner that makes no misstatements, and yet out of his stirring of the cauldron issues an odor and a significance. This is why people read the Mirror. It gives off an evanescence that leads somewhere. Just before the Russian revolution, Reedy was uncannily speculative and querulous about something doing over at that arc of the planetary curve. Occasionally he makes a bum guess, but most of the time when he says that a certain rathole or a certain horizon is worth watching then something generally appears thereat or thereabouts.

Every once in a while Reedy is smitten with a terror that he is writing too high and it goes over the heads of his people. His way of overcoming this danger is to ride on the surface cars and talk his editorials to motormen and conductors.

From week to week this girthy gargantuan down at St. Louis insists on cross-examining Death and Love in their relationship to the events of the day and their connections with the advance of man and the mastery of the race over the broad earth. He is sophisticated and intimate with all our oldest sins—and yet he keeps a grip on the illusions of youth and the dreams that lead men on to danger and women to travail. He will turn from writing of financial imperialists playing buzzard to the war and change to writing of the riot of joy and imagina-

---

12. Masters' *Spoon River Anthology* made its first appearance serialized in Reedy's magazine.

13. Mrs. Arthur Aldis of Chicago had established an outdoor theater and art center at her Ravinia home which grew into the summer location for the Chicago Symphony Orchestra concerts. It was also a center for numbers of midwestern literary aspirants.

14. Lord Dunsany, Irish dramatist and member of the Abbey Theatre group.

tion in the new music drama of "Jack and the Beanstalk." From the output of writing poured into the Mirror during the Reedy career there could be collected a series of essays, sketches and kitkats that would make books worth standing alongside of Maeterlinck and Emerson. Nor is Marcus Aurelius more serious nor the white slave, Epictetus, more sure in grasp of what in life is worth living.

Some day we shall have a real biography of William Marion Reedy. These are the random New Year jottings of one who has read his paper thirteen years.

The *Ulysses* Affair

From 1918 to 1921, at the instigation of Ezra Pound, Margaret Anderson's *Little Review* undertook the serialization of parts of James Joyce's *Ulysses*, and the project continued until an issue of the *Review* was seized by the U.S. Post Office and the publishers were fined $100 for mailing obscenity. The magazine was not located in Chicago after 1917, but *Ulysses* nevertheless quickly attracted the attention of the city's literary wits and precipitated a serio-comic quarrel between the *Daily News* and the *Tribune* book pages—Ben Hecht and Keith Preston for the former and Burton Rascoe for the latter. All concerned struck attitudes of superiority to their opponents; Hecht and Preston particularly enjoyed twitting the former University of Chicago undergraduate for his youth, which caused Rascoe to adopt an even loftier and more pontifical tone than usual. He was in a somewhat embattled position on the *Tribune* anyway, since he wished to forward the cause of much of the new writing but faced the unyielding conservatism of his paper in doing so. His answer was to make himself a critical sponsor especially for the new American writing, arguing the faddishness of favoring European effort, an argument consistent with the *Tribune's* own chauvinism. Hecht and Preston, in turn, positioned themselves as being far above any such narrowness and caused Rascoe to bait them back with their own homegrown origins.

Hecht began the fray with a long and generally enlightening comment on Joyce's work entitled "Boob Babble" and included the specially pointed paragraphs presented here to justify his headline. Rascoe was the boob. He immediately replied in a brief paragraph appended to a long article on another subject. Preston intervened at this point with a witty commentary on *Ulysses* itself, somewhat apart from the fray, and Hecht published a letter attacking Rascoe. Rascoe concluded the interchange with an article defending himself against the imputations of Hecht's letter and so had the last word.

Ben Hecht: From "Boob Babble"

The response of the faithful to the art of James Joyce has convinced me that my suspicions were a credit to the general intelligence of the race. The response of the faithful to the art of James Joyce has been the unmistakable hee-haw, the never to be confused neigh of derision and alarm which the true and well bred Philistine ass emits in the presence of his betters.

In the eyes of the faithful—a faithful, mind you, capable of getting the subtleties of Bloc, of digesting firmly the arpeggios of Kreymborg, of encompassing sensitively the spectric hoaxes of Arthur Ficke and Witter Bynner perpetrated under the names of "Anne Knish" and "Emmanuel Morgan" [15]—in the eyes of the superdelicious minority, James Joyce has proved himself, by the composing of "Ulysses," an incoherent and meaningless writer. Ah, to be able to dash off some foreign and sardonic phrase at this point or some tart, epigrammatic morsel in Greek! For the situation has an epic flavor, a universal kittenishness to it. Arise, ye Tartarians of Chicago and Gary and Oak Park and Benton Harbor and 57th street! Come forth, ye Jack Daltons, ye Burton Rascoes, ye J. Nicholas Beffells! [16] Joyce incoherent, garbled, damfoolish, impossible to read, a hoaxer or an idiot! Well may the artist, harassed by the imbecilic yappings of the O. Henry school of art lovers, turn the glass eye of agony upon the faithful, with the classic exclamation, "Why do you act this way, Burtus?" [Chicago *Daily News*, July 3, 1918]

Burton Rascoe: From "The Intellectual Autobiography of Francis Hackett"

James Joyce is to be congratulated. He has found an ardent champion for his "Ulysses" in a bright if not quite literate Chicago police reporter.

---

15. The list of names is a reference to American avant-gardists. The "Spectric Hoax" was a brief-lived sensation instigated by Bynner along with Ficke and Marjorie Allen Seiffert, both midwesterners.

16. The University of Chicago campus and a small bohemian settlement were both centered on 57th Street. Hecht adds two abusive cognomens to Rascoe's own name to suggest the latter's provincialism.

That the most honest newsman mistakes Joyce for something he is not, does not matter. And though the two columns of childish patter by this ambitious hotfoot was scarcely less incoherent than "Ulysses," which it presumably was about, it was ungenerous of the waggish editor of the "Daily News" book page to caption it "Boob Babble." [Chicago *Tribune*, July 6, 1918]

Keith Preston: From "The Periscope"

Why do the heathen rage? What makes the wild cat wild? Why has B. R. of 7 South Dearborn street,[17] with a low blood curdling whoop sneaked up and used the death maul on James Joyce and his gallant defender? We don't understand B. R. in this any more than we do when he talks of the "paucity of the Greek vocabulary," which is to say the lack of salt in the ocean, or the "jargon of Quiller Couch," whom we consider a penman of sorts. But at any rate B. R. has put James Joyce on the war map. "The Periscope," with strict neutrality, proposes to explain Joyce to the man in the street. If we can make him safe for democracy, so much the better. Incidentally, still speaking as the man up a tree to the man on the street, we shall put in a word for the rights of self-determination of the smaller magazines, notably The Little Review.[18]

"Ulysses," by James Joyce, appears monthly in The Little Review, a small but spunky magazine devoted to fast colors and loose verse, poetic prose and prosy poetry. The title "Ulysses" denotes a wanderer and was selected by Mr. Joyce to show that his tale wanders. The hero, Stephen Dedalus, is also a classical reference. Daedalus was the first aviator and Mr. Joyce's Stephen is flighty. Daedalus invented the labyrinth in which was stabled the famous Minotaur, half bull and half human. Mr. Joyce's tale has been compared to a labyrinth, but is not generally believed to contain any bull. The inventiveness of Stephen Dedalus is shown in numerous colorful epithets, spot green, oyster gray, and the like.[19] Mr. Joyce is not ordinarily hard to follow, though the reader will miss certain typographical landmarks, as quotation marks. The English is clear and vigorous, though impolite. From this

17. The then address of the Chicago *Tribune*.
18. Preston salts his vocabulary with the World War I catchwords of the day, "safe for democracy," "self determination," etc.
19. Euphemisms for Joyce's "snot green" and "gob gray" required by contemporary newspaper usage.

fact the ignorant and salacious reader may look askance at Mr. Joyce's Latinity. This is generally of great purity, except where goulashed by the licentious compositor.

"Ulysses" may be briefly described as a train of thought derailed at intervals. For example, let us suppose that the hero, Stephen Dedalus, starts out to buy a sausage (Mr. Joyce is now residing in Austria-Hungary, where it takes a hero to capture a sausage). Observing on the way a white horse, he will instantly be reminded of a redheaded girl. Naturally enough it will occur to him that woman's crowning glory is her hair. But the morning glory thereof is less glorious than the evening glory! (A few reflections on curl papers.) Stumbling over a dog, Stephen will be reminded of his sausage, but as he quickens his pace a passing wagon will splash him with clay—which leads him to reflect on imperial Caesar, dead and turned to clay (reflections on pipe clay and imperials).[20] Ultimately, of course, he will arrive at the butcher shop and obtain his sausage, which will prove the opening link of a new chain of meditation. The story moves by fits and starts, fits of abstraction and starts of surprise. It progresses also by episodes and dashes.[21] The dashes are usually short, but Mr. Joyce has been known to do the hundred word dash upon urgent occasions. [Chicago *Daily News*, July 10, 1918]

Burton Rascoe: From "Do, Re, Mi, Fa, So, La"

(The following from the Daily News of Wednesday is so sweet and pathetic that it deserves some circulation.) "Dear Sell: I am going to tell the teacher on Burty Rascoe and see if she can't be prevailed upon to coax him back to the classroom. For, despite a tendency toward academic hysteria, me and Steve Crane and Rudge Kipling, and Art Machen and Charlie Dickens and all other police reporters in good standing feel convinced that there is promising material in this still flushed and pensive undergraduate. Burty's habit of flying into a rage and slapping the wrists of people with whom he seeks to argue is indeed a regrettable symptom of juvenilia. Nevertheless I feel quixotically certain that, given a diet of red meat and a few more lessons under some rigorous schoolmarm, Burty would be able to understand James

---

20. Imperial, a particular cut of the beard.
21. Joyce used dashes in the place of quotation marks.

Joyce. Yours, with Huysmanian bitterness. 'A poor but honest police reporter'"

It has not occurred to the honest newsman that I have omitted to argue with him for the reason that his notions are so vague and erratic as to admit of no argument. We no longer argue with the man who proclaims that the earth is flat: we either tolerate him with mild amusement, pity him, or send him to the booby hatch. Margaret Anderson, and Keith Preston, Llewellyn Jones and *jh*, John Dos and Mr. Gus Oomplatz.[22] These red blooded, full chested, tobacco chewing Broncho Billies tell me, variously in effect, that honesty is the best policy, a rolling stone gathers no moss, and birds of a feather flock together.

Preston's contribution is the only one I can regard with any sympathy—and it I can actually rejoice in—for the reason that Preston treats the whole thing as an elaborate joke and indulges in a shrewd bit of kidding at the expense of his confreres and of Joyce. This, no doubt, is the ultimate wisdom in a critique of such a subject. True enough, Preston hints that he is hep to Joyce, but he betrays himself in the same paragraph by revealing that he so far misunderstands my by no means esoteric prose as to credit me with finding serious fault with Quiller-Couch's English. If he doesn't get me, I entertain suspicions about his understanding of Joyce.

As for the others, they all point out ludicrously what was obvious from the first installment—viz.: that Joyce is attempting to record those shifting uncorrelated visual, olfactory, tactile and auditory impressions and associations we all have but which never get into speech or print. They do not point out what relation this jumble of uncorrelated material has to do with art. From not one of them do I get a hint as to the character of Stephen Dedalus, his relationship to his surroundings, or even what he is by way of being or doing. [Chicago *Tribune*, July 13, 1918]

The *Tribune* Book Page

The Chicago *Tribune* had maintained a regular page of book reviews and literary comment as a Saturday feature that, over the years, was to

22. The last is a derisive nickname for Hecht. Llewellyn Jones was the current editor

be edited by a variety of persons. For the most part, it was a wholly conventional newspaper department both in style and attitude. Before Burton Rascoe's accession to its editorship, it had for some time been under the charge of Elia Peattie, one of whose causes was her antagonism to literary innovation in general. In such a conservative atmosphere Rascoe's post was not easy. During his two years of editing the page (he was eventually dismissed for a carelessly slighting reference to Christian Science), Mrs. Peattie and other traditionalists continued to flourish there, but in some of his own writing Rascoe was to alter the tone in a deliberate effort to find acceptance for some of the new authors of the day. His tactic was to support American contemporaries against any supposed inferiority to European contemporaries and especially to defend James Branch Cabell during the time that *Jurgen* was being prosecuted by the New York Society for the Suppression of Vice.

Rascoe had begun newspaper work early in life. He had been a student for two years at the University of Chicago, and from there he became first a reporter for the *Tribune* and later a general features manager, work that led to the book page and to its editorship in 1918. After leaving Chicago in 1920, he was attached to the New York *Tribune* and the *Bookman* magazine and later proceeded to a career as an independent writer. Much of the best of his criticism is reprinted in *A Bookman's Daybook* (1929), and he was the author of two lively volumes of autobiography, *Before I Forget* (1937) and *We Were Interrupted* (1947).

Burton Rascoe: From "On a Certain Condescension in Our Natives"

A situation somewhat different now obtains from that which once caused James Russell Lowell with admirable restraint to write: "It is not merely the Englishman; every European admits in himself some right of primogeniture in respect to us, and pats his shaggy continent on the back with a lively sense of generous unbending.

The German who plays the bass viol has a well-founded contempt, which he is not always nice in concealing, for a country so few of whose children ever take that noble instrument between their knees. . . . The

---

of "The Friday Literary Review," "jh" is Jane Heap of the *Little Review*. "John Dos" is not identifiable. The name may be a misprint for "John Doe."

Frenchman feels an easy mastery in speaking his mother tongue, and attributes it to some native superiority of parts that lifts him high above us barbarians of the west. The Italian prima donna sweeps a courtesy of careless pity to the overfacile pit which unsexes her with the *bravo!* meant to show a familiarity with foreign usage.

They are not foreigners, in especial, now who slander us, though it was only recently that the scholarly A. B. Walkley left off reading his Bohn's *Handbook of Classical Quotations* long enough to counsel Englishmen to forget, in the interest of the duty which Great Britain and the United States are allied in fulfilling, the disagreeable fact that America is the raucous region of vulgarity and illiteracy that it is. These unpleasantries we condone, assenting in the general belief that from Mr. Walkley's unapproachable standards they are justified. Further, we are purring over the nice things the French are saying about us—their insistence that with Poe, Whitman and Emerson, at least, we have given great names to literature, and their assurances that reciprocal literary relations are now being fostered between the two countries.

What we are beginning to bear with indifferent fortitude is the self-alienation of many of our native born, the assumption of superiority by the very "hicks" among us. We have Iowans who annoy us with boarding-school French when they could be nearly as intelligible in English. We have Chicagoans who affect the contraband English of Boston in preference to their less anomalous patois of State Street.

We meet those who will have in their libraries nothing except English editions and those to whom Mark Twain is a vulgar bounder they would not think of reading. We have collectors (through agents) of Italian *objets d'art* (as they invariably refer to them) who would shudder on being apprised that ceramics have, in this country, been developed to a remarkably satisfying degree of esthetic perfection. There exists a wide acquaintance (through postcards and imported folios) with the paintings and sculpture of the Louvre, the Uffizi and the Dresden galleries among those who have never spent an hour at a time in the Art Institute.

Everywhere is to be seen the partial accomplishment of that amusing desire of human beings to seem otherwise than they are. And just now to be an American, above all a Midwest American, with a liking for American books, American art, American language, and American traditions is to be a pariah to the gentleman who is eager to forget that he was born on a Nebraska farm, the young lady who has spent three years at an Eastern finishing school, and the matron whose salon is furnished with an astonishing admixture of the bizarre of all periods. . . .

Elsewhere among the critics hypermetropy is evident. They can see Anatole France, probably the greatest literary figure on the European continent, but they cannot see James Branch Cabell, who is under their noses. The viewpoint of the two men is much the same; they have the same tolerant irony, the same refinement of taste, the same sanity of judgment and much the same subtlety of expression. They can see Gilbert Chesterton's huge bulk in Fleet Street, but they cannot descry Frank Moore Colby, who is cleverer, at their elbow. They pass up our most cosmopolitan writer and our most discursive essayist, James Huneker—but that may be ascribed to jealousy.

H. L. Mencken, whose *A Book of Burlesques* strikes with fine precision many notes as fundamental as themes from Swift, Molière and Aristophanes, is unread save by a few and is avoided mention by those who write of books. But Stephen Leacock, a Canadian clown, whose burlesques are no more rereadable than the jokes of vaudeville, is invited to give lectures at American universities.

A bearded Bengalese in a kimono,[23] whose translated poems read like paraphrases of Ossian, is taken seriously; an American experimenting in unrhymed verse is greeted with derision. Europeans are accorded praise by our critics for the very virtues they account as vices in an American. An Icelander, a Polynesian, a Spaniard, a Pole, a Peruvian, a Turk, has by the very fact of his being such, a carte blanche at our tables, while an American, by the very fact of being such, must beg his bread. Our generous hospitality knows no gauches excepting home-folk.

Burton Rascoe: From "Olla Podrida"

Now that we are assured, after persistent demands for it, that we have an indigenous American poetry, why not turn our attention to the development and recognition of an indigenous American philosophy? We have indigenous American philosophers, certainly, of a peculiarly high order of intelligence, acerb, keen, given to quick and sure analy-

---

23. The reference is to Rabindranath Tagore, whose work was being boomed by Ezra Pound in *Poetry* magazine.

sis, capable of precise evaluations, and gifted with a picturesque and explicit charm of expression.

I have no reference here, of course, to the professorial and didactic products of German metaphysics and philology, to Thorstein Veblen, John Dewey, Doctor Sidis, and numerous other collegiate philosophers who are no more indigenous to America than are palms to Lincoln park, but to geniusnesses the like of which are produced nowhere else, to Ed Howe, Ring Lardner, George Ade, and above all to Will Rogers.

My choice as the premier indigenous philosopher of America is Dr. Rogers, who twirls a mean lariat and ropes fallacies and steers with equal expertness and expedition. His latest treatise, though a slim, scant volume which can be read in twenty minutes, nullifies, renders superfluous, I think, all the hundreds of bulky tomes and pamphlets which have been written about the settlement of the war. In his "Peace Conference" [Harper] we have profound, paragraphic ideas, succinctly put, imprisoned in language that holds and delights the eye. Any one of them, were he capable of engendering it, would occupy Dr. Veblen to the extent of 600 pages. And in the matter of grammar, Dr. Rogers, though indigenously nonconformative, would have a shade the best of it.

I trust that Dr. Rogers will soon leave the topical and deal with the cosmic questions, great though his services are to the race in the former direction. I feel that there are larger and less ephemeral matters than the peace squabble which demand his elucidation. I eagerly await his next book; and all my other books on the league of nations, the problems of the big four, etc., meanwhile, go into the coal box against next winter's rigors.

The unthinking may assert that Dr. Rogers is a humorist rather than a philosopher. To which I reply that by the same token were La Rochefoucauld, La Bruyere, and Socrates humorists rather than philosophers.

The *Chicago Literary Times*

Ben Hecht was born in New York City in 1894 but at an early age was taken to Racine, Wisconsin, by his parents, who were attempting to reroot their small business in that city. After high school graduation he made his way to Chicago, where he found a place as cub reporter on the Chicago *Journal*. He moved to the *Daily News* in 1914 and began association with the literary interests on that paper reflected in Sell's and Hansen's book page in 1916. He served as foreign correspondent in 1919 and on returning to the *Daily News* began a daily column, "1001 Afternoons in Chicago," which he maintained for two years. During 1923 and 1924 he edited and published the weekly *Chicago Literary Times* and wrote much of its contents. His brash irreverence had found considerable expression during his *News* years on its book page. The *Literary Times*, where he was associated with Maxwell Bodenheim, became an almost wholly personal sheet filled with Hecht's and Bodenheim's opinions of the moment and such other excursions as those included here. In 1924 he concluded this work and departed for his later career centered largely in New York and Hollywood.

He had originally patterned his attitudes from his admiration for H. L. Mencken, who published stories of his in the *Smart Set*, and from a close personal friend named Sherman Duffy, a Rabelaisian, Phi Beta Kappa graduate of the University of Chicago who served the *Journal* and later the *Tribune* as sports editor. Hecht published nearly thirty volumes of fiction, drama, and essays. His early novel, *Fantazius Mallare*, gained a *succès de scandale*, and *The Front Page*, written with Charles MacArthur, attained notable theatrical success among his plays. His short stories are assembled in *The Collected Stories of Ben Hecht* (1945), and he was the author of an autobiography, *A Child of the Century* (1954).

From "Cabaret Folk Songs that Articulate the Amorous Soul of the Americano"

[The following two pieces appeared in the *Literary Times* without a signature. Such absence of attribution in the paper ordinarily indicated that Hecht was the author, and these two items are presented in that light.]

• • •

If it is true that the heart of a nation expresses itself in its popular songs—

If it is true that the spiritual preoccupation of a people finds its simplest outlet in the ballads they sing and applaud—

We offer the following careful summary of the fifteen songs which today are the chief musical expression of the United States as a cross section of the Republic's aesthetics. . . .

3. Babylon—(By Harry Williams and Neil Moret). The singer, resting his caravan by an ancient temple in the desert beneath the crescent moon, hears through the creeping shadows the voice of a vision informing him that when he was a King in Babylon and she was a Christian slave she gave him unfailing love.

4. Whoa, Tillie, Take Your Time—(By Creamer and Layton). The singer informs Tillie, who is a dancing fool, that she has all night in which to dance and should therefore be more careful of what she shakes, lest she know not what she breaks.

5. You've Got To See Mama Ev'ry Night (Or You Can't See Mama at All)—(By Billy Rose and Con Conrad). The singer informs her daddy dear that his behavior recently has been amorously unsatisfactory and that if he doesn't come to see her every night and kiss her right upon each visit she will deprive him of her company altogether. She climaxes her admonition with the warning that she doesn't want the kind of man who works on the installment plan.

6. Runnin Wild—(By Joe Grey and Leo Wood and A. Harrington Gibbs). The singer confides he has quarreled with his gal, but that far from being consumed with grief over the matter and sitting home, he's going to show her who's wrong. He is, therefore, he continues, running wild and has lost control and is painting the town red and enjoying himself beyond anyone's conception. . . .

9. Louisville Lou (That Vampin' Lady)—(By Jack Yellen and Milton Ager). The singer, rehearsing the claims of the world's successful vampires, announces that Louisville Lou, who has a kiss as potent as the kick of a mule, is by all odds the outstanding Lorelei of her day. Miss Lou, the singer ecstatically confides, has charms which inspire delirium in all male beholders. As a final boast of the lady's incredible accomplishments, the singer hurls the warning that all men wishing to preserve their integrity had better keep far away from Louisville Lou. . . .

13. Lonesome Mama Blues—(By Welker Brown, E. Nickel and Billie Brown). The singer laments the mysterious departure of her man who, for no reason she can think of, has ridden off in a Pullman. As a result she is laid low with a malady known as the lonesome mama blues. In the midst of her sorrow, however, she feels that no matter how far he

may stray with other women he will never find another one so good and kind as herself. She, accordingly, supplicates God upon her knees to restore her lovin' man to her lonesome arms. . . .

15. He May Be Your Man (But He Comes to See Me Sometimes)—(By Lemuel Fowler). The singer relates the manner in which Miss Minnie Lee alienated the affections of Sadie Snow's affinity. The gentleman, despite Miss Snow's epic love for him, was unable to resist the oscillation of Miss Lee's shimmy. And to add insult to injury Miss Lee tauntingly reminds Miss Snow that the Lothario involved might legally be hers, but he paid frequent and surreptitious visits to the Lee menage. Further, Miss Lee gloatingly points out, the fellow is unable to put her out of his mind even while kissing her rival, Miss Snow. On top of all this, Miss Lee concludes with a threat that before she is through with the man she will have won him over entirely for her own purposes.

Rhyme of the Literary Don Juan

> I always was a well read chap,
>> But yet I found that brains
> And culture were a handicap
>> In copping out the Janes.
>
> I used to stand by full of woe
>> And watch the dames hurray
> For dumbbell Sheiks who didn't know
>> De Gourmont from Zane Grey.
>
> But now the little goose hangs high;
>> I've got the fillies sewed
> By merely learning to apply
>> The Literary Code.
>
> I've given up the stupid task
>> Of making love before;
> I simply come right out and ask,
>> "Oh, have you read George Moore?"
>
> And if the lady answers, "Nay,"
>> I send her from the shelf
> "The Story Teller's Holiday"
>> And call for it myself.
>
> I figure that a dame who reads

M. Huysmans and Ben Hecht
 Without more selling talk must needs
  Know just what to expect.

And if the cutie's head is turned
 By Sherwood Anderson
(At least so far as I'm concerned)
 She's practic'lly undone.

The competition may be close,
 But show me any Sheeb
Who can hold against a dose
 Of Nietzsche and vers libre.

Seduction is a waste of time;
 Just hand them culture's best—
Pierre Louys and Bodenheim.
 Let Nature do the rest.

And when the going's not so well
 Try Dreiser in a pinch,
And faithful Mr. James Cabell
 To bring them to a clinch.

Dear Father Francois Rabelais,
 God bless his merry soul.
Can help me knock most any day
 A filly for a goal.

Petronious and Ezra Pound,
 Doc Mencken and Tridon
Are excellent First Aids I've found
 One can rely upon.

I always was a well read chap,
 But it did me little good.
The culture that I had on tap
 Ne'er got me what it should.

Until one day it came to me
 To turn my learning loose
And try to put its properly
 Marked passages to use.

And now I know the ways of love,

My treasured books I find
Are low and vile procurers of
    The chaste and modest mind.

No filly ever fell for me,
    But since I changed my line—
Now once into my library
    And Gad! the gal is mine.

Tough Town

Chicago's newspapers altered in character in the years between the world wars. Hearst's efforts to establish a daily in Chicago shrank to unimportance. The morning *Tribune* and the evening *Daily News* largely divided the field between themselves until the appearance of Marshall Field III's *Sun* (later the *Sun-Times*) in 1941, but wit played only a small part in them. Depression, crime, war, scandal, and politics were the staples. The advent of Langston Hughes' "Simple" pieces in the Chicago *Defender* was the first sign of renewal in long years. They appeared in a weekly newspaper of national scope originated by Robert S. Abbott and characterized by vigorous social concern. Hughes' column reflected this state of affairs, but like his predecessors he was to make a good deal more of the material at hand than was customarily seen in it. The world of racial depression and social conflict was a hard place, and Hughes made his Simple an accurate reflector of it. However, he moved his writing strongly toward a tough-minded but tempered concern with human reality and interest that struck a note to be heard in other contemporary urban wit.

For the earliest Chicago humorists, the city and its life, as such, had often presented themselves as literary occasions, wit fulfilled in the language and literary form it found for clothing its subject. The heyday of Field, Ade, and Dunne was colored by the creation of imaginative worlds, the city somewhat transformed by language in an inclusive creative act. The earlier twentieth century betrayed difficulty in holding this synthesis together. The urban subject, as in Lardner, seemed alien to sympathetic shaping, and in turn, in the writing of others, wit sought more congenial quarters.

In Langston Hughes, as in Nelson Algren and Mike Royko, the urban subject has been restored to a primary place, but one requiring wit to take this subject on its own terms. All are "humorists," but their humor is often acerbic, often somewhat nonplussed. They are truth tellers. Wit in them becomes equipment for surviving in the contemporary city, which is hard-bitten and much-suffering at the same time. Mike Royko sees his character of Slats Grobnik, of the Division Street Polish community, as a being at once clown, victim, and slob, and the range of his column's tone seldom if ever slides away from the predominant drabs of the city's "neighborhoods." But that range equally seldom fails to show the color of life. If his subjects (what Royko in a book title called "Slats Grobnik and Some Other Friends") recall Lardner's dim view of the average man and his nature, the spirit of his work avoids Lardner's consequent air of superior distance. His tone more often suggests the irony than the comedy of existence.

Nelson Algren stands somewhat apart in that his identification is more clearly literary than journalistic. However, it is his work, in one of its currents at least, that has done much to form the mixture of comedy, grim realism, and irony that Hughes and Royko share. Like them, he sees the city as an incongruous blending of human resource and frustration, far as yet from recognizing or even knowing its own nature, and as anomalously directed in even its best efforts.

[James] Langston Hughes

Hughes (1902–1967) was born in Joplin, Missouri, and almost immediately began a peripatetic way of living that would continue for decades and include residence in cities and towns in New York, Ohio, Mexico, Kansas, Illinois, and Colorado before his settling more or less permanently in New York's Harlem district. He visited France, Italy, and Haiti as a young wanderer, graduated from Lincoln University in Pennsylvania, published three books of poems, a novel, a book of short stories, a volume of autobiography, and established three different theatrical groups (often concerned with the production of his own plays) before introducing his "Simple" stories into his column in the Chicago *Defender*, "Here and Yonder," in 1943. These accounts of the thoughts and doings of Jesse B. Semple were themselves to extend into five volumes that were interspersed with much other publication during the later decades of Hughes' life. Hughes' character, beginning as a witty observer of and commentator on a segregation-ridden America and referred to only as "my simple minded friend," speedily developed into a personage in his own right, and one with a name of his own to account for his unflattering nickname. Hughes himself was only incidentally a Chicagoan, but he was vividly aware of the complex tone of American Negro life in big cities, and Simple includes Chicago in his purview in addition to Harlem, his chief abode. Like Finley Peter Dunne before him, Hughes began with a real-life original for his character and proceeded to relate him to a particular locale and culture; and like the young George Ade he possessed a sharp eye for the particulars of the existence he surveyed. The result was a mingling of wit, realism, social criticism, and broad humor in a wholeness of temper that, in the *Defender* and later the New York *Post*, added a new and substantial chapter to American newspaper humor. Hughes published nine volumes of poetry which are sampled in *Selected Poems* (1959). The six volumes of Simple stories are similarly selected in *The Best of Simple* (1961). He was the author of two volumes of autobiography, *The Big Sea* (1940) and *I Wonder as I Wander* (1956), and with Arna Bontemps edited *The Poetry of the Negro, 1746–1949* (1949).

Feet Live Their Own Life

"If you want to know about my life," said Simple as he blew the foam from the top of the newly filled glass the bartender put before him, "don't look at my face, don't look at my hands. Look at my feet and see if you can tell how long I been standing on them."

"I cannot see your feet through your shoes," I said.

"You do not need to see through my shoes," said Simple. "Can't you tell by the shoes I wear—not pointed, not rocking-chair, not French-toed, not nothing but big, long, broad, and flat—that I been standing on these feet a long time and carrying some heavy burdens? They ain't flat from standing at no bar, neither, because I always sets at a bar. Can't you tell that? You know I do not hang out in a bar unless it has stools, don't you?"

"That I have observed," I said, "but I did not connect it with your past life."

"Everything I do is connected up with my past life," said Simple.

"From Virginia to Joyce, from my wife to Zarita, from my mother's milk to this glass of beer, everything is connected up."

"I trust you will connect up with that dollar I just loaned you when you get paid," I said. "And who is Virginia? You never told me about her."

"Virginia is where I was borned," said Simple. "I *would* be borned in a state named after a woman. From that day on, women never give me no peace."

"You, I fear, are boasting. If the women were running after you as much as you run after them, you would not be able to sit here on this bar stool in peace. I don't see any women coming to call you out to go home, as some of these fellows' wives do around here."

"Joyce better not come in no bar looking for me," said Simple. "That is why me and my wife busted up—one reason. I do not like to be called out of no bar by a female. It's a man's perogative to just set and drink sometimes."

"How do you connect that prerogative with your past?" I asked.

"When I was a wee small child," said Simple, "I had no place to set and think in, being as how I was raised up with three brothers, two sisters, seven cousins, one married aunt, a common-law uncle, and the minister's grandchild—and the house only had four rooms. I never had no place just to set and think. Neither to set and drink—not even much my milk before some hongry child snatched it out of my hand. I were not the youngest, neither a girl, nor the cutest. I don't know why, but I don't think nobody liked me much. Which is why I was afraid to like anybody for a long time myself. When I did like somebody, I was full-grown and then I picked out the wrong woman because I had no practice in liking anybody before that. We did not get along."

"Is that when you took to drink?"

"Drink took to me," said Simple. "Whiskey just naturally likes me but beer likes me better. By the time I got married I had got to the point where a cold bottle was almost as good as a warm bed, especially when the bottle could not talk and the bed-warmer could. I do not like a woman to talk to me too much—I mean about me. Which is why I like Joyce. Joyce most in generally talks about herself."

"I am still looking at your feet," I said, "and I swear they do not reveal your life to me. Your feet are no open book."

"You have eyes but you see not," said Simple. "These feet have stood on every rock from the Rock of Ages to 135th and Lenox. These feet have supported everything from a cotton bale to a hongry woman. These feet have walked ten thousand miles working for white folks and another ten thousand keeping up with colored. These feet have stood at altars, crap tables, free lunches, bars, graves, kitchen doors, betting windows, hospital clinics, WPA desks, social security railings, and in all kinds of lines from soup lines to the draft. If I just had four feet, I could have stood in more places longer. As it is, I done wore out seven hundred pairs of shoes, eighty-nine tennis shoes, twelve summer sandals, also six loafers. The socks that these feet have bought could build a knitting mill. The corns I've cut away would dull a German razor. The bunions I forgot would make you ache from now till Judgment Day. If anybody was to write the history of my life, they should start with my feet."

"Your feet are not all that extraordinary," I said. "Besides, everything you are saying is general. Tell me specifically some one thing your feet have done that makes them different from any other feet in the world, just one."

"Do you see that window in that white man's store across the street?" asked Simple. "Well, this right foot of mine broke out that window in the Harlem riots right smack in the middle. Didn't no other foot in the world break that window but mine. And this left foot carried me off running as soon as my right foot came down. Nobody else's feet saved me from the cops that night but these *two* feet right here. Don't tell me these feet ain't had a life of their own."

"For shame," I said, "going around kicking out windows. Why?"

"Why?" said Simple. "You have to ask my great-great-grandpa why. He must of been simple—else why did he let them capture him in Africa and sell him for a slave to breed my great-grandpa in slavery to breed my grandpa in slavery to breed my pa to breed me to look at that window and say, 'It ain't mine! Bam-mmm-mm-m!' and kick it out?"

"This bar glass is not yours either," I said. "Why don't you smash it?"

"It's got my beer in it," said Simple.

Just then Zarita came in wearing her Thursday-night rabbitskin coat. She didn't stop at the bar, being dressed up, but went straight back to a booth. Simple's hand went up, his beer went down, and the glass back to its wet spot on the bar.

"Excuse me a minute," he said, sliding off the stool.

Just to give him pause, the dozens, that old verbal game of maligning a friend's female relatives, came to mind.

"Wait," I said. "You have told me about what to ask your great-great-grandpa. But I want to know what to ask your great-great-grand*ma*."

"I don't play the dozens that far back," said Simple, following Zarita into the smoky juke-box blue of the back room.

In the Dark

"What you know, daddy-o?" hailed Simple.

"Where have you been so long lately?" I demanded.

"Chicago on my last two War Bonds," answered Simple, "to see my Cousin Art's new baby to which I am godfather—against his wife's will, because she is holy and sanctified."

"What is the trend of affairs in Chicago?" I inquired.

"Balling and brawling," said Simple. "And me with 'em."

"Did you take in the DeLisa?"

"No, I did not take in the DeLisa," said Simple, "but I went to the Brass Rail, also Square's, also that club on 63rd and South Park which jumps out loud. Also the Blue Dahlia."

"You got around, then."

"Sure did! I went to a couple of them new cocktail lounges, too, what don't have no light in 'em at all hardly. Chicago has the darkest bars in the world. So dark it is just like walking into a movie. Man, you have to stop and pause till you can see the bar. The booths are like Lovers' Lane, man. I thought my eyesight was failing the first time I went in one. Everything's the same color under them lightless lights. Ain't no telling whiskey from gin with the natural eye."

"You were probably intoxicated," I said.

"I was expecting to get high," said Simple, "but I did not succeed. The glass was thick that night and the whiskey thin. But I met a old chick who looked *fine* setting there in the dark, although I couldn't of seen her had she not had on a white hat. I asked her what her name was and she told me Bea.

"'But don't get me wrong, King Kong, because I told you my name,' she said, 'I am a lady! My mama calls me Bea-Baby at home.'

"I said, 'What does your daddy call you?'

"She said, 'I has no daddy.'

"I said, 'You must be looking for *me* then.'

"She said, 'I *heard* you before I saw you so I could not have been *looking* for you. You abstract attention to yourself. But since you asked me, I drink Scotch.'

"So I ordered her some Teacher's. But that girl was thirsty! She drunk me up—at Sixty-Five Cents a shot! I said, 'Bea-Baby, let's get some air.'

"She said, 'Air? I growed up in air! I got plenty of air when I were a child. Sixteen miles south of Selma there weren't nothing but air.'

" 'Selma is far enough South, but *sixteen miles south of there* is too much! How long you been up North, girl?'

" 'Two years,' she said, 'and if I live to be a hundred, I will be up here seventy-five more.'

" 'You mean you are not going back to Selma?'

" 'Period,' she said.

" 'In other words, you are going to stay in Chicago?'

" 'Oh, but I am,' she said.

" 'Well, we are not going to stay in this bar seventy-five years,' I whispered. 'Come on, Bea-Baby, let's walk.'

" 'Walk where?' she hollered, insulted.

" 'Follow me and you will see,' I said.

" 'I will not follow you, unless you tell me where we are going.'

" 'I will not tell you where we are going, unless you follow,' I said.

"But when we got out of that darker-than-a-movie bar, under the street lights on Indiana Avenue, I got a good look at her and she got a good look at me. We *both* said 'Good-by!' In that dim dark old dusky cocktail lounge, I thought she was mellow. But she were not! I thought she was a chippy, but she were at least forty-five.

"And the first thing she said when she saw my face was, 'I thought you was a *young* man—but you ain't. You old as my Uncle Herman.'

"I said, 'I done had so many unpleasant surprises in my life, baby, until my age is writ in my face. *You* is one more unpleasantness.'

"I thought she said 'Farewell,' but it could of been 'Go to hell.'

"Anyhow, she cured me of them dark Chicago bars. *Never make friends in the dark*, is what I learned in Chicago."

"I am glad you learned something," I said.

"Thank you," said Simple. "Now, come on let's have a beer to welcome me back to Harlem. Not to change the subject, but lend me a quarter. I'm broke."

"I'm broke, too."

"Then you can't have a beer, daddy-o," regretted Simple. "What is worse, neither can I."

Nelson Algren

Algren (1909–1981), originally named Nelson Ahlgren Abraham, was born in Detroit, but his family soon moved to Chicago, where he grew up. He graduated from the University of Illinois in journalism in 1931 and launched into the depression years on an extended migratory jaunt that was reflected in two of his novels and numbers of the short stories he began publishing in 1933. By the middle thirties he was re-settled in Chicago and steadily at work as a writer except for military service abroad in the Second World War. His novel, *The Man with the Golden Arm*, won the first National Book Award and was made into a successful movie, though one the author himself had small use for. His long prose poem, *Chicago, a City on the Make*, first appeared in 1951 and pictured the city as a tired strumpet sought for and fought over by the "promoters" who wanted her for their own purposes, the "do-gooders" who wanted to reform her, and the "poets" who alone re-sponded to and cherished her real nature.

This mixed sense of local reality, one reflected from the start in Al-gren's fiction, has influenced later Chicago writers. In particular, Algren, Mike Royko, and Studs Terkel have recognized one another in dedications and credit lines in their various publications and, without constituting any sort of "school," reflect a common and contemporary urban awareness. Algren published nearly a dozen books of fiction, nonfiction, and poetry, most notably the novels, *Never Come Morning* (1942) and *The Man with the Golden Arm* (1949). His short stories are sampled in *The Neon Wilderness* (1947), and he speaks at length about himself and his writing in *Conversations with Nelson Algren*, edited by H. E. Donahue.

How the Devil Came Down Division Street

Last Saturday evening there was a great argument in the Polonia Bar. All the biggest drunks on Division[1] were there, trying to decide who

---

1. Division Street was a main artery of the North Side Polish community.

the biggest drunk of them was. Symanski said he was, and Oljiec said he was, and Koncel said he was, and Czechowski said he was.

Then Roman Orlov came in and the argument was decided. For Poor Roman has been drunk so long, night and day, that when we remember living men we almost forget Poor Roman, as though he were no longer really among the living at all.

"The devil lives in a double-shot," Roman explains himself obscurely. "I got a great worm inside. Gnaws and gnaws. Every day I drown him and every day he gnaws. Help me drown the worm, fellas."

So I bought Poor Roman a double-shot and asked him frankly how, before he was thirty, he had become the biggest drunk on Division.

It took a long time, and many double-shots, for him to tell. But tell it he did, between curses and sobs, and I tell it now as closely to what he told as I can. Without the sobs, of course. And of course without any cursing.

When Roman was thirteen, it seems, the Orlovs moved into three stove-heated rooms in the rear of a lopsided tenement on Noble Street. Mama O. cooked in a Division Street restaurant by day and cooked in her own home by night.

Papa O. played an accordion for pennies in Division Street taverns by night and slept alone in the rooms by day.

There were only two beds in the tiny flat, so nobody encouraged Papa O. to come home at all.

Because he was the oldest, Roman slept between the twins, on the bed set up in the front room, to keep the pair from fighting during the night as they did during the day. Every day Teresa, who was eleven and could not learn her lessons as well as some of her classmates, slept with Mama O. in the windowless back bedroom, under a bleeding heart in a gilded oval frame.

If Papa O. got in before light, as happened occasionally early in the week, he crawled uncomplainingly under Roman's bed until Roman rose and got the twins, who were seven, up with him in time for Mass.

If Udo, who was something between a collie and a St. Bernard and as big as both together, was already curled up beneath the front-room bed, Papa O. slugged him with the accordion in friendly reproach— and went on into the back bedroom to crawl under Mama O.'s bed. In such an event he slept under a bed all day. For he never crawled, even with daylight, into Mama O.'s bed. Empty or not. As though he did not feel himself worthy to sleep there even when she was gone.

It was as though, having given himself all night to his accordion, he must remain true to it during the day.

For all manner of strange things went on in Papa O.'s head, as even the twins had become aware. Things so strange that Teresa was made ashamed of them by her schoolmates, whenever they wanted someone to tease.

This, too, was why no one, not even the twins, paid Papa O. any heed when the family returned from Mass one Sunday forenoon and he told them someone had been knocking while they were away.

"Some*body* was by door," he insisted. "I say 'Hallo.' Was no*body*." He looked slyly about him at the children. "Who plays tricks by Papa?"

"Maybe was Zolewitzes," Mama O. suggested indifferently. "Mama Z. comes perhaps to borrow."

That Sunday night it was cold in all the corners. Papa O. was gone to play for pennies and drinks, Mama O. was frying *pierogi*, the twins were in bed, and Teresa was studying her catechism across the table from Roman, when someone knocked lightly twice.

To Roman it sounded like someone at the clothes-closet door; but that was foolish to think, since the twins were in bed. Yet, when he opened the hall door, only a cold wind came into the room from the long gaslit passage.

Roman, being only thirteen, did not dare look behind the door. Far less to speak of the clothes closet.

All that night a light snow fell, while Roman O. lay wakeful, fancying he saw it falling on darkened streets all over the mysterious earth, on the pointing roof tops of old-world cities, on mountain-high waves of the mid-Atlantic, and in the leaning eaves of Noble Street. He was just falling off to sleep when the knocking came again. Three times, like a measured warning.

The boy stiffened under the covers, listening with his fear. Heard the hall door squeak softly, as though Papa O. were sneaking in. But Papa O. never knocked, and Papa O. never sneaked. Papa O. came home with the accordion banging against buildings all down Noble Street, jingling his pennies proudly, singing off-key bravely, mumbling and laughing and stumbling. Papa O. never knocked. He kicked the door in happily and shouted cheerfully, "What you say, all peoples? How's t'ings, ever-body?" Papa O. pulled people out of bed and rattled pans and laughed at nothing and argued with unseen bartenders until somebody gave him sausage and eggs and coffee and bread and hung the accordion safely away.

Roman crept, barefooted, in the long underwear Mama O. had sewed on him in the early fall, to the hallway door.

The whole house slept. The windows were frosted and a thin line of ice had edged up under the front window and along the pane. The family slept. Roman shoved the door open gently. The tenement slept. Down the hall the single jet flickered feebly. No one. Nothing. The people slept.

Roman looked behind the door, shivering now with more than cold.

No one. Nothing. All night long.

He returned to bed and prayed quietly, until he heard Mama O. rise; waited till he knew she had the fire going in the big kitchen stove. Then, dressing with his back to the heat, he told Mama O. what he had heard. Mama O. said nothing.

Two mornings later, Papa O. came home without the accordion. It did not matter then to Mama O. whether he had sold it or lost it or loaned it; she knew it at last for a sign, she had felt the change coming, she said, in her blood. For she had dreamed a dream, all night, of a stranger waiting in the hall: a young man, drunken, leaning against the gaslit wall for support, with blood down the front of his shirt and drying on his hands. She knew, as all the Orlovs knew, that the unhappy dead return to warn or comfort, to plead or repent, to gain peace or to avenge.

That day, standing over steaming kettles, Mama O. went back in her mind to all those dear to her of earth who had died: the cousin drowned at sea, the brother returned from the war to die, the mother and father gone from their fields before she had married.

That night she knocked on Mama Zolewitz's door. Mama Z. sat silently, as though she had been expecting Mama O. for many evenings.

"Landlord doesn't like we should tell new tenants too soon," Mama Z. explained even before being told of the knocking, "so you shouldn't say it, I told. It was a young man lived in this place, in your very rooms. A strong young man, and good to look at. But sick, sick in the head from the drink. A sinner certainly. For here he lived with his lady without being wed, and she worked and he did not. That he did not work had little to do with what happened, and the drink had little to do. For it was being unwed that brought it on, at night, on the New Year. He returned from the taverns that night and beat her till her screams were a whimpering. Till her whimpering became nothing. A strong young man, like a bull, made violent by the drink. When the whimpering ceased, there was no sound at all. No sound until noon, when the police came with shouting.

"What was there to shout about? I could have told them before they came. The young man had hanged himself in the bedroom closet. Thus it is that one sin leads to another, and both were buried together. In unsanctified ground, with no priest near."

Mama O. grew pale. Her very clothes closet.

"It is nothing to worry," Mama Z. told her neighbor sagely. "He does not knock to do harm. He comes only to gain a little peace that good Christian prayer for him may give. Pray for the young man, Mama O. He wishes peace."

That night after supper the Orlovs gathered in prayer about the front-room stove, and Papa O. prayed also. For now that the accordion was gone, the taverns must do without him. When the prayer was done, he went to bed with Mama O. like a good husband, and the knocking did not come again.

Each night the Orlovs prayed for the poor young man. And each night Papa O. went to bed with Mama O. for lack of his accordion.

Mama O. knew then that the knocking had been a sign of good omen, and told the priest, and the priest blessed her for a Christian. He said it was the will of God that the Orlovs should redeem the young man by prayer and that Papa O. should have a wife instead of an accordion.

Papa O. stayed at home until, for lack of music, he became the best janitor on Noble Street. Mama Z. went to the priest and told of her part in the miracle of the poor young man, and the priest blessed Mama Z. also.

When the landlord learned that his house was no longer haunted he brought the Orlovs gifts; and when the rent was late he said nothing. So the priest blessed him equally, and in time the Orlovs paid no rent at all, but prayed for the landlord instead.

Teresa became the most important person in her class, for it became known that a miracle had been done in the Orlov home. Sister Mary Ursula said the child looked more like a little saint every day. And no other child in the room ever had her lessons as well as Teresa thereafter.

The twins sensed the miracle and grew up to be fast friends, doing all things together, even to wearing the same clothes and reading the same catechism. Udo, too, knew that the home was blessed. For he received no more blows from the accordion.

Only one sad aspect shadowed this great and happy change: Poor Roman was left bedless. For with Papa O. home every night like a good husband, Teresa must sleep between the twins.

Thus it came about that the nights of Roman Orlov became fitful and restless, first under the front-room bed and then under the back-room bed. With the springs overhead squeaking half the night as likely as not. The nights of Roman's boyhood were thereafter passed beneath one bed or the other, with no bed of his own at all. Until, attaining his young manhood and his seventeenth year, he took at last to sleeping during the day in order to have no need for sleep at night.

And at night, as everyone knows, there is no place to go but the taverns.

So it was, being abroad with no place to go and the whole night to kill, that Roman took his father's place. He had no accordion for excuse—only lack of a bed. He came to think of the dawn, when the taverns closed and he must go home, as the bitterest hour of the day.

This is why he still calls the dawn the bitterest hour: he must go home though he has no home.

Is this a drunkard's tale or sober truth? I can only say he told it like the truth, drinking double-shots all the while. I only know that no one argues about who the biggest drunk on Division is if Roman O. is around.

I only know what Mama O. now tells, after many years and Papa O. in his grave and the twins scattered: that the young man who knocked was in truth the devil. For did she not give him, without knowing what she did, a good son in return for a worthless husband?

"I'm drownin' the worm t'night," Poor Roman explains, talking to his double-shot. "Help me drown the worm t'night, fellas."

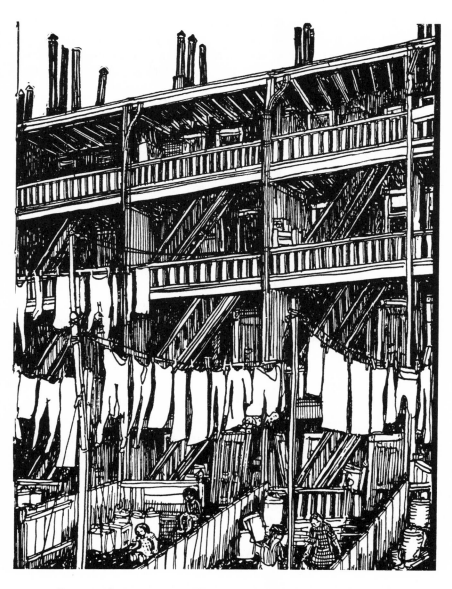

From an illustration by Herman Rosse for Ben Hecht's *1001 Afternoons in Chicago*.

Does the devil live in a double-shot? Is he the one who gnaws, all night, within?

Or is he the one who knocks, on winter nights, with blood drying on his knuckles, in the gaslit passages of our dreams?

Mike Royko

Royko was born in 1932; his growing up involved the closest kind of scraping through Chicago's neon wilderness, including intermittent schooling, arrests, and an embattled period at Montefiore High School, a depository for North Side toughs. At the same time it led to an early interest in writing and its practice, to close familiarity with a city where his father operated a tavern and his mother a small tailoring business, to study at Wright Junior College, to service in the Air Force (where he had his first experience with journalism), and, in 1954, to work on North Side neighborhood newspapers. In 1956 he joined the City News Bureau, first as reporter then as assistant editor, and in 1959 he became a reporter for the *Daily News*. He emerged there as columnist in 1963, continuing until the *News*'s termination in 1978. Since that time he has been a featured writer for the Chicago *Sun-Times* and its syndicated wire service.

His work is an unpredictable mixture of the tough and the sympathetic, with a constant resource in its hard-fibered, cogent style. He chiefly concentrates on the warp and woof of Chicago living, viewing it at close range—an observer mostly inured to its roughness but aware of an intricate life in it easily lost in the daily encounter. His line of perception and his attitude toward direct experience with Chicago's ordinary lives he shares, in part, with Nelson Algren. Irony is a staple of his wit. Sometimes it is directed at the meannesses, the all-too-common commonness of the city dweller of high or low place; often it points to the power and authority of a city government that cannot do without wholesale jobbery as its prime source of political strength; sometimes it considers the more general pretensions of hypocrisy, or status, or power, and sometimes the fazed self-recognition that life creates for the writer himself. Royko can be arrogant and impatient. He trades in shock, but shock for the sake of perception. He is a dealer in what is, and he has become a power in Chicago journalism.

Out of it all there stems an original and major voice, one wanting the city taken on its own terms, knowing those terms to be hard ones. He has published a major study of one of Chicago's most compelling citizens in his *Boss*, an account of Richard J. Daley and his mayoralty. The book is an unsparing revelation of power politics, but it also comprehends the kind of governing personality shaped by a world that could hardly be governed by a gentler individual. Royko is a writer and wit in a sharp, even classic, mode, whose subject is necessarily that of a hustling, turbulent, and often irrational reality. Selections from his columns, written for the most part as a daily feature, appear in *Up Against It* (1967), *I May Be Wrong But I Doubt It* (1968), and *Slats Grobnik and Some Other Friends* (1973).

When Slats Caught Santa

Those of us who grew up in a big city can sometimes feel we missed out on the typical American Christmas.

The schoolbooks always showed it in a setting where people got syrup from maple trees, took sleigh rides, cut their own Christmas tree in the forest and cooked in big farm kitchens.

Yet, you never read the reminiscences of somebody like my friend Slats Grobnik. The scene of his childhood—a second-floor flat above a tavern with the L tracks in back—is never shown on postcards.

But Slats has warm memories.

The Grobniks never cut down their own Christmas tree. They got theirs from Leo the mover, who sold trees in an empty lot next to his moving store.

Buying a tree from Leo took more skill, really, than chopping one down in the forest, because Leo was an early pioneer in creating artificial trees. But you never knew when you got one.

Leo used to spend half of his time in his garage, drilling holes in the trunks of scrawny trees, and gluing branches in to fill out the bare spots.

He'd hold up a tree, away from the glow of the street light, and say:

"Look'dis beauty. The trunk's straight as broomstick."

"It ought to be," Mr. Grobnik would say, "since the trunk happens to be a broomstick, you no-good thief."

The Grobniks never went for a sleigh ride, although Mr. Grobnik rode in a few paddy wagons, but they had a family tradition that was something like a sleigh ride.

Every Christmas eve in the middle of the afternoon, Mrs. Grobnik would bundle up Slats and his brother Fats, and they would ride a streetcar to the plant where Mr. Grobnik worked.

When he came out they would greet him and the whole family would ride home together on the streetcar.

It was partly sentiment, but it was mostly a way of making sure Mr. Grobnik didn't stop and blow his Christmas check on Division St.

In the evening, Slats and his brother would hang their stockings. The first year Slats was old enough to do this, he looked at the oil stove in the parlor and said:

"I heard on the radio where you are supposed to hang your stocking by the fireplace. How come we ain't got a fireplace, pa?"

Slats' father explained that if they had a fireplace, and if somebody as fat as Santa could come down through it, any two-bit burglar in the neighborhood could do the same, and that's why they didn't have one.

"How's he going to get in then?" Slats asked.

"We'll leave the kitchen door unlatched," said Mrs. Grobnik, "like we do when your father goes on Division St."

Slats pointed out that Bruno, their red-eyed, black-tongued dog, would probably bite Santa, because Bruno liked to bite everybody, even the Grobniks.

Mr. Grobnik sat Slats on his knee and told how reindeer would hold Bruno at bay until Santa got the stockings stuffed. "Reindeers got horns sharp as razors," Mr. Grobnik said, "and Bruno's no fool."

Satisfied, Slats and his brother Fats would hang their stockings by the oven on the kitchen stove, the closest thing they had to a fireplace, and get into bed.

Actually, Slats used one of his father's size 16 work stockings. He later explained. "I figured a guy who had to make that many stops in one night wouldn't have time to measure nobody's feet."

And in the morning, the stockings would be loaded to the brim, and by the time they sat down to Christmas dinner, so was Mr. Grobnik.

Like all kids, Slats had to find out one day that there was no Santa. He still remembers.

He was awakened during the night by the sound of somebody moving about in the kitchen.

Slats crept from his bed, hoping at last to catch a glimpse of Santa.

But there, by the kitchen stove, stood his father in his long underwear, his arms loaded with gifts.

Slats bounded through the kitchen into his parents' bedroom, howling:

"Ma, get up quick—pa's filching every damn present Santa left for us!"

So that's when his parents decided—when Slats picked up the phone and started yelling for the cops—that he ought to know the truth.

Ma's Quiet Tax Revolt

Every April 15, when taxes are due, I think of my mother.

That probably sounds strange because most people think of their mothers at such times as Mother's Day or Christmas.

I do that, too. But also on April 15 because long before anyone mentioned a "tax revolt," my mother waged one.

She did it quietly, and nobody but her children knew about it, but she did it.

For about 20 years, while earning a taxable income running her own small business, she didn't pay a nickel of income tax.

She didn't use loopholes. She wouldn't have understood them.

Ma just didn't bother to file a return all those years. She simply ignored the existence of the Internal Revenue Service.

I know that sounds like outright tax evasion, rather than a tax revolt, but the distinction has to do with motive.

If a well-to-do person doesn't pay because he wants two Cadillacs instead of one, that would be evasion.

But if there just isn't enough for both you and the government, that amounts to self-defense.

As my mother explained it:

"I need it more than the government does. Besides, they'd probably waste it anyway."

You couldn't argue with that. During many of those years, she supported her family in her tiny tailor shop, sitting at a sewing machine 12 hours a day, six days a week. And that brought in just enough to get by.

If she paid taxes, she would have had to work 14 hours a day. Enough is enough, Congressmen don't work that hard, except when they are weaving new tax loopholes for the rich.

And none of the money was wasted. It was spent on the ingredients for large pots of soup, oil for the stove in the parlor, and repairs on the old Singer sewing machine. But if the government got it, it would just design another military transport plane that can't fly.

As to the possibility that she would be caught and prosecuted, since it was a criminal offense, she said:

"I'll tell them to put me in prison. If they won't let me support myself, then they can support me."

But she wasn't caught, and now it is too late, so I can admit that Ma got away with a pretty good one.

And why not? We are told of millionaires who pay no income tax, thanks to loopholes created for them by Congress.

J. Paul Getty, one of the world's richest men, is said to pay only $5,000 or so on an annual income of more than $50 million.

If true, Getty pays only one-tenth of one-tenth of one-tenth of one-tenth of his income. My mother would have gladly paid under those terms. It would have amounted to about 30 cents.

The laws are so crafty that if a rich heiress puts $1 million into municipal bonds, she gets back about $50,000 a year—tax free.

But if a scrub lady sweats to save $1,000 and puts it into a savings and loan, she gets back about $50 a year—and has to share the $50 with the federal government.

The loopholes are for the rich. For the ordinary person, the loophole turns into a noose.

Despite this, we hear Treasury Sec. John Connally saying of tax reform: "It leaves me cold." Then he launches a widely publicized crackdown on the storefront tax preparers. You bet, because they are cheating for the hand-to-mouth crowd. But there's no crackdown on millionaires.

We hear the Vice-President carp about a welfare mother chiseling an extra dollar or two, but he doesn't say a word about the big real estate write-offs, oil depletion, and those who pay only one-tenth of one-tenth of one-tenth of one-tenth.

If the tax laws are reformed, it will amount to merely throwing a few crumbs in the direction of the ordinary worker. The cake will remain right where it is.

What this country needs, for genuine reform, are a few million people who had my mother's attitude.

It is a foolish dream, of course, but let us imagine for a moment that a few million hard-pressed people said: "Sorry, there's not enough for both of us, so put me in jail."

The computers would catch them. But where would they find enough judges and prosecutors to try them?

And where would they find a jury of their peers to convict them? You would need a jury composed of J. Paul Gettys to find guilty a man who said:

"Sure, I didn't pay taxes. I have to work two jobs to barely support my family. Go get it from H. L. Hunt."

If that happened on a big scale, we would have tax reform, and we'd have it faster than you can say IT&T.

But it won't happen, because few of us have enough courage. I got my check in on time, and I probably paid more than old man Getty. Ma would be ashamed of me.

San-Fran-York on the Lake

It has finally happened, damn it.

A decent, potbellied working man's city is now wearing a turtleneck sweater, long sideburns and a suave look on its face.

And its nose is stuck in a brandy snifter.

The economists and sociologists can explain why it happened. All I know is that it has.

The merchants tell it as well as anyone, with their accounts of the past Christmas season.

Leon Carteaux, Loop jeweler: "It's been different this year. Those who used to shop for costume jewelry wanted something in good gold; those who weren't accustomed to quality were asking to see the better items."

Frank Armanetti, liquors: "They're buying better quality in everything, not worrying about saving 50 or 75 cents on a bottle. We're running short, especially in fine wines."

Dick Innocenti, camera dealer: "Our low-priced cameras didn't sell well. The top of the line sold."

Shelby Young, Allied Radio: "There's been a move toward quality products, more expensive products, on every level of sound equipment."

Siegfried Shattil, art dealer: "This December was the best month we've ever had."

That's the story everywhere. The most expensive pipes, ski equipment, home pool tables, fur rugs, wine racks, men's casual clothing, women's casual clothing and anything else you don't really need. That's what sold.

A town that used to think that six cylinders and a stick shift belonged to a thinking man has put on an imported Irish wool cap and is zipping around in a pseudo-sports car.

It's wearing a razor-cut hair style for six dollars and is gobbling up French food faster than the restaurants can overprice it.

Chicago Man has become a dandy right out of the ads. Not long ago, the only distinctive look a Bear fan had was his booze-blurred eyes at the end of the game. Today he dresses out of Abercrombie and Fitch.

Chicago Man might have a well-trimmed beard. He won't drink plain water unless it's on the rocks. Everybody looks like George Hamilton or Norman Ross.

Chicago Woman defies description, with her thighs stylishly bared to 30 mph arctic winds while her torso is wrapped in an artificial Abominable Snowman fur coat.

And it's not just the individual. It's the mood of the city right up (or down, if you prefer) to City Hall. Luxury items have priority over the bread-and-butter projects. Did we really need that $86,000,000 Civic Center more than a few other things?

The city can't get real estate developers even to think about low-cost housing. They want to build top-rent high-rises with carpeting on the balconies and an indoor parking space for every man.

Gracious and stylish living, that's what has Chicago in its grasp. I don't know if my daddy can whip your daddy, but he has a home wine cellar. And my mommy has joined a health club.

It is not a paint-flecked-pants town anymore. The city of the three-flat with flowered wallpaper and linoleum in the parlor, the lunch pail, the shot-and-beer and count-your-change, has become something else: San-Fran-York on the Lake.

Tomorrow is Carl Sandburg's birthday. You remember him. He was named after a high-rise development.[2]

He's dead but he got out of town long before it went to hell in a martini mixer. To observe his birthday, I'm updating his 1916 poem, "Chicago." You know, the one about "Hog Butcher for the World . . . Stormy, husky, brawling . . . City of the Big Shoulders."

Chicago

Hi-Rise for the World
Partygoer, Stacker of Stereo Tapes,
Player with Home Pool Table and the Nation's Jets;
Dapper, slender, filter-tipped,
City of the Big Credit Card:
They tell me you are wicked, and I don't believe them; for
I have seen your painted men tossed in jail every time
they try luring the farm boys.
And they tell me you are crooked, and I answer: Yes,
it is true, but now you steal with the ballpoint pen
and contract, and that's no fun.
And having answered so I turn once more to those who
sneer at this my city, and I join in the sneer and
say to them:
Come and show me another city with razor-cut head
singing so proud to have a Mustang and a white
turtleneck and reservations for dinner.
Fierce as a poodle with tongue lapping for dog yummies.
Wig-headed,
Skiing,
Spending,
Twisting,
Tipping,
Purchasing, discarding, repurchasing,
Under the big restaurant canopy, burgundy sauce

2. Carl Sandburg Village, a complex of skyscraper apartments and town houses, is a feature of the city's rebuilt Near North Side.

282 *Chicago's Public Wits*

all over his mouth, giggling with white capped teeth.
Under the terrible burden of Consolidated Monthly
Payments, giggling as a disk jockey giggles,
Chuckling even as a smooth salesman chuckles who
has never lost a sale,
Bragging and chuckling that on his wrist is a
battery-operated watch and under his ribs a moroccan
leather belt.
Giggling!
Giggling the silly giggle of the fourth martini
at lunch: half naked, but not sweating, and if
sweating, not offending; Proud to be Hi-Rise
for the World, Partygoer, Stacker of Stereo Tapes,
Player with Home Pool Tables and Jet Handler to the
Nation.

Alinsky Not in Their League

The City Council paid a great tribute to the late Saul Alinsky a few days ago. It refused to name a city park after him.

An independent alderman had suggested that one of the many un-named little parks in Chicago be called Alinsky Park and equipped with a soapbox because of Alinsky's devotion to free speech.

The other aldermen, who also believe in free speech, except when the mayor tells them to shut up, didn't like the idea.

Alinsky would have been pleased. Their reaction meant they are still aching from the many kicks he gave them. It meant they remember who formed the toughest, most effective community organizations in Chicago. Alinsky's most recent creation—the Citizens Action Program (CAP)—gave Assessor Parky Cullerton heartburn, and now it is leading the fight against the Crosstown Expressway.

The aldermen's reaction got me to wondering who our many parks and playgrounds are named after, besides Presidents such as Lincoln, Grant, Washington, and Jackson.

Once you get past the world-famous names, the locally prominent Indians, and some of the city's early settlers and businessmen, you find that our politicians are fond of honoring the people they like best—themselves.

On the near West Side, for instance, you have the Sain Playground and the Touhy Playground.

For years, Ald. Harry Sain and County Comr. John Touhy ran the 27th Ward, and they ran it well. On election day they made sure that every bum on W. Madison St. voted, at least once.

They also prospered as insurance men. Businessmen in the ward were eager to place their insurance with the Touhy and Sain Agency. If they didn't, they might need insurance.

Then there is Connors Park, on the Near North Side, named after the late State Sen. William (Botchy) Connors.

One of Connors' admirers said of him: "Botchy was the kind of guy who would give you the shirt off his back. Of course, then he'd take the suit, pants, and shoes off you."

On the South Side, there is the Meyering Playground, named after a former alderman and sheriff, William Meyering.

Meyering was the guardian of Cook County's law and order in the days when Al Capone was our most famous citizen.

Roger Touhy, the gangster, once provided this thumbnail description of Sheriff Meyering, while testifying in federal court.

"A fixer," Touhy said.

The South Side also has a Micek Playground, named after the late Frankie Micek, who was a ward sanitation-office superintendent for 21 years, before rising to alderman.

When he passed away, Ald. Micek was eulogized by Mayor Daley as having been a "dedicated and devoted servant of the people." Later, one of his fellow aldermen added the lofty praise: "Frankie always did what he was told."

McGuane Park, in the Mayor's neighborhood, is named after Mr. Daley's old friend and political crony, John McGuane.

McGuane was a park commissioner and, for a brief time, he was the assessor. He never got in trouble as assessor, and he was replaced by Parky Cullerton, who wasn't as lucky.

On the West Side, we have the Horan Playground, named after the late Al Horan, a noted politician.

Mr. Horan was boss of all the Municipal Court bailiffs, and he was known for never having hired anyone who had committed an infamous deed, such as failing to deliver a precinct or being a Republican.

There is a Pietrowski Playground, on the far South Side, named after County Comr. Lillian (Shoutin' Lil) Pietrowski. Miss Pietrowski is known for her shouting.

Then we have Gately Park and Gately Stadium on the far South Side. These were named after a former president of the Park Board. Park commissioners like to name parks after themselves.

Although James Gately was in charge of the parks, he had a fondness for concrete, as do many Chicago political figures. And he once made the remarkable observation that:

"You can have too much grass."

To which the city's high-rise dwellers, parking-lot operators, and bit contractors said: "Amen." After all, grass isn't the only thing that's green.

Dent Leads to a Wipe-Out

The stoop-shouldered man and his wife came out of the restaurant and walked to their car in the parking lot. He unlocked her door, went around to get in on his side, stopped, and stared at his car.

In the door was a dent. It wasn't a big dent, but it was enough so he saw it immediately.

"Goddamn it," he hissed.

His car was new. It was in the $4,500-to-$5,000 bracket. The paint glowed with Blue Coral wax.

He shook his head and muttered. His wife finally leaned across the seat and asked what was wrong.

"Come on and look," he said.

She got out and shook her head.

"This jerk did it," he said, pointing to the big, black car next to his.

"How do you know?" she said.

"This spot was empty when we got here. He's got to be inside eating. This goof did it all right."

To demonstrate, he used his arm to duplicate the way the other car's door would have swung open.

"See?" he said. "If he opened the door hard, and didn't pay any attention, it would hit right . . . HERE!" He swung his arm so his hand touched the dent.

He stood with his hands on his hips, a Bogart-like grimace on his face, staring at the dent. In his eyes, it got bigger and deeper. He could almost see the rust spreading.

"Damn it," he said, running his hand over the dent, the only imperfection in the sleek metal.

The car meant something to him, silly as that can be. It was the only new car he had ever liked, and one of the few he had ever owned. Not only was it new, but it was an imported, foreign job, known for its road-racing handling, classic lines, craftsmanship, glamour.

It was the kind of car he had wanted as a young man, but couldn't afford. Now it was a balding man's toy. But it had a dent in it.

If the dent had come while roaring around an Alpine hairpin turn, pursued by enemy agents in black fedoras, that would have been a different matter. But that couldn't happen, because most of his driving was done on the Kennedy Expressway, dreaming of mountain roads and spies.

Not that it was an expensive dent. For $35 or $40, most body shops would take care of it. But that meant taking it in, leaving it for a day or two. And $35 is $35. Just because an idiot couldn't open his door with care.

That's one of the curses of modern, big city, parking-lot life. Careless strangers can $40 you to death with dents.

Two kinds of people use parking lots. One kind will get in or out of a tight space inch by inch, cranking the wheel, carefully angling the car to avoid making contact. They open the door with care, squeeze their bodies in or out—anything to avoid crunching the next guy's door.

Then there are those who lurch forward, backward, banging, bumping. They fling open the door, sending chips of paint flying, leaving behind one after another of $40 dents.

A person can baby his car, drive like a Wisconsin farmer, vow to get ten years out of his new wheels. But it's a matter of time until he walks out of the place he works, or a restaurant or a shopping center, and finds a $40 crease in the tin. And someday, when he trades it in, the salesman will look at that one dent and say: "A real dog you got here."

The man in the restaurant parking lot thought about those things, then exhaled with resignation, and started to get in his car.

But then he got back out and looked around the lot. Nobody was in sight.

Smiling wickedly, he leaned over and grabbed the windshield wiper on the other car. He gave it a yank. With a loud crack, the whole thing broke off.

Then he went to the other side and tore off the other wiper.

He fumbled through his pockets and found a piece of paper, on which he wrote: "Next time, you SOB, be careful whose car you dent." He put the note on the windshield, and weighed it down with the broken wipers.

Then he got back in his car, carefully backed out of his parking space, and drove away, feeling a little better.

It's a true story. Don't ask me how I know.

Bill Granger

In addition to the syndicated wits from Chicago who are relatively well known, there are other journalists—perhaps not as popular—whose work entertains local and national audiences. It might be fitting to end our collection with Bill Granger's "Talkin' Chicawgo," which first appeared in *The Chicagoan* (December, 1973), a short-lived monthly magazine of the city's life.

After a career as a popular local journalist and TV critic for the *Sun-Times*, Granger, who was born in 1941, has recently turned his attention to the writing of mystery novels. His latest one, *Sweeps*, appeared in 1980. He follows in the tradition of the debunkers of the Chicago myth who also seem—at the same time—to be apologists for it.

Talkin' Chicawgo: A Basic Language Primer on How to Tell an Outsider from One of Us

Chicago is the only city in the country where the very common language of the people is enthroned. Before Richard J. (Dick) Daley became DaMare, it was expected that the higher one went in government, the better one talked. After all, Mayor Kennelly didn't *dese* and *dose* his way through office. But with Daley came the revolution of the common language. Suddenly it was in for bright people to talk about *clout* (which means political influence, with implications of impropriety). Even Mayor John Lindsay of New York used, and misused, the word. Now it has lost almost all value.

Our language continues to reach for new platitudes of success, to misquote the mayor, and one becomes sensitive to those outsiders who do not know how to talk Chicawgo (where the "o" is nearly silent).

We who remember the gangways and prairies of our youth laugh to scorn the effete suburbanite who still thinks *cophouses* are precinct stations. They are *district* stations. A *precinct* is what you hold back on election night until Downstate is counted; a *district* is where you get protection. Also, a *gangway* (literally the "going way") is where one lurks; and a *prairie* is where one plays softball of the Chicago 16-inch variety.

One learns that the oldest joke in the city is this snappy exchange: *Does dis bus go todaLoop? No, it goes beep-beep.* Learning this, one promptly forgets it.

In Chicago, it is always the El even when it goes underground briefly. The *Trib* and the *Times* are the morning papers in town; the *News* and the *American* (or even the *Herald*, but never *Today*) are the afternoon papers. In Chicago, with its heavy German-Polish-Irish-Scandinavian mix, *ya* is both you and yes, as in *ya guys* and *ya, I know dat*.

To talk Chicawgo, you must learn streets, the street names that do not appear in Leonard's pocket guide.

It is *Crawford*, not Pulaski, even in Chicago, and even if you're Polish.

It is *The Congress*, not the Eisenhower Expressway (the first known example of congressional dominance over the executive).

It can be *Roosevelt* (with emphasis on the *ROOO*) but the market is called *Twelfth Street* or *Maxwell*.

DaLoop is vaguely downtown. Many non-Chicagoans believe that *DaLoop* is named for the elevated structure girdling the downtown district. Actually, it was named for the loop of ground-level railroads that surrounded "downtown" before the turn of the century.

Neighborhoods: It's called *East Side* not "The East Side"; it's still *Rogers Park* even when you're in West Ridge; and it's *Kenwood* down by 40th Street, no matter where the University of Chicago tries to relocate it.

The North Sider comes from either parks or intersections. Where ya from? *Logan Square, Belmont-Ashland. Portage Park.*

The South Sider, perhaps reflecting the Irish background, comes from parishes. Even if he's not a Catholic. Ask Bill Singer, the well-known alderman, where he was raised and he will say, *Philip Neri*. Others grew up in *John o' God, Vis, St. Pete's* and *Holy Angels*.

The West Sider. Yes. Well, now we have a problem. I talked to an old West Sider one day and I asked him where he grew up.

"'Round Kraflin Karp," he said.

At that moment, a beautiful young lady walked into the joint (we were in a saloon, although that is not a Chicago word; we call them taverns or bars here). My friend spun around and said, "Kate a kool at the drawb! Gib tobbles, huh?" "Huh?" I responded.

What this West Side relic was speaking was Kraflin Karp slang, a kosher pig-latin language spoken by the mostly Jewish residents around Franklin Park (or Kraflin Karp) some 20 years ago. ("Take a look at that broad," is what he said. "Big bottles, huh?")

Now we must explore the ersatz-Chicagoan who tries to talk DaMare's English but can't quite pull it off.

I was stunned and shocked when I saw *Boss* recently at the Forum theater in Summit. There was this New York actor on the stage, pretending he was the mayor of Chicago. It was a very clever parody, but he gave himself away when kept referring to "youse guys." "Youse" is New York; *ya* or *yaas* is Chicago, just as New York's "toity-toid" becomes *turdy-turd* 700 miles west.

The pseudos say "White Sox Park" and da natives say *Comiskey*. The outlanders say "O'Hare" and the real folks say, *O'Hara*.

Few white Chicagoans know they are referred to as *gray dudes* by some blacks or that *my main man* is "my best friend" or that *fine as wine in the summertime* once was an expression of a mellow scene perceived.

The Chicago talking game can be played by anyone—against anyone. Take television newscasters. Len O'Connor talks Chicawgo, of course; Joel Daly doesn't. Floyd Kalber is getting there, but Fahey Flynn has been there a long time. Carl Greyson is usually there, although he has these odd lapses into a parody of a British accent.

But the most successful exponent of Chicago talk is, of course, DaMare. Dr. Raven McDavid, a University of Chicago linguist who has listened to Hizzoner on occasion (as, indeed, everyone has), says that Daley talks differently to different groups. "He can speak well when he wants to," is the way McDavid phrased it. But when he is talking Irish

Soul, Daley has no peer as a Chicawgo talker. Will we ever forget *da wunnerful people of dis great city*? It is doubtful.

And can we ignore the special Chicago scatology? No way. *Asshole* seems to be a unique Chicago pejorative. Anyone can be one. In fact, a recent book on popular psychology might better have been called *I'm OK—You're An Asshole* for the Chicago audience. One is an *Asshole* for making a left turn in front of you, dumping his garbage in the alley, leaving his TV on late at night, getting muscled due to an overdue juice bill, or for just walking down your street at night.

Basically, to talk Chicawgo, you have to live here, keep your ears open, and never, never ask if a bus goes todaLoop.

If ya do, I'll come on by your house and break both your legs.